T0094665

Faith on Trial

RELIGION AND THE LAW IN THE UNITED STATES

Mark J.T. Caggiano

Skinner House Books
BOSTON

www.skinnerhouse.org

Printed in the United States

Cover design by Kathryn Sky-Peck
Text design by Jeff Miller
Author photo by Chris Lang Photography

print ISBN: 978-1-55896-876-9
eBook ISBN: 978-1-55896-877-6

6 5 4 3 2 1
25 24 23 22 21

Cataloging-in-Publication information on file with the Library of Congress

Contents

To my children, with love.

Introduction

I USED TO BE A LAWYER. That changed, but here I am still writing about the law. Why? Because the law can be interesting—and because it really matters.

A decade ago, on my way to a career change, I was attending Harvard Divinity School. During my last year of seminary, I was in the required senior writing seminar. We spent two semesters researching and drafting our final projects. There were two coincidences of significance in the course. First, my class that year was made up of almost all of the Unitarian Universalist students (my denomination) and almost all of the Black students.[1] The other coincidence was that two students were researching the same topic: the role of religious speech in U.S. society. The same topic, however, led to directly opposite conclusions.

---

[1] The Black students included both American and non-American students.

1

One student resolved that religious speech should not be considered in matters of public policy. The other student argued that religious speech, essentially one's religious viewpoint, was an unavoidable part of U.S. political life; I was the second student. We had to present our topics to the wider group, sounding out issues and ideas with the input of others. The shared subject split the group in half. The Unitarians sided with my classmate, also a Unitarian, while the Black students, from various Protestant denominations, sided with me. It was a bit awkward.

In retrospect, I have come to understand this difference as a fundamental aspect of those respective traditions. Liberal, white, suburban religious folk (in my admittedly limited experience as a liberal, white, suburban man), have often tried to separate their faith from other areas of concern: politics, social groups, etc. Conversely, Black people identify in national polling as more consistently religious and more religiously observant than other groups.[2]

This is not to declare one group liberal and the other illiberal, but to suggest that the idea of "liberalism" can be both problematic and limiting. If we were to define liberalism as "a tradition of rebellion against inherited authority that seeks to free individuals and communities from bondage of the body,

---

[2] For example: "While the U.S. is generally considered a highly religious nation, African-Americans are markedly more religious on a variety of measures than the U.S. population as a whole, including level of affiliation with a religion, attendance at religious services, frequency of prayer and religion's importance in life." From "A Religious Portrait of African Americans," Pew Research Center, pewforum.org/2009/01/30/a-religious-portrait-of-african-americans/.

mind, and spirit,"[3] we would in turn need to reconcile liberalism as a reaction to authority while also understanding it as an embodiment of authoritative traditions reflecting an accretion of liberalism's past responses. In this way, liberalism's rebellious phase has tempered, rendering it a movement within an existing culture rather than a struggle toward systemic change.

The "liberal" individual hoisting the banner of freedom must consider the enduring constrictions imposed on society through liberal byproducts such as capitalism. The "Protestant work ethic" of Max Weber encapsulated and privileged a social framework of merit. This self-congratulatory cultural trope becomes a lynchpin of liberalism and capitalism, as well as embracing overt religious and implicit racial superiority. Perhaps salvation of the term "liberal" arises from yoking the linguistically related concepts, *liberal* and *liberating*, while acknowledging them as not always being historically consonant.[4]

As for the disagreement regarding the proper place for religious speech, I would not describe this as a difference between an ability to compartmentalize parts of one's life, but as a difference of opinion over the appropriateness of doing so. The old saying that one should not talk about money, religion, or politics in polite company is not a universal view, particularly when it comes to religion. And so, the "liberal" tendency to divorce religious language from the lexicon of public discourse may arise

---

[3] Sofía Betancourt, Dan McKanan, Tisa Wenger, and Sheri Prud'homme, "Claiming the Term 'Liberal' in Academic Religious Discourse," *Religions* 11, no. 6 (2020): 311. doi.org/10.3390/rel11060311.

[4] Bettancourt et al., 311.

from the habit of bridling against undesirable expressions of authority while at the same time unconsciously wearing preferential social treatment like a comfortable cloak.

The premise of my senior year research project was that religious speech should be expected in political conversations. Not only because such speech is clearly permissible for legal reasons but also because such speech is often at the core of peoples' identities. Expecting one another to segregate the political from the religious is to ask many citizens to leave their most cherished values outside the halls of government.

That is not to suggest that religious views should automatically win any debate over social policy. But it would be a mistake to fight the wrong battle. A crisp philosophical expectation about public policy in this case runs directly contrary to the fundamental rights protected by the United States Constitution: rights of freedom of speech, freedom to petition government, and freedom of religion. The question is not whether such speech is legally permissible, because it is. The question is why some groups of people, the liberal and progressive religious folks, have exited the conversation while others, such as Evangelical Christians, have often made it the cornerstone of their political involvement.[5] A central purpose of this book is to inform and to engage with reli-

---

[5] Establishing a definition of Evangelical Christianity could take up an entire book. I use the four-part definition espoused by the National Association of Evangelicals and developed by Prof. David Bebbington in the 1980s: 1) the need for a "born again" conversion experience, 2) the active expression of the gospel through missionary work and social reform, 3) the use of the Bible as the ultimate authority, and 4) the centrality of the sacrifice of Jesus Christ making human salvation a possibility. From "What is an Evangelical?" National Association of Evangelicals, nae.net/what-is-an-evangelical.

gious people across the political and social spectrums so that they might become more effective in joining public conversations and making themselves heard. And if they learn something along the way, all the better.

I have spent my adult life studying religion and the law. As a lawyer for decades, I have argued in the courts and have researched the law extensively for clients and out of personal interest. Later in life, I switched careers and became an ordained minister, a pastor at a church outside of Boston, Massachusetts. I now preach on Sundays and study scripture, philosophy, and history the rest of the week to make those sermons possible— and occasionally palatable. In many ways, however, little has changed across those seemingly different careers. The law is about the rules of society. Religion, if I may be so bold, is about the rules of life.

How religion and the law mesh, or clash, is therefore of some importance. People may seek to reconcile what they must do under the law with what they ought to do under their religions, beliefs, or personal philosophies. Sometimes that balancing process is simple and straightforward. At other times, there is conflict on a fundamental level.

Some behaviors that may be encouraged under a religion might be prohibited under the law, such as taking certain illegal drugs or engaging in polygamous marriages. And activities permitted under the law may be forbidden in a particular faith community. Drinking alcohol, working on the Sabbath, seeking an abortion: depending on the religious background of a person, these actions may be either utterly sinful or completely acceptable. The laws of the United States are, in theory, of general applicability but may result in conflicts with particular religious beliefs and traditions.

The First Amendment of the United States Constitution directly addresses the question of religion in American society: "Congress shall make no law respecting an establishment of religion, or prohibiting the free exercise thereof. . . ." When the time came to set out a list of foundational rights, the framers of the Constitution put the question of religion first, taking up that subject before even freedom of speech, which follows in the next clause of the First Amendment. Religious freedom and worries over religious strife were important matters for those early Americans. Religion and its complexities remain important today, though perhaps to differing degrees and with varying points of emphasis. And religious groups that historically fought for protections for religious minorities, that is, themselves, may now be less inclined to do so for others, having achieved places of greater social acceptance.

Indeed, one particular challenge over the span of U.S. history has been the protection of minority religious views. It is not surprising that the beliefs of the majority need less protection, not because of their lack of importance but because challenges to them are less likely to arise. Smaller religious groups face greater obstacles. Unpopular faith traditions encounter higher scrutiny. And new religions, perhaps splitting off from more familiar or established denominations, may on the one hand garner hostility from their religious cousins and on the other hand arouse suspicions from an uninformed public.

Broadly speaking, the First Amendment was created with these concerns in mind. But the simplicity of those sixteen words in the so-called Establishment and Free Exercise Clauses belies the many complexities that various religious groups and individuals have faced throughout U.S. history. Legal decisions based on these clauses have evolved over the past two centuries, in keeping with the shifting framework of the federal government. There had been until recent years a modern "progressive" focus on protecting religious minorities from the effects of hostile legal requirements or the unintended consequences of federal and state laws. Lately, however, the use of the term "religious freedom" has become a rallying cry for a certain segment of the political spectrum. Rather than protecting minority religious groups from majority religious expectations or prejudices, calls for religious freedom have at times become a means for shielding religious beliefs from the perceived intrusions of secular society. The perception of majority versus minority is instead secular versus religious.

Even the civil rights of individuals have been transmogrified to serve the needs of corporations and business interests. Concerns for religious freedom have been used to justify securing federal and state funding for religious schools or activities.[6] Religious freedom becomes a means for allowing religious believers and their businesses to abstain from government expectations, such as providing their employees mandatory medical insurance that includes abortion and birth control services, or to deny the provision of goods and services to consumers living disapproved

---

[6] Trinity Lutheran Church of Columbia, Inc. v. Comer, 582 U.S. ___; 137 S. Ct. 2012 (2017). Note: these underlined blank spaces refer to cases where the Supreme Court has not yet assigned its own pagination. Where this occurs, I add the Supreme Court Reporter (S. Ct.)'s pagination for reference.

"lifestyles."[7] The boundary between religious beliefs and social obligations has blurred to the point where it may be difficult to pass seemingly neutral laws without repeatedly clashing with expectations of faith.

Religious progressives and those of the so-called "mainline" liberal traditions have often chosen to shy away from public religious controversies. For liberals—whether religious or political—religion may be thought of as a private matter, not a topic for open discussion, which is a major change from the historic place of religion in society.[8] Making moral claims in the public square is therefore seen as at best vulgar grandstanding and at worst political manipulation. There are philosophical underpinnings to these more secular perspectives, ones often linked to Thomas Jefferson's famous call for a wall of separation between church and state.

Conversely, religious progressives may suspiciously view courts or political processes as the tools of an unjust society, ones unlikely to be of use in creating a new way forward. A religious progressive would focus more on the "liberating" aspects of reform, more consistent with the tenets of liberation theology, and without deference to the potentially problematic facets of historic liberalism such as capitalism and meritocracy. And like liberals, progressives are more likely to speak in broad political

---

[7] Respectively, Burwell v. Hobby Lobby Stores, Inc, 573 U.S. 682 (2014); Masterpiece Cakeshop v. Colorado Civil Rights Commission, 370 P.3d 272 (2016).

[8] As a New England pastor, I can attest to the general reluctance of New Englanders to profess faith publicly or even among close friends. It makes membership growth a challenge.

language, invoking justice or decrying inequality, rather than expressing articles of faith.

I realize this is a sweeping assertion and that progressive voices speaking in religious terms have existed for many years, such as Rev. Martin Luther King Jr., and are currently making themselves known, such as Revs. William Barber and Nadia Bolz-Weber. This is not, in my experience, the natural mode of religious liberals and progressives. MLK was not a lone voice, but in the 1960s he was occasionally a lonely one.

Failing to show up to a debate rarely means that you have won it. Instead, the views of liberal and progressive religious folk have become faint, if not silent, often replaced with secular political positions carefully couched in non-religious terms. The precision of language has become the presiding virtue of conversation while an opportunity to speak on a deeper, more spiritual level is lost.

In one sense, the high ground has been claimed by liberals and progressives as to the desired moral results, and yet moral *language* within the conversation has become one-sided in opposition to that claim. There are clear moral concerns about racism and income inequality, discrimination over gender, gender identity, and sexual orientation. Those concerns not only can be discussed in religious terms but, I would argue, *must* be if they are to be afforded the same weight and seriousness in a nation that retains a strong affinity for religious language, if not always religious practice. Transcendent values need the power and heft of transcendent language.

Why distinguish this as a religious imperative? Why not approach it from the angle of secular values? Freedom of religion is a fundamental right protected under the United States Constitution. Freedom of *philosophy*, as in the freedom to act upon one's life philosophy rather than to practice one's religion, is not expressly protected.[9] Freedom of speech may seem to cover much of the same intellectual ground, but it notably does not provide protection for practices and behaviors; you can claim you want to fight climate change but putting up those solar panels is another matter entirely. "Secular humanism" is not generally classified as a religion under the law, though humanistic religion could receive similar protections.[10] And a desire for freedom *from* religion is far less of a legal right than might be imagined. Arguably, freedom of *conscience* is not as well protected.

This book is intended as an examination of freedom of religion in the United States. It will follow the evolution of this area of U.S. law, in a hopefully user-friendly fashion, so that people of faith may gain an appreciation for the legal landscape. Specifically, the goal is to present an understanding of the law and its history so that religious liberals and progressives may enter public debates over social policy prepared to speak in terms of both law and faith. I do not mean to suggest that religious con-

---

[9] Put another way, what one believes may be protected either as religion or as speech, but one's behaviors are offered protection under the First Amendment only if religious.

[10] See, e.g., Torcaso v. Watkins, 367 U.S. 488, 495 n.11 (1961). Maryland could not require public officeholders to affirm a belief in God: "Among religions in this country which do not teach what would generally be considered a belief in the existence of God are Buddhism, Taoism, Ethical Culture, Secular Humanism and others." Compare to Kalka v. Hawk, 215 F.3d 90 (2000), in which the failure to permit a humanist prison group was found not to be clear violation of First Amendment religious rights. If this seems confusing, more details will be forthcoming in later chapters. More *clarity* is another story entirely.

servatives might not benefit from this book, and welcome the increased readership, but those groups have generally been at the forefront of the religious "values" conversation for decades.

To begin, the historical context for the First Amendment will be sketched out, followed by a review of the development of U.S. law through court cases and various statutes. This will be a 101-level review of legal basics, though it is a complex area of the law even for legal professionals. This will be followed by a case study, a lawsuit against a group of 1970s snake handlers whose story ties together many aspects of this area of the law prior to dramatic legal changes in the 1990s. (It is also one of my favorite cases.) After that, I will examine the legal treatment, and mistreatment, of specific religious minorities across the nineteenth-century United States: Jews, Catholics, and Latter-day Saints, also known as Mormons. Specific legal cases and statutes will serve as the backdrop for discussing the creation of religious rights over that time period and the balancing of religious freedom with public safety, the latter being a concern which may conflict with the exercise of religious belief.

The following chapters will consider how important historical events overlap with significant changes in the religious population of the United States and in the laws protecting religious expression. After the American Civil War, the Constitution was dramatically transformed. Specifically, amendments to the Constitution concerning race and citizenship also created major shifts in religious rights, broadening their scope and spurring new modes of thinking. Next, religious responses to the tumult of the early twentieth century play a significant role in the evolution of this area of the law, such as the religious travails of

Jehovah's Witnesses. This fertile environment for change culminates in what might be described as progressive protections of religious freedom, particularly in the 1960s and 1970s. But a shifting political landscape in the 1980s and 1990s will lead to pushback and, more importantly for this book, to a reinterpretation of religious rights from a story of a progressive protection to one of conservative retrenchment.

Ultimately, the question for religious liberals and progressives—the "liberal" versus the "liberating"—is how to engage with the moral challenges of the day while, I would argue, expressing those responses in religious terms. This might be best understood as a matter of fluency: learning to speak and to advocate using language expressing core religious values that is recognizable to the wider society. It is no coincidence that Rev. Dr. Martin Luther King Jr. expressed his responses to racial, social, and economic challenges in religious terms. And it is no wonder that progressives and liberals alike have historically turned to the language of religion and the values of faith to confront injustice, from the Social Gospel movement and the civil rights era to the current waves of protests over racism, immigration reform, and a wide spectrum of social concerns. Separating church from state is by no means the same as separating religious values from social action.

It is paramount that religious liberals and progressives cultivate and refine an ability to articulate the need for moral changes within the political system. That goal will require an understanding of the law as well as a moral vision for the world. Not an exclusive moral vision; not an "us versus them" environment of winners and losers. There is a dire need for effective action within a troubled society. Organizing for change is one means of response. Advocating for change based upon shared moral principles and a sense of faith is another, one often lacking from many liberal and progressive religious folks. The project of this book is to help encourage that next step, a step made repeatedly throughout a long and progressive history of effective social action and timely moral leadership. The arc of history does not always or easily bend toward justice. Sometimes to get matters moving, it needs a good and righteous whack.

CHAPTER 1

How to Describe a Wall

A WALL OF SEPARATION between church and state, or perhaps religion and the law, requires a degree of imagination. What is meant by this idea? Regardless of whether one is for or against something, it is worth taking a moment to picture what is being sought after or fought against.

Imagine a wall. It could be tall and sturdy, soaring above protectively. It could be steel and stone, studded with spikes and wrapped in barbed wire. It could be elegant wrought iron, easy to see through to the other side. It could be a white picket fence, homey and well tended, marking the boundaries of a house rather than the borders of one's territory. Appearances can be deceiving.

Imagine the purpose of the wall. Good fences are said to make good neighbors, but could the same be said for walls? Is it to show the tidy outlines of a home? A way to keep a spirited dog from running away or dangerous animals from getting in (or out)? Is it like the Berlin Wall, built in theory to keep outsiders away but just as likely to lock others in? Is the wall for defense and protection? Or is it a boundary showing where a different set of rules apply?

Keep off the grass. No trespassing. Employees only. More than one description may apply.

In the chart below, there are spheres of influence suggested, places where religion and the law might operate and hold sway. These could interact in differing ways, places, and times. Completely separate spheres of religion and law are hard to find, except perhaps in the confines of a believer's mind. Even that clean separation becomes muddied the moment a religious belief becomes expressed. Whether as speech or in writing, when religion enters the world it may become subject to the law. And while the law may expressly protect such speech, there could be ways, places, and times in which even that freedom is limited. This is before even considering specific religious practices, rituals, and other behaviors.

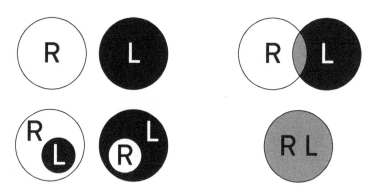

The relationship between religion and the law can be imagined as separate, overlapping, controlled, or co-equal, which views may vary in an individual, a community, or society.

How to Describe a Wall

There are many ways for religion and the law to overlap. Marriage is one area in which religion in the United States works in conjunction with government. Clergy can perform marriages which are registered at courthouses, county offices, and municipal registries. Clergy do not obtain their authority to marry in a religious sense from the states, but the recognition of those religious marriages by the state allows various legal rights to flow to religiously married couples. Those legal rights were among the key reasons same-sex marriages were recognized. The balance between the religious and legal aspects of marriage varies by country and by culture. For example, in the sixteenth century, English marriages were solemnized by Anglican clergy while contemporaneous Dutch marriages were civil arrangements. English Puritan colonists embarking from Protestant Holland similarly viewed marriage as a civil matter because it was not understood as a Biblically sanctioned sacrament like baptism or communion.

One concern arising from the legalization of same-sex marriage in the United States was the prospect of clergy being forced to perform marriages that conflicted with their religious beliefs. That is an unlikely legal result given the breadth of First Amendment protections against compelled behavior, as will be seen in subsequent chapters regarding Jehovah's Witnesses and the Pledge of Allegiance or prayer in public schools. In a similar vein, clergy could not be required to perform religious marriages for same-sex couples. A particular religious tradition is not required to perform such marriages, or any marriages, or to marry any and all comers. But as civil institutions, the states, unlike religious traditions, must allow these marriages. Nevertheless, this prospect may remain a matter of consternation, if not likely occurrence, for those who prefer a specific, religiously based formulation of marriage, which definition the U.S. Supreme Court has rejected since 2015.[11]

The contrary worry might be religious expectations invading civil matters, anxieties about creeping theocracy arising outside the pages of speculative fiction like *The Handmaid's Tale*, which might only be "speculative" for those blotting out antebellum United States history. Within a religious mindset or community, however, the transcendent sense of the beliefs of a religion may readily extend outside the laws of the land. For example, a conscientious objector may choose to follow the expectations of faith rather than the demands of society for military service. Immigration law that prohibits aiding or sheltering migrants might violate sincerely held beliefs about helping the stranger, leading to resistance and protests. The requirements of a religion might necessitate confrontation of the law, and, barring an exception, the religious believer might then be prosecuted, fined, or imprisoned. The law does not need to accommodate every religious impulse or directive, but there are modern trends discussed later in this book that may limit national and local government in significant ways.

The law somehow encircling religion may seem a more likely, though uncomfortable, image for people of faith. Yet this may be a problem for those of a religious mindset rather than one recognized in the world. The law does not control belief, in the sense of what one is permitted to think, though a totalitarian regime might try to break into even such a personal stronghold. Dis-

---

[11] Obergefell v. Hodges, 576 U.S. 644 (2015).

comfort over the idea of the law as paramount may be a way of calling out to society that "You're not the boss of me," while for practical purposes the requirements of the law remain. And, conversely, a belief that religion should stand beyond the confines of the law may clash with society's need for an orderly structure, a social framework in which the public peace and social equality must be maintained regardless of the requirements of any one religious tradition. One might retort, "Religion, you're not the boss of *us*."

Finally, religion and the law may be imagined as perfectly overlapping. This may seem a strange result if the two areas are understood as having nothing in common—the sinful City of Man and the righteous City of God distinction made by Augustine. But in a sense, religion and the law could be understood as being co-equal, overlapping seamlessly in the lives of religious people within a society. How religion plays out for a person internally, or mentally, would be unhindered by the law while the outward expression of that religion through behavior would be subject to legal scrutiny of varying degrees. Of course, if religion has no bearing on the world or the people in it, would the law ever need to intrude upon such a private and perhaps innocuous matter of one's mental state? And yet should religion ever be so disengaged from the world or a society?

The law is also more than a means for inhibiting religion. For instance, if religion and the law are entirely separate, as with the first figure, what protections exist to assure that religion may be practiced freely? The law can also prohibit discrimination and persecution. Religious practices may only exist in some contexts if the law steps in to guarantee such freedom. Drawing a diagram is theoretical. But establishing and maintaining the balance of rights within a society will most likely be the true measure of how well the law protects the freedom of a religion as well as assuring freedom from any one religion.

Moreover, if religion is to be deemed beyond the control of the law, how will it contend with lawless activity that might undermine the free exercise of religion? Augustine was notably writing his *City of God* work after Rome was sacked by the Visigoths (and not for the last time). Blame for the tragedy was being laid at the feet of upstart atheistic Christians because the empire had strayed away from traditional Roman values.[12] Traditions may hold firm or evolve. Resorting to them in times of trouble can be a comfort, a caution, or an excuse. And those traditions may be propped up in turbulent times, which begs the question of their ultimate strength in the face of challenge or their ongoing relevance in times of change.

Another way of understanding this dynamic is to contrast three pairs of ideas: church and state, religion and the law, and faith and politics. Church and state could be seen as representing distant institutions, monolithic fortresses contending over territory like medieval popes and kings. With such a "zero sum" sense of territory lost and gained, any blending of church and state could be viewed as an invasion, a worrisome development particularly if the ascendant "church" is not one's own. That concern may well have been the motivation for quickly amending the U.S. Constitution in 1789 to protect both existing religious

---

[12] Christians were deemed atheists because they refused to believe in the gods, instead choosing to believe that only one existed.

institutions from federal intrusion and religious behavior from federal oversight. This was by no means a divorce of church and state on the state and local level, but merely assurance that the national government would stay out of the religion business.

"Religion" and "the Law" are remote concepts, as compared with church as embodied in denominations and buildings or the state as understood through the government and politicians. Religion as a set of ideas and the law as a philosophical subject are topics for our musings and occasional reform efforts. Religions evolve, laws are amended. The interplay of religion and the law shifts in emphasis along varying perspectives: the centrality of religion in one's life, the warmness or hostility one holds for religion or the law, etc. And yet society needs order, peace, and tranquility. Law and religion can each provide a facet of those sought-after qualities and can conceivably work harmoniously toward those shared goals.

And then comes faith and politics. Politics hovers around the state and the law; it might talk about them in earnestness or scorn. But politics cannot readily be equated with the state without slipping into some brand of authoritarianism. And politics cannot be understood as the law because it is a shifting landscape, a chameleon becoming what it needs to appear to be to endure for another election cycle. Faith can be just one more color added to that political camouflage, an opportunistic duck blind hiding many underlying flaws. And yet religious language is common in political rhetoric, telegraphing any number of social policies (e.g., abortion, birth control, etc.).

But true faith is not that. It inhabits the social and spiritual core of people concerned with the world and the people around them. Placing a wall between faith and politics is fundamentally at odds with the expression of values of these people.

That does not mean that the state should bow down to any church. Nor does it imply that religion should rule over the law, or that the law should shackle religion. Order, peace, and tranquility are important, but those desired ends should not serve as excuses to subjugate church or state, religion or the law. The freedom to believe and to practice a religion is paired with the freedom to speak, to communicate about those beliefs and practices.

And so the wall of separation is not about silencing the religious, or those opposed to religion. The image of a wall is perhaps unsuited to the task of maintaining a balance between these important but often competing qualities. If we instead imagine these paired ideas—church and state, religion and the law, faith and politics—as being kept in a healthy equilibrium, it may seem less like battle lines being drawn and more like the careful give and take needed to protect order, promote peace, and achieve tranquility in a healthy and occasionally happy society. The scales of justice may be a more apt metaphor. Whether that is a workable mechanism is another story.

CHAPTER 2

The Legal Basics

HOW TO EXPLAIN THE LAW? You might think it would be a straightforward matter, like recalling memorized lessons about algebra or grammar. That common sense would carry the day.

Not really.

I often and only half-jokingly explain that the answer to every legal question is the same: *it depends.* It depends on where you are. It depends on who was involved. It depends upon matters terribly great and ridiculously small.

An example: a college classmate was getting ready to move out of state. He was selling off his car, a serviceable old heap not much to look at. Notably, it had a manual transmission. He was contacted by a buyer, a new driver looking for a first car. The deal was struck, the money exchanged for keys and papers.

Soon afterwards, the seller gets a call from the buyer: the car would not work, so he was demanding his money back. The seller went and checked out the car, realizing that the new driver had burned out the clutch. The seller declined to give back the money. The buyer filed a lawsuit in small claims court. After looking over the documents and hearing both sides, the judge announced that the *buyer* had prevailed. When asked about the result by the baffled seller, the judge explained that if the buyer had driven the car into a wall, he would still get his money.

Why? In what alternate reality does this make sense? The clue to the result is in the description: "new driver." The buyer had just obtained a drivers' license at the minimum age, which is 16½ in Massachusetts. But the minimum age for making legally binding contracts is 18. Minors cannot make contracts, which is why the seller should have sold the car to a parent or guardian of the driver. Whether the seller could have counter-sued the buyer for damaging the clutch is another story.

For some, that result may scream injustice. It may run counter to common sense, whatever that means.[13] Alter the story slightly and imagine a used car lot. An unscrupulous sales representative is passing off a junker to a new minor driver. The driver gets his money back, which seems more just. The law is not about making the story sound good. It is about rules that make sense prospectively, looking forward while also responding to past problems. If the results start trending against the underlying intention of the laws, the courts have some maneuvering room, but

---

[13] Common sense is often defined as sound judgment derived from experience, but that implies a standard set of experiences leading to a similar set of conclusions. My working definition of common sense is *current* sense, how I would decide something now based upon what I believe. Those beliefs are generally controlled by where and how I grew up, where I currently live, who I choose to be with and listen to, and what I was taught in school and in life. In other words, "common sense" is not much of a common measurement.

generally the fix would come from the state legislature or Congress. Or not.

Judges typically apply the law as the law is (though the Supreme Court often takes on cases where the law is unclear and therefore will be effectively made through their decisions). And when there are ambiguities or unfair results, there are some possibilities for relief, often referred to as equitable relief. At this point, the label "judicial activism" occasionally gets trotted out by the losing side, so it is worth examining the broad strokes of the U.S. legal system.

Speaking in painfully broad generalities, modern legal systems tend to be based either on common law, such as in the British tradition, or on civil law, such as in the French tradition (more distantly derived from the Romans). The pervasive reach of these two systems is an enduring imposition of colonialism and continues in modified and hybrid forms around the world. There are also religious legal systems, such as Canon, Jewish, and Islamic law, but those are not often broadly used outside of religious contexts, though there are notable exceptions best addressed in someone else's book.

A civil-law system typically relies upon a code of laws, generally a set of books akin to a legal encyclopedia. What law applies in this case? Well, let me pop open to the right section . . . minors and legally binding contracts, page X. Those specific laws are applied and cover most situations. Exceptions would be set out in the law via catchall provisions or in overriding constitutional documents. There might be some flexibility in their application by a particular court, but the example of that variation of result is not necessarily used for other similar cases—it could be a guide, but not a controlling precedent. Different judges might not make the same exception from the rule. In one sense this is even handed, if the same rules are applied, but not if exceptions exist that are made only in some situations. And no, I am not aware of any late-breaking trends in European Union bureaucracy or unfolding Icelandic jurisprudence: thus the warning of "painfully broad generalities."[14]

The common-law system was and often is far more organic. England had no comprehensive legal code, but a patchwork of royal edicts and parliamentary acts responding to various situations. "Common law" filled the gaps. These are the product of decisions that judges and legal authorities have generated over centuries to fill in the wide range of situations not covered by a specific piece of legislation. A statute would apply if one existed, but even then the application could often be modified for unexpected issues, novel situations, or inequitable results. You killed his cow, but she was eating your crops, and so forth. Even ancient Roman laws could be invoked as examples for interpreting a novel case.

The U.S. legal system follows this more eclectic approach. Think about the U.S. Constitution. One would guess that it was intended to cover the important stuff, it being the foundational document of a nation. And yet, if you were to read the Constitution closely, you would search in frustration for some legal basics.

For example, there is nothing in the Constitution about murder, rape, or arson. The Fifth Amendment prohibits the *government* from taking anything without just compensation, but no

---

[14] My apologies to the people of Iceland for using them as an object lesson; they seem quite nice.

one else is covered by that rule, so theft seems to be permitted. Before you consider going out and wantonly pillaging, you must realize that a scrum of intersecting and conflicting legal systems already existed in the original thirteen colonies of the United States. The Constitution explained the relationship of the federal government to the states, which were functioning with fierce independence under their own legal systems prior to the formation of the new national government.

American lawyers face entire buildings filled with legal cases, along with statutes and regulations, that all must be considered and applied (computers help). Each of the now 50 states has its own set of laws and regulations which stand in complex relationship to the federal laws and regulations set forth by Congress and the various federal agencies. That complexity has to be navigated by the courts, judging whether an area of the law is exclusively state or federal in nature, or if there have to be accommodations made for both. And then there are the territories, the District of Columbia, military law, international treaties, etc. "It depends" is putting the complexity of the United States legal system mildly.

This ongoing process of judicial assessment is similarly important with respect to the First Amendment and religious freedom. Historically, the First Amendment did not apply to the individual states, only to the federal government. States could, for example, establish state churches that were funded by tax dollars. Plymouth was founded as a religious colony by the Pilgrims, who as "pilgrims" were fleeing the English church. This established church predated the Constitution, as well as the Commonwealth of Massachusetts, and was accommodated in the new federal system. The church system in Massachusetts remained in place until 1833, the last to be disestablished. More on that later.

U.S. law can seem somewhat chaotic from the outside, but it has a logic and a consistency for those trained in its operation and merits. The Constitution is an overarching authority. Federal laws from Congress can cover areas of life far beyond the Constitution's explicit content, but those laws cannot typically intrude into what the Constitution protects or prohibits—no one gets to quarter troops in your house under the Third Amendment.[15] The same is true of federal regulations, rules generated by federal agencies which must in turn also comply with federal law and the Constitution. This is a rough pyramid of authority, which is interpreted by the courts in legal cases that in turn may serve as helpful guidance or authoritative direction in subsequent lawsuits. That is a lot to manage, but we are only getting started.

The states have their own legislatures and court systems. Some areas of the law are typically state rather than federal. You generally get married or divorced under state law, not federal.[16] You buy a car, sell a house, and rent an apartment under state law, not federal. But Federal law may in turn control the emissions from that car and impose civil-rights prohibitions against housing discrimination.

Much of our day-to-day lives are state-based physically. And, not surprisingly, the web of laws we find ourselves working under

---

[15] Yes, someone mentioned you, Third Amendment. No, the War of 1812 is over. Go back to bed.

[16] Though constitutional restrictions under federal law may limit the states, which cannot, for example, deny same-sex couples, mixed-race couples, or interfaith couples the right to marry.

is often state-specific. Cross state lines and it changes. But deal with some federal-only issue, like immigration or the military, and state law may be displaced.

Important for our present purposes, civil rights are covered by both state and federal law. State constitutions typically have sections mirroring the First Amendment's religious protections, with often additional protections or different considerations. If you were discriminated against at your job due to your race, ethnic background, or religion, you could find options for redress at the state or federal level. Which to choose is a special realm of an employment lawyer's expertise, but generally speaking there is a lot of overlap. That being said, the U.S. Supreme Court has the ultimate authority when interpreting the U.S. Constitution and when interpreting federal statutes and regulations. State supreme courts similarly have ultimate authority in construing their state constitutions and local laws, except where state and federal law conflict (i.e., the feds typically win).[17]

Even a basic description of U.S. law is unavoidably complicated.

Because of this degree of overlapping legal territory, the state courts will often consider legal cases that could also have been in the federal courts. There are reasons to "make a federal case" out of some situations, but there are also equally valid reasons for trying to keep something local. Expense of travel to the fed-

---

[17] As the federal Constitution puts it (Article VI, cl.2): "This Constitution, and the laws of the United States which shall be made in pursuance thereof . . . shall be the supreme law of the land; and the judges in every state shall be bound thereby, anything in the Constitution or laws of any State to the contrary notwithstanding."

eral court, local sympathies among judges, existing state cases favoring a desirable result: there are many reasons why you might like to keep your case out of the federal system.

For example, the *Masterpiece Cakeshop* case involved whether a baker has the right to refuse to design a wedding cake for a gay couple seeking to marry. *Masterpiece Cakeshop* was reviewed in the Colorado state court system, after making its way through the Colorado civil rights administrative commission, only to be appealed to the U.S. Supreme Court near to the end of the legal road. The issues in the case as finally decided by the state court opened the door for an appeal to the federal system because it potentially involved First Amendment rights, and specifically the Free Exercise Clause rights, of the baker.

The *Masterpiece Cakeshop* case was considered by two sides of a political debate as a moment to determine respectively the civil rights of the gay couple or the religious freedoms of the baker. The case could also have been resolved more narrowly as a freedom of speech matter without any resolution of the religious rights allegedly violated—my money was on that result. The Court might have decided that the baker could not be compelled to speak, assuming that designing and decorating a cake in a certain way counts as speech. The Supreme Court indeed decided on the baker's behalf, but on an extremely slender legal basis: the improper decision-making of the Colorado Civil Rights Commission. The Supreme Court effectively did not reach the underlying dispute with the couple seeking to buy a wedding cake.[18]

---

[18] Masterpiece Cakeshop v. Colorado Civil Rights Commission, 584 U.S. ___; 138 S. Ct. 1719 (2018).

The Legal Basics

If a court can resolve a case procedurally, meaning on a dreaded "technicality," it often will do so. This is not because judges like dodging political bullets (though sometimes . . .). If the statement of a case is unclear, if the complaint is decades old, if the parties are in the wrong state or the wrong court system, it makes sense to get that out of the way before people have spent years of time and lots of money arguing over the dispute. And, not insignificantly, before judges have spent many working hours dealing with a messy case that does not have clear sight lines toward a decision.

Without question, politics intrude upon the legal system, but that same system's greatest strength comes from the process being performed out in the open. The decisions are public, the proceedings generally open to all. Lawyers and judges can be politically partisan in their lives, but when it comes to the legal system, they are typically far more ethical than a cynical public gives them credit for. And they are far more traditionalist than their politics might suggest—the traditions of the law and the courts, not a predetermined partisan result under the law or in the courts. The law, at its best, is beyond politics.

Whether liberal or conservative, a lawyer should be capable of assessing a matter objectively, regardless of how they or their client might want things to turn out. Lawyers then, by the nature of the profession, slip out of that mindset of clinical objectivity into a mode of advocacy, at times even against their own political leanings. Even if they think a client has only a 50 percent chance of winning, that is still a chance and still within the ethical obligations of the lawyer. Lawyers need to be able to understand the many sides of an argument and the prospects of losing, even as they prepare to argue from one particular perspective.

If only these intellectual skills of lawyers were more commonly developed and applied.

In the area of religious rights, the highest authority is the U.S. Constitution and specifically the first two clauses of the First Amendment. Then there is a relatively recent and critically important federal statute, the Religious Freedom Restoration Act of 1993 (RFRA).[19] It was passed by Congress effectively to overrule the Supreme Court, which did not end up going as Congress planned.

RFRA, which will be discussed in greater detail, might be best described as a "liberal" effort to protect religious minorities. But the statute's general applicability and far-reaching language, essentially requiring every federal law and regulation to take into account religious rights, has made it a tool for religious groups, minority or not, to avoid the effects of federal laws. There are also state versions of the RFRA statute, but not in every state, nor in the same words, nor with the same legislative emphases. And we have not even considered the Religious Land Use and Institutionalized Persons Act of 2000 (RLUIPA), a statute of great legal import with a mildly absurd acronym.[20]

Whew.

And thus, overlapping laws, both state and federal, complicated by jargon-filled regulations and overseen by competing constitutions, require careful analysis and competent legal representation. This ever-shifting landscape of legalities further supports my one and only piece of confident legal advice to the gentle reader: *it always depends.*

---

[19] 42 U.S.C § 2000bb et al.

[20] 42 U.S.C § 2000cc et al.

CHAPTER 3

Handling Snakes

ANYONE WITH A PASSING FAMILIARITY with the Bible knows that a snake makes an early appearance. Adam and Eve have an encounter with a serpent, and it does not end well. And there are other occasions when snakes appear. For example, Moses and his followers have to deal with snakes on the Exodus from Egypt. Jesus calls upon his followers to be as wise as serpents and as innocent as doves. Snakes are symbols of both wisdom and danger in the Bible, and so how one handles a snake matters.

In the Gospel of Mark, there also *may* be a reference to snakes. Open a Bible to the closing chapter of Mark and there could be one of three endings (or multiple ones). In the first, Mary Magdalene and other women discover an empty tomb when they expected to find Jesus's body. They leave the scene in terror and amazement, the resurrection of Jesus alluded to but not yet confirmed. A second version extends the text briefly, describing the delivery of this news about the empty tomb to Peter and the others and a proclamation by and through Jesus of eternal salvation.

The third ending is seen in the King James Version. Some scholarly sources suggest it was added a century or more after the writing of the original (and shortest) version of the Gospel of Mark. This longer ending supplies more detail, specifically as to the coming of signs: "And these signs will accompany those who believe: by using my name they will cast out demons; they will speak in new tongues; they will pick up snakes in their hands, and if they drink any deadly thing, it will not hurt them. . . ."[21]

Notably, those who are to follow Jesus would be known by having certain abilities arising from their faith and acting as signs for others to follow. Safely handling snakes and drinking poison would therefore be significant representations of God's power. And so, from this description in the Gospel of Mark, certain religious groups have adopted the handling of snakes and the ingestion of poisonous substances as practices to be performed, as the Spirit moves.[22]

---

[21] The New Revised Standard Version sets out the endings and flags them as the "Shorter" and the "Longer."

[22] Some could be troubled that the Biblical verse from which these actions derive might not appear in the oldest version of the Gospel of Mark. How did it get there? Was it from the hand of the author or tacked on by someone long afterwards? And if it is not original, what meaning should it have? Other ancient texts claim to be from the disciples of Jesus, like the so-called Gospel of Thomas and the Gospel of Mary, but they are not accepted as canonical texts. Some religious texts made the editorial cut, like the Gospel of Mark; others did not, like the Gospel of Mary. And still others are in some Bibles but not others. I had a church reader search in vain for the Book of Sirach in his King James Version of the Bible. We had an interesting chat about "apocrypha," and I got a funny sermon story. Win-win.

Literary and historical concerns aside, these practices sketched out in the Gospel of Mark are dangerous—so dangerous that someone might get injured or die outright. Which leads to a fascinating episode the Supreme Court of Tennessee reviewed in *Swann v. Pack*, an example of the Gospel of Mark playing out in the world. The *Swann* court offered some history about a particular Southern church:

> The Mother Church [of the Holiness Church of God in Jesus Name] was founded in 1909 at Sale Creek in Grasshopper Valley, Tennessee, approximately thirty-five miles northeast of Chattanooga, by George Went Hensley. Hensley was motivated by a dramatic experience which occurred atop White Oak Mountain on the eastern rim of the valley during which he confronted and seized a rattlesnake which he took back to the valley and admonished the people to "take up or be doomed to eternal hell."[23]

The Holiness Church spread throughout the South and Southeast.[24] According to the defendants in *Swann*, the handling of snakes and the drinking of poison are not acts of faith but confirmation of the Word of God through the acknowledged signs set out in the Gospel of Mark. A congregant needs to be "anointed," which is not an act of the church but an encounter with the Holy Ghost. It is not a test of faith, or even of sincerity. As the lead defendant, Pastor Pack described it:

---

[23] State Ex Rel. Swann v. Pack, 527 S.W.2d 99, 105 (1975) (citations omitted).

[24] Snakehandling and Freedom of Religion, State ex rel. Swann v. Pack, 527 S.W.2d. 99 (Tenn. 1975), 1976 Wash. U. L. Q. 353 (1976).

It comes from inside . . . If you've got the Holy Ghost in you, it'll come out and nothing can hurt you. Faith brings contact with God and then you're anointed. It is not tempting God. You can't tempt God by doing what He says do. You can have faith, but if you never feel the anointing, you had better leave the serpent alone.

The events leading to the case of *Swann v. Pack* are consistent with these practices. At a service on April 7, 1973, snakes were being handled and poison (strychnine) was being drunk. One person was bitten by a snake and lived while two drank poison and died. At the funeral for one of the deceased, Pastor Pack attended and handled snakes.

Thereafter, the District Attorney for Cooke County in Tennessee sought an injunction to prevent any further handling or displaying of poisonous snakes or using strychnine or other "poisonous medicines."[25] As an alternative remedy, the authorities sought to shut down the church entirely, padlocking it if necessary.

The Supreme Court of Tennessee held that the Holiness Church was a constitutionally protected religious group, but such protection has limits. For example, in the 1878 case of *Reynolds v. U.S.*, the federal government sought to halt the practice of polygamy by the Church of Jesus Christ of Latter-Day Saints, colloquially known as the Mormons.[26] The U.S. Supreme Court in *Reynolds*

---

[25] *Swann*, 103. Note, for anyone reviewing the underlying case, the term "prayer" is used, a term for pleading the court rather than God. This might seem a surprising usage to the non-lawyer.

[26] Reynolds v. U.S., 98 U.S. 145 (1878).

held that while religious beliefs and opinions have strong protection under the First Amendment, religious behavior may be subjected to greater control. This is a key free-exercise clause that has held through to the present.

A practice may be backed by sincere belief, but the consequences of such action are the concern of government. Plural marriage, or polygamy, had long been unacceptable in the United States and Europe, even though there are numerous references to the practice in the Bible.[27] The nineteenth-century Latter-day Saint revival of polygamy as a Biblically sanctioned practice was curtailed under *Reynolds*, to the legal effect that a claim of a religious practice was not a defense against criminal prosecution.

U.S. courts have also invoked the example of "sati" as a religious tradition nonetheless subject to being banned. The practice of sati, or suttee, involved the wife of a Hindu man throwing herself on his funeral pyre.[28] Religious behaviors that threaten the life, health, or well-being of believers, or the public, are subject to higher scrutiny.

As the U.S. Supreme Court held in a later case, *Davis v. Beason*:

It was never intended or supposed that the [First] amendment could be invoked as a protection against legislation for the punishment of acts inimical to the peace, good order and morals of society. . . . To permit this would be to make the professed

---

[27] King Solomon is said to have had 700 wives and 300 concubines. 1 Kings 11:3.

[28] The practice of sati was banned by the Parliament of India in 1987. See the Commission of Sati (Prevention) Act, 1987.

doctrines of religious belief superior to the law of the land, and in effect—to permit every citizen to become a law unto himself.[29]

Belief and opinion are protected as "religion" but the practices, or "cultus" as referred to in *Davis*, does not receive the same freedom.[30] Freedom to believe is not the same as the freedom to act. It is worth noting, however, that the image of "good order and morals of society" bears a striking resemblance to European values, and protection of the "peace" requires the policing of Asian or African practices. A court's framing of these specific practices often relied upon religious, ethnic, and cultural revulsion as much as legal reasoning. Again, polygamy is squarely sanctioned in the Bible if not in the nineteenth-century United States.

With the holdings in *Reynolds* and *Davis* in mind, the Supreme Court of Tennessee restricted the religious practices of the Holiness Church and the congregation. This was done even though snake-handling practices were based on religious scripture, just like the polygamous marriages of the nineteenth-century Latter-day Saints. It is arguable, however, that the Tennessee case was an even more severe case and therefore a more likely situation for imposing such restrictions.

The *Swann* court struggled with the scope of the problem, trying in theory to limit the reach of its ruling. The case was not criminal in nature but an effort to stop a public nuisance, that is, anything that endangers life or health, gives offense to the senses,

---

[29] Davis v. Beason, 133 U.S. 333, 342 (1890).

[30] *Davis*, 338.

violates the laws of decency, etc.[31] The court therefore needed to tailor its decision to stop the nuisance-causing aspects of snake handling and poison drinking. However, the "endangers life or health" aspect of the practices effectively made this impossible. As the court wryly noted, "Most assuredly the handling of poisonous snakes by untrained persons and the drinking of strychnine are not calculated to increase one's life span."[32] Tailoring the remedy was therefore difficult to achieve when the religious practices are inherently dangerous, both to the public who might enter the church and for children who are a part of the congregation.

The underlying trial judge for *Swann* enjoined the handling of snakes, though he allowed the drinking of strychnine which had led to the deaths of two congregants. The appeals court modified the snake-handling provision to prevent "the handling, displaying or exhibiting dangerous and poisonous snakes in such manner as will endanger the life or health of persons who do not consent to exposure to such danger." Upon review of the matter, the Supreme Court of Tennessee chose to ban everything.

The *Swann* court could have limited these practices in some manner, such as restricting them for members only or requiring they be performed without the presence of children. It could have imposed a consent requirement, however that might have played out in a fervent worship service of the spirit. The court reasoned that it would have to limit some aspect of the Holiness Church's religious freedom, whether the religious right to raise

---

[31] *Swann*, 113.

[32] *Swann*, 113.

children in a certain way or to evangelize to non-members. Instead, it ordered the practices to stop, snakes and poison alike, there being no reasonable way in the mind of the court of removing these nuisances as protentional threats of harm. That is perhaps true.

But there is an inkling of something else in the tone of the court: embarrassment. It is evidenced by gratuitous side comments about the strange practices of the church—men kissing each other on the lips, no use of traditional medicine, and no drinking of coffee, tea, or carbonated beverages. Those religious behaviors were not at issue, but the *Swann* court arguably uses them to paint a vivid image of weirdness in the context of the United States in 1975. And such a sense of cultural oddity, of otherness, will be a peripheral theme in other cases. That same mindset may have curtailed the court from searching terribly far for compromise in its blanket decision, which the U.S. Supreme Court declined to review.[33]

After the decision, Pastor Pack and two church members spoke to a *New York Times* reporter about their church's ways and history.[34] The reporter voiced a broad concern in the article that the *Swann* decision implied a threat to religious freedom on the eve of the nation's Bicentennial celebrations. The implications of *Swann* may have suggested a judicial tightening around questions of freedom of exercise, or it may have signaled a growing fatigue of the U.S. Supreme Court and other judges having to hear such thorny religious cases.

---

[33] *Swann*, 365.

[34] Lisa Alther, "They shall take up serpents," *New York Times*, June 6, 1976, nytimes.com/1976/06/06/archives/they-shall-take-up-serpents-serpents.html.

Handling Snakes

But the worry of the *Swann* court, that the state had the right to guard against the creation of widows and orphans, may have been borne out. After the decision, Pastor Pack described to the *Times* reporter the practice of snake handling: "Anyone who participates in the serpent handling, we don't tell them what to do, but we'd rather if they're going to handle serpents and get bit, just to trust the Lord even if it takes them to the hillside to be buried."[35]

---

[35] Ibid.

CHAPTER 4

Disestablishment

"Antidisestablishmentarianism" was once reputed to be the longest word in the English language, barring chemical names and other jargon. It was therefore a high-water mark for elementary school spelling bee hopefuls. But what exactly does it mean? Those who oppose the withdrawal of public financial support for, or official recognition of, a state-approved church.

Chop off the prefixes and suffixes from that unwieldy word and you are left with "establish." This legal term is front and center in the First Amendment of the Constitution. It may not seem as personally meaningful as protecting the free exercise of religion, but prohibiting Congress from establishing a religion was critically important to the original colonies. Not that these states were against established religion. Several had already established their own and sought to resist these being toppled.

New England states like Massachusetts, Connecticut, New Hampshire, and Vermont had established Congregationalist churches, while other states like New York, Virginia, Georgia, and the Carolinas established, or perhaps reestablished, the Church of England. Some states like Rhode Island and Pennsylvania, which had large populations of Baptist and Quaker settlers who had often clashed with other established churches, did not establish churches at all.

An established church was supported by taxes. You did not have to be a member of the church to be taxed for its support, a point of great frustration for minority religious groups like the Baptists, Quakers, and Universalists. These religious traditions differed in varying ways from the Congregationalists and Anglicans on matters of religious doctrine. Baptists, for example, did not believe in the baptism of children but rather supported "believer's baptism," or the baptism of adults. Universalists, as the name implies, taught universal salvation of souls, a stark point of disagreement with traditional Congregationalists of the Reformed tradition.

This taxation system led to paying for something you neither used nor ever wanted. The goal of the system was to support a public institution of moral learning and the ministers of these established churches were the designated teachers. Supporters of the system saw this as meeting the goal of instilling proper values in a community. Not surprisingly, opponents pointed out that what was being taught as "moral" was not always consistent with their own religious traditions.

The restriction in the Constitution was a hedge against the new federal government stepping in and establishing a federal church. The colonies that became the original states were not exactly kindred cultures, particularly religiously. They could be described as culturally and religiously remote cousins more than closely knit siblings. The federal system was designed not to intrude too deeply into the powers of those member states. The Tenth Amendment reflects this concern: "The powers not delegated to the United States by the Constitution, nor prohibited by it to the States, are reserved to the States respectively, or to the people." This amendment has in some ways been effectively edited out of the Constitution by the post-Civil War amendments, but it was intended to limit the federal government's reach and to enshrine the existing prerogatives of the various states.

The hoped-for protection against federal involvement in religious matters, however, did not account for the evolution of the sentiments of citizens. As the states developed and religious backgrounds became more diverse, resentment grew against supporting a religious institution not one's own. Perhaps the examples of Rhode Island and Pennsylvania, without established churches, served as ongoing tax-free reminders. And some of the leading figures of the American Revolution became strong voices for religious freedom and against established churches.

Thomas Jefferson famously called for "building a wall of separation between Church and State."[36] Jefferson was from the Commonwealth of Virginia, which had established the Church of England before the war. In 1776, on the eve of the American colonies declaring independence, Virginia adopted its Declara-

---

[36] Thomas Jefferson, "Letter to a Committee of the Danbury Baptist Association," January 1, 1802.

tion of Rights, which included religious freedom as one of its essential values:

> That religion, or the duty which we owe to our Creator, and the manner of discharging it, can be directed only by reason and conviction, not by force or violence; and therefore all men are equally entitled to the free exercise of religion, according to the dictates of conscience; and that it is the mutual duty of all to practise [sic] Christian forbearance, love, and charity toward each other.

The astute reader might notice certain assumptions in the text. "All men" suggests a narrowing of the field, though some might argue that at that time "men" was intended to include everyone. That modern suggestion of kindly intent, however, would gloss over women having few legal rights at that time and enslaved Africans and Indigenous people possessing practically none.

The final call for the practice of "Christian forbearance, love, and charity" may seem odd within a document calling for freedom from such specific expectations. It is reminiscent of a story about a British negotiator working with Jewish settlers and Palestinian Muslims before the founding of the State of Israel. The discussions were going nowhere and the British man exclaimed in frustration, "Can't you settle your differences like good *Christians!*" "Christian" is used as a generic term of virtue rather than a specific religious tradition that might imply differences across denominations. At least, that is *one* way to hear it.

The Declaration of Rights, even with its limitations, was a point of progress toward religious freedom and became a building block for further development of this desire for religious freedom. It was used by Thomas Jefferson as a resource from which the Declaration of Independence was drafted. As for the later debates over disestablishing churches, the Declaration may have also offered the seeds of change: "Governments are instituted among Men, deriving their just powers from the consent of the governed, [and] That whenever any Form of Government becomes destructive of these ends, it is the Right of the People to alter or to abolish it. . . ."[37]

The New England states were historically strong supporters of established churches.[38] As Massachusetts drafted its post-Revolution constitution in 1780, its leaders were reminded of their duty to instill morality in society. "Rulers should encourage [religion and virtue] not only by their example, but by their authority . . . [and] should have power to provide for the institution and support of the public worship of God, and public teachers of religion and virtue."[39]

And here is the relevant part of the text of the Massachusetts Constitution of 1780 as adopted:

---

[37] "Declaration of Independence: A Transcription," National Archives, archives.gov/founding-docs/declaration-transcript.

[38] See, e.g., Nathan S. Rives, "'Is This Not a Paradox?' Public Morality and the Unitarian Defense of State-Supported Religion in Massachusetts, 1806–1833," *New England Quarterly* 86, no. 2 (June 2013): 232–265. doi.org/10.1162/TNEQ_a_00277.

[39] Rives, 236 (from a sermon by Simeon Howard to the legislature).

Disestablishment

As the happiness of a people and the good order and preservation of civil government essentially depend upon piety, religion, and morality, and as these cannot be generally diffused through a community but by the institution of the public worship of God and of the public instructions in piety, religion, and morality: Therefore, To promote their happiness and to secure the good order and preservation of their government, the people of this commonwealth have a right to invest their legislature with power to authorize and require, and the legislature shall, from time to time, authorize and require, the several towns, parishes, precincts, and other bodies-politic or religious societies to make suitable provision, at their own expense, for the institution of the public worship of God and for the support and maintenance of public Protestant teachers of piety, religion, and morality in all cases where such provision shall not be made voluntarily.[40]

Again, the "teachers" in question would be Congregationalist ministers preaching in Congregationalist churches supported by taxes drawn from Congregationalists and non-Congregationalists. This was akin to supporting a public school. Massachusetts had founded the first public school in 1635, the Boston Latin School, which still exists. And while there was no question that "piety, religion, and morality" were to be taught as set down in 1780, the questions of who did so and what was included in those lessons would fester in Massachusetts for at least the next 52 years until Massachusetts' disestablishment—and even long after.

---

[40] "Massachusetts Declaration of Rights—Article Three," Massachusetts Law Updates, blog.mass.gov/masslawlib/legal-history/massachusetts-declaration-of -rights-article-3/.

Congregationalists encouraged reading the Bible and therefore literacy was supported by public institutions. Just as there
was no wall at that time separating church from state, there was
no wall separating church from school. The religious push toward
literacy caused the need for publicly funded education, which
may in hindsight appear as a "liberal" goal. Churches served as
schools as well as town meetinghouses. In early New England,
the only publicly supported building in a town might have been
the meetinghouse, which served as the seat of religion, government, and education. As those New England towns developed
and as the population became more diverse, the overlapping
responsibilities came into question.

In 1833 Massachusetts was the last state to disestablish its
church, meaning no further state funding of churches or their
ministers. Leading up to that event, religious groups either supported or dissented from the Standing Order, as it was called.
The Standing Order referred to the system of taxation, the supported churches, and the connection between church and parish, the latter meaning the geographic area served by the church.

Some groups, like Quakers and Baptists, had doggedly sought
exemption from paying taxes that supported Standing Order
churches, even petitioning the English king for help. In 1728,
their efforts resulted in the Five Mile Act. Quakers and "Anabaptists" would be freed from paying religious taxes or going to jail
for failing to pay them. This act required that they attended
another church within five miles of their homes, a decidedly
strong way of encouraging Sunday attendance. Quakers were
further expected to swear an oath to the King that they accepted
the doctrine of the Trinity and the divine inspiration of the

Bible.[41] If such a demand for an oath based upon required religious doctrines appears intrusive coming from the government, the treatment of the Church of Latter-day Saints in a later chapter may seem openly hostile (spoiler: it was).

The tug-of-war between the Congregationalists versus Anglicans, Baptists, Quakers, and Universalists continued in Massachusetts for decades. The pressure that arguably brought about the end of the Standing Order, however, came from within the Congregationalists. Doctrinal disputes had erupted between two groups, the so-called Trinitarians and Unitarians. The term "Unitarian" was initially intended as an insult, for to deny the validity of the Trinity—the Father, Son, and Holy Ghost—was seen as a rejection of a basic element of Christian faith.

Unitarianism was far more than a dispute over the formulation of the Trinity. Unitarians adopted a rational approach to religion and in doing so grew suspicious of religious doctrine that relied solely on faith. For example, the term "Trinity" does not appear in the Bible and the phrase "Father, Son, and Holy Ghost" appears once in the Gospel of Matthew. The early Unitarians did not necessarily reject any of those three entities, or even their organization, but many could not accept the assumptions made about them without either support in the Bible or arriving at those same conclusions through reason.[42]

---

[41] William McLoughlin, *New England Dissent 1630–1883: The Baptists and the Separation of Church and State, Volume I* (Cambridge: Harvard University Press, 1971).

[42] See, e.g., Conrad Wright, *Three Prophets of Liberal Religion: Channing, Emerson, and Parker,* (Boston: Skinner House, 1986), 57. From William Ellery Channing's Baltimore Sermon of 1819.

In the same vein, Unitarians sought self-improvement and supported moral cultivation as the pathway to salvation. Calvinist Congregationalism had long taught that salvation came through faith in God alone and that "good works" and charity had no bearing on the matter.[43] Only God knew if you were saved and there was no way of discovering that fate in this life. Unitarians rejected both salvation through faith alone and the lifelong anxiety it often inspired in sinners, who worried whether they and their loved ones would spend eternity in hell. While the name "Unitarian" suggests a narrow dispute, the weightier difference was arguably the change in expectations of behavior and what needed to be taught to achieve and cultivate heavenly virtue.[44] And so, if the preacher and teacher under the Standing Order was offering lessons from the Unitarian perspective, a Trinitarian[45] might take offense. And they did.

The trajectory of disestablishment took a different form in the early nineteenth century, as Unitarians and Trinitarians internally struggled to control Standing Order churches. Central to that struggle was control over an American institution that was ancient even then: Harvard College (now Harvard University). Founded in 1636, Harvard is the oldest college in the United States. Recall that Congregationalists valued literacy

---

[43] "John Calvin: Reply to Sadoleto" in *The Protestant Reformation*, ed. Hans Hillerbrand (New York: Harper Perennial, 1968), 162.

[44] Wright, *Three Prophets of Liberal Religion*, 78.

[45] Congregationalists following the Calvinist tradition preferred to be called "Orthodox." See McLoughlin at 1195. There are also occasional references to this term in legal cases of that time. But with Greek Orthodox and Russian Orthodox churches being more familiar to a modern audience, the sensibilities of this more historically distant group must be placed aside.

and learning because of their central focus on reading the Bible. They also required learned ministers to propagate the faith and to teach religion and values in the churches. And Harvard trained ministers.

Originally a stalwart of traditional thinking, Harvard liberalized over time in keeping with Enlightenment philosophy and other new perspectives coming out of Europe. In 1805, Harvard selected Henry Ware, a liberal Unitarian, to become the professor of divinity of the college, much to the consternation of the Trinitarians. In 1816, the Harvard Divinity School was founded. It signaled a distinct shift from traditional Calvinism to the new Unitarian outlook.

These high-visibility disputes among ministers and theologians perhaps did not have much impact on the day-to-day expectations of churches. Taxes were still being collected and minister's salaries paid. Control over those churches was a different phase of the struggle, as reflected in a legal dispute known as the "Dedham case."

Dedham, Massachusetts, had a Standing Order church, but a dispute erupted when time came to choose a new minister in 1818. The Dedham parish chose Alan Lamson, a recent graduate of the Unitarian-leaning Harvard Divinity School. The parish does not equate to the church (i.e., the congregation), however, and the Trinitarian members of the congregation did not want Lamson, a Unitarian, in their pulpit. A council of outside parties, which consisted mostly of Unitarians, was convened to consider the question. Eventually, the Trinitarians grew frustrated with the process and its seemingly inevitable conclusion. The dissident church members walked out, taking the church silver, funds, and records and setting out to build a new, more ortho-dox church.

This church fight became a divorce in most senses of the term. The legal case of *Baker v. Fales* was filed, and the Unitarians within the parish sought relief by the hoary practice of *replevin*, an ancient legal way of saying "I want my stuff back." They were looking for the return of the records, the silver, and a not incon-siderable amount of money.

The decision ultimately required the return of all three in 1820, but by that point the Trinitarian dissidents had been excommunicated from the church, leaving them without any legal standing within the Standing Order institution. This dis-placement led to the Trinitarian Congregationalists having to seek permission from the state to withdraw from the parish tax system their forebears had created and that they had relied upon for centuries. The irony thickens.

They were treated in the same manner as if they were Quak-ers or Baptists, an unexpected and karmic result that led to flag-ging interest among orthodox Calvinists in continuing support for the Standing Order. It is all well and good to receive parish taxes to support the expenses of the church, but bearing the bur-den without receiving the benefit became a less attractive result. The Trinitarians as a group did not give up on the Standing Order quite yet, but as the influence of Unitarians grew in Massachu-setts churches, so did the shift of Trinitarians away from the institution of a state-established church.

The Unitarians, however, held firmly on to that position of support. It is perhaps surprising to imagine such a perspective in a group that turned to reason as the basis of its religious engagement, as if reason would support such an uneven system. And yet the Congregationalists themselves had been dissident Puritans seeking to escape the control of the Church of England only in turn to impose the Standing Order enshrining their own control. After winning the race, it is often hard to give up the prize. And the Unitarians had successfully wrested away control of many Standing Order churches and of Harvard.

Moreover, Unitarians of the time were passionately concerned with moral cultivation and social progress. This emphasis in their religious lives helped to foster many of the progressive movements of the nineteenth century, such as the abolition of slavery and the pursuit of women's suffrage. With all those good works remaining to be accomplished, one might argue, the Standing Order could serve as a statewide pulpit from which to teach such moral messages, which were to Unitarians the means of salvation for individuals and society alike.

The question resulting from this dispute between the Standing Order factions is about what is being protected. Those in power, in the majority, or in ascendance suggest that "Religion" is being promoted rather than "a religion."[46] It is hard to argue that morality, ethics, and virtue are bad for society. But if that moral instruction takes the form of a particular religious tradition, other moral, ethical, and virtuous people have reason to be upset if they happen to be dissenters from the doctrines of that one tradition. Even as the Quakers were forced to swear oaths accepting the doctrine of the Trinity, so other religious groups may be placed in an uncomfortable position of acquiescence. Either

---

[46] E.g., Rives, "Is This Not a Paradox?" 250.

accept the Standing Order as it takes shape under the control of another religious group or reject the system to preserve one's spiritual integrity while incurring varying degrees of social and economic costs.

Even after the final disestablishment of the last state-funded churches in 1833, the struggle to disentangle religious majority control over moral education would continue in the context of public schools. This ongoing societal dispute particularly fueled tensions between old European enemies: Catholics and Protestants.

CHAPTER 5

Drafting the Bill of Rights

BEFORE CONSIDERING the creation of the Bill of Rights, a moment to consider the creation of an idea for a new nation, an idea that admittedly starts out with certain limitations and progresses from there. What the early United States was is not the same as what the United States has become: bigger, more centralized, more diverse, etc. These changes may be a point of pride or a source of frustration, depending on one's perspective.

In discussions about religious rights, there is occasionally an assertion that the United States was founded as a Christian nation. A more accurate assessment might be that the United States was founded as a nation filled with Christian settlers or, actually, various groups of Protestants. Catholics[47] and Jews[48]

---

[47] The Colonial Williamsburg Foundation, "Catholics in British America," The American Revolution, ouramericanrevolution.org/index.cfm/page/view/p0155.

[48] Jonathan D. Sarna, "The Impact of the American Revolution on American Jews," *Modern Judaism* 1, no. 2 (1981), 149.

were few in number, respectively 25,000 and 2,500 out of approximately 4,000,000 people in late eighteenth-century America. These small numbers likely relate to the limited rights of Catholics and Jews to emigrate to, or to take up residence in, many of the states.

There was also probably a large number of Muslims in colonial America, all likely enslaved West Africans. Other Africans would have held traditional religious beliefs depending on their tribe or area of origin, whether Yoruba, Igbo, etc. It would be difficult however, to determine any religious census, though estimates of Muslim enslaved peoples alone range into the tens of thousands.[49] And there were Indigenous peoples' religious traditions of long-standing presence and little legal standing.[50] Needless to say, these were not religious voices present in the debates.

Catholics and Jews faced varying degrees of hostility and limitations of rights. Enslaved people were treated as legal objects, that is, chattel, and held few if any rights. Indigenous people were in legal limbo when they were not the subject of open hostilities. Again, declaring that the United States was founded as a nation

---

[49] Michael A. Gomez, "Muslims in Early America," *The Journal of Southern History* 60, no. 4 (1994): 682.

[50] Indigenous peoples' religious traditions were not protected, which should not come as a shock in light of overall treatment of Indigenous people. Military power was even used to prevent the performance of religious rituals. A century after the Bill of Rights was promulgated, the Commissioner of Indian Affairs issued rules with the goal of stamping out "demoralizing and barbarous" customs, meaning cornerstone religious practices of the Lakota community, including the Sun Dance and Ghost Dance. See John Rhodes, "An American Tradition: The Religious Persecution of Native Americans," *Montana Law Review* 52, no. 1 (1991). This dispute leads to the Wounded Knee Massacre in 1890 and the death of 250 Lakota.

of Christians makes many assumptions, about who was present at the negotiation tables and about who mattered in those
closed-door conversations.

And, to embellish this argument, the United States could be
specifically described as a nation founded by and for free white
Protestant males who owned property. For example, under the
Massachusetts Constitution of 1780, the following could vote:
"every male inhabitant of twenty-one year of age and upwards,
having a freehold estate of the value of sixty pounds."[51] The subsequent Naturalization Act of 1790 specified that foreign born
individuals could become citizens of the United States if they
were "free white person[s]." Most Black people could not legally
vote until the Fifteenth Amendment was ratified in 1870, women
until the Nineteenth Amendment was ratified in 1920, and Indigenous people until the Indian Citizenship Act of 1924. A land
containing a diverse range of people was the setting for a new
government founded by and for a small group of men.

Clearly, the colonial era decision makers were capable of
restricting rights to a small minority, replicating an aristocratic
system based on land, wealth, and race rather than lineage.
And yet those people, that scant handful of men, chose not to
do so for religion. They adopted a series of constitutional provisions that, in their historical context, were intended to provide a
strong degree of protection for religious rights, specifically protection *from* the new United States government. In practice, this
would become a complicated legacy for religious groups like

---

[51] Mass. Constitution of 1780, Part the Second, I, 2, II. Sixty English pounds
sterling would be worth approximately $11,000 in 2020.

Jews, Catholics, and Latter-day Saints, as will be seen. But the intent was broadly to protect individual rights of religious conscience. As one writer suggests about early United States ideals:

> The Declaration of Independence laid emphasis not only on the worth of the individual but on the individual's right to determine his or her own religious beliefs and to act on those beliefs. Indeed, the individual gained a religious freedom that had never before been known on such a large scale at any time or place in history.[52]

Why was this the case? Likely because the various states had contended over religious freedom in many ways. Much like in England, American Catholics were held in low esteem. At one point before the American Revolution, they were forced to flee from the previously welcoming shores of Maryland to the still hospitable borders of Pennsylvania. Quakers and Baptists were driven southward from Puritan Massachusetts to Rhode Island, established by Roger Williams, a dissident preacher who also founded the First Baptist Church in America. In other words, these men were creating a system of religious rights to protect themselves from *each other*.

While the notion of separation between church and state is often attributed to Thomas Jefferson, much of the intellectual energy behind these rights came from his fellow Virginian, James Madison, who has been called the Father of the Consti-

---

[52] Derek H. Davis, *Religion and the Continental Congress 1774–1789: Contributions to Original Intent* (Oxford: Oxford University Press, 2000), 151.

tution. Madison was ostensibly an Episcopalian but studied at the College of New Jersey, later known as Princeton, which was founded as a Presbyterian institution. Presbyterians often found themselves in the role of dissenting church, under the Church of England, in the Episcopalian South, and even in the Congregationalist North. This frequent experience of minority status cultivated their support for religious rights. And that freedom-seeking culture among the Presbyterians likely molded the sensibilities of a young Madison.

Madison was involved in the drafting of the Virginia Declaration of Rights of 1776. Original language by George Mason called for the state's government to "tolerate" the religious rights of individuals. Tolerate: a verb used to imply that something unwelcome or unpleasant is to be endured or allowed to exist, like a rash. Rather than use "toleration" as the measure of freedom, Madison instead proposed a successful amendment to the Declaration that protected the "free exercise of religion, according to the dictates of conscience."[53]

In order to secure ratification of the 1787 Constitution, Madison and other fellow Federalists had promised to seek amendments to protect, among other civil rights, religious liberty. In 1789, in keeping with this promise and the sentiments of the Virginia Declaration, Madison drafted the first set of amendments to the then newly adopted Constitution. These were eventually referred to as the Bill of Rights. However, when they were offered, the amendments were little more than the proposals of

---

[53] Virginia Declaration of Rights, collected in *Constitutional Debates on Freedom of Religion: A Documentary History*, eds. John J. Patrick and Gerald P. Long (Westport: Greenwood, 1999), 38.

a concerned representative of the people trying to keep a difficult promise.

Imagine that.

In the first session of Congress, the newly selected representatives and senators had gathered to establish the basic requirements of a new nation. The individual states had their own governmental infrastructure, such as court systems and taxes, but the federal government was in its infancy. At that historical moment, the United States consisted of only eleven of the original thirteen colonies who fought in the war. Rhode Island and North Carolina had yet to ratify the Constitution. Some of these ratification votes were close ones, as suggested by the Federalists' pledge to seek amendments. Massachusetts ratified with a vote of 187–168, New Hampshire 57–47, New York 30–27, and Virginia 89–79. The tight Massachusetts vote in particular may have been swayed toward acceptance by the promise that amendments protecting various rights would be considered by the new Congress.

Conversely, Rhode Island had yet to vote, perhaps as a consequence of the U.S. Constitution having no express provisions protecting religious freedom. Rhode Island's 1663 royal charter provided that "No person within the said colony, at any time hereafter shall be any wise molested, punished, disquieted, or called into question, for any differences in opinion in matters of religion. . . ."[54] The state arose as a haven from religious intolerance and the prospect of handing away any aspect of such freedom to the federal government, even in theory, may have been

---

[54] Patrick and Long, 16.

unappealing. It might be observed that while both Massachusetts and Rhode Island were seeking protection from the federal government, Massachusetts was effectively protecting its existing *system* of religious establishment while Rhode Island was protecting free exercise of religion by *individuals*. This is perhaps confusing from a modern perspective because the First Amendment as drafted was not intended to affect the states. That all changed after the American Civil War with the Fourteenth Amendment, which has been relied upon to apply First Amendment protections against the states, as will be discussed in greater detail in subsequent chapters.

Similar concerns were championed by a group of writers from various states known as the Anti-Federalists, such as Patrick Henry of Virginia. They were concerned that the new Constitution did not contain express protections of individual rights, took too much control away from the states, and risked concentrating power in the new role of "President" that could become monarch-like. Federalists supported greater central control, as the name implies, but some, like Madison, were sympathetic to the concern about religious liberty.

In light of such debates, and the close ratification votes, Madison offered a speech to the newly formed Congress on June 8, 1789, proposing a list of amendments to the Constitution of 1787.[55] He expressly did so on behalf of these others who were

---

[55] Madison proposed interspersing the various changes directly into the text of the Constitution, a process also known as interlineation. Some members of Congress saw this proposed process as beyond the language provided in Article V of the Constitution regarding amendments. Perhaps more concerning, it was confusing to follow. The Bill of Rights would eventually be separated and

concerned about the lack of overt protections of liberty in the Constitution, which concern he chided as "mistaken in its object but laudable in its motive."[56]

This mildly negative judgment of those questions may have been more rhetoric for an audience than heartfelt belief. Madison had notably and consistently championed religious rights and the separation of church and state in his home state of Virginia. As he stated in his "Memorial and Remonstrance Against Religious Assessments," a text against reestablishing a church in Virginia, "it is proper to take alarm at the first experiment on our liberties . . . the same authority which can establish Christianity, in exclusion of all other Religions, may establish with the same ease any particular sect of Christians, in exclusion of all other Sects?"[57]

At the first session of Congress, with regard to religion, Madison proposed inserting into the Constitution, "The civil rights of none shall be abridged on account of religious belief or worship, nor shall any national religion be established, nor shall the full and equal rights of conscience be in any manner, or on any pretext, infringed."[58] Madison further sought to amend the Constitution to limit the ability of the *states*: "No State shall violate the equal rights of conscience, or the freedom of the press, or the trial by jury in criminal cases. . . ."

---

appended as a list, which editorially speaking was a more convenient model for posterity.

[56] Patrick and Long, *Constitutional Debates*, 61.

[57] Patrick and Long, 50.

[58] Patrick and Long, 61–62.

Congress agreed to consider the amendments, tasking a committee to further pursue the matter so that other business before the body could be pursued. The committee submitted back to Congress a revised version of the provision regarding religion: "no religion shall be established by law, nor shall the equal rights of Conscience be infringed."[59]

Madison's proposal regarding controlling the states' right to legislate regarding "equal rights of conscience" did not survive. Any effort to use the Constitution to impose controls by the federal government upon the various states would have been a controversial move, noting that such amendments would need to be ratified by those states. One of the primary arguments against a Bill of Rights was that the federal government *had no power* to infringe upon such rights, whether of the states or individuals. By this line of thinking, the powers of the federal government had been specifically enumerated in the Constitution and all other power rested elsewhere, whether with the states or in the hands of the people. This mindset was later bootstrapped by the Ninth and Tenth Amendments, protecting the legal rights of the people and the states respectively. These amendments are now fleeting constitutional afterthoughts, of little seeming effect.

As one speaker in that 1789 Congress, Roger Sherman of Connecticut, noted, "the amendment [regarding a national religion is] altogether unnecessary, inasmuch as Congress had no authority whatever delegated to them by the constitution to make religious establishments," and he therefore moved to have

---

[59] Annals of Congress, 1st Session, 757.

the proposed provision stricken out.[60] Daniel Carroll of Maryland, one of the few Catholics in Congress, disagreed: "[M]any sects have concurred in opinion that they are not well secured under the present construction," and that he was much in favor of the adoption as it would "tend more towards conciliating the minds of the people to the Government than almost any other Amendment he had heard proposed."[61]

Benjamin Huntington of Connecticut invoked his neighbor Rhode Island to express his support for the language, seeing Rhode Island "enjoying the blessed fruits" of such liberty. But he also lodged a concern, that the language proposed for supporting religion should not be used by those *opposing* religion. "He hoped, therefore, the amendment would be made in such a way as to secure the rights of conscience, and free exercise of the rights of religion, but not to patronize those who professed no religion at all."[62] This seems to have been an effort to protect state patronage of established churches against those unwilling to pay the related taxes.

The stories of these various men play a significant role in how they understand these arguments over setting forth civil rights in the U.S. Constitution. Religious outsiders like Daniel Carroll, a Catholic, perceived a clear need. Benjamin Huntington, a Connecticut Congregationalist, accepted a theoretical need but drew the line at a practical application that might intrude upon the existing system of taxes supporting established churches. Mas-

---

[60] Annals of Congress, 757–758.

[61] Annals of Congress, 758.

[62] Ibid.

sachusetts voiced similar concerns while Rhode Island sought more definitive expressions of religious rights. The circles being drawn around the areas of influence of religion and the law were being suggested based upon the personal experiences of those very few men in the room.

Madison, himself influenced by the religious-freedom loving Presbyterians, sought to explain his understanding of the proposed protections for rights of conscience. He thought the meaning of the words to be, "that Congress should not establish a religion, and enforce the legal observation of it by law, nor compel men to worship God in any manner contrary to their conscience." Such restrictions on federal power had been sought by various states. And as the Constitution was framed to enable the Congress to make laws, it would be reasonable to limit that power to prevent Congress from infringing on rights of conscience or to establish a national religion.

Note that these accounts of the debate among the members of the First Session of Congress is the account of an observer. It was most likely a clerk furiously scratching down the dialogue with a feather quill. It would most likely have been abbreviated, and the highlights may reflect what one person thought more important than the rest. Which is a hazard of history.

Madison focused on the terms "conscience" and "right of conscience." What did he mean? Looking to his extended writing on the subject of religious rights, "Memorial and Remonstrance Against Religious Assessments," Madison is referring to an unalienable right, one subject to neither society nor government. That one's duty to the Creator may only be directed by reason and conviction and that religion must be left to one's individual "conviction and conscience."[63] Conviction could imply either faith or choice, while conscience suggests reason as the mental faculty by which that faith is born out or such choices are made. Madison was seeking to protect religious rights and may also have been seeking to craft a right of freedom from religion, as one's conscience dictated.

The House voted to send the following proposed amendment to the Senate for consideration: "Congress shall make no law establishing religion, or to prevent the free exercise thereof, or to infringe the rights of conscience." The Senate deliberated over this language from September 3 to September 9, 1789. There is no record of those debates as the Senate deliberated in secret. The final text transmitted back to the House was: "Congress shall make no law establishing articles of faith or a mode of worship, or prohibiting the free exercise of religion."

The Senate language is quite different and sharply curtailed, reducing the scope of protection against establishment and striking out the reference to rights of conscience. The limitations on establishing articles of faith or modes of worship could have allowed for the creation of a national religion, provided creed and the liturgy were not specified. This result would have been inconsistent with the tenor of the debate in the House. The Senate sought to prevent the choice of a specific religious denomination, effectively leaving open the possibility of a generic, federal religion.

A joint committee of the House and Senate met to reconcile the two proposals. The final language was adopted and merged

---

[63] Patrick and Long, *Constitutional Debates*, 50.

with several other amendments on freedom of speech, freedom of the press, and others. The provision remains unchanged in the Bill of Rights: "Congress shall make no law respecting an establishment of religion, or prohibiting the free exercise thereof. . . ."

The revision of the House amendment by the Senate, deleting the term "rights of conscience," suggests that the Congress sought to pinpoint the practice of religion generally rather than the right to reason freely about religion. That may seem a subtle distinction, but if the protection applies to the choice made rather than to the means for choosing, then the right protects religion rather than one's philosophical or ethical process. Again, while freedom of speech protects the ability to express an opinion, religious freedom takes the extra step toward protecting behaviors and modes of worship, as well as religiously motivated actions.

On balance, the House debates and the series of language changes suggest that the Congress sought to protect "religion" in broad terms and to protect the particulars of religious exercise. No national religion dictated by Congress. But "free exercise" of religion would be protected.

What does that mean for those who want religious values but not religious specifics? What does that mean for those seeking freedom from the religious expectations of the majority? Freedom to be left alone? These questions have not been satisfactorily answered even to the present day.

CHAPTER 6

Legal Misfits in the United States: Jews, Catholics, and Latter-day Saints

A JEW, A CATHOLIC, AND A MORMON walk into a bar . . .
What popped into your head? Anything at all?

As befits a joke, this series of religious identities should some-how follow a drumbeat pattern, one of well-worn expectations commonly held by one group about, or against, another. This list would follow a set of stereotypes of these three groups, gener-ally negative ones. Those stock images are sadly not confined to jokes but have spilled over into social policy, legal disputes, and even laws passed by legislative bodies. The United States has, at times, been a difficult environment in which religious communi-ties have sought to live and to assimilate.

What does it mean not to fit in? Some aspect of one's person-ality, appearance, or behavior does not mesh with the group, the community, or the society. When such ill-received qualities are attributed generally to a religion rather than embodied in an individual, the lack of fit arises from prejudice, the prejudging of a person due to stereotypic assumptions about their identity.

Many religious groups have struggled to become a part of the fabric of American society. Three are notable either because of the enduring nature of the prejudice against them or the vehemence of historic responses against the group. These are Jews, Catholics, and Latter-day Saints. Jehovah's Witnesses have also had notable difficulties and Muslims are currently struggling as pronounced targets of bigotry. Some legal cases involving each will be discussed in later chapters. During the formative time of the nineteenth-century United States, however, Jews, Catholics, and Latter-day Saints faced pervasive and sustained prejudice.

Jews in the United States

Early Christians were persecuted by Roman emperors when bad events required handy scapegoats. In that tragic tradition, European kings more than occasionally laid the blame upon the Jewish people. Anti-Semitic tendencies are often a legacy of certain Christian views about Jews, amplifying or distorting aspects of the New Testament. Even the term "New Testament" suggests a displacement of the "Old Testament," a religious perspective known as supersessionism. This term describes the assumed replacement of Jews by Christians as the chosen people of God. In this way, religious cousins became estranged during the early years of Christian expansion. Later, European history would become rife with pogroms, ghettos, and other forms of Jewish persecution.

In the American colonies, anti-Semitism existed but was less prevalent owing to small numbers of Jews emigrating. At the time of the Continental Congress, there were an estimated 1,300 to 3,000 Jews in the United States, less than 0.1 percent of the population.[64] The American colonies were by no means a hospitable place for Jews, but relatively speaking they were often better than European alternatives—the frying pan is a marginally safer place than the fire.

In 1654, twenty-three Jewish refugees arrived from Brazil to the port of New Amsterdam in the New Netherlands, later known as New York City. These refugees were fleeing the invading forces of Portugal, who had seized the South American port of Recife from the more religiously tolerant Dutch. Most of the fleeing Jews returned to Europe, but a few made their way north.

Peter Stuyvesant, the leader of the New Netherlands, was not pleased with this development. He was an elder in the Reformed Church and the son of a minister. He had previously blocked public worship by emigrating Lutherans, and he harbored no more fond feeling for the Jewish refugees, calling them "deceitful" and "repugnant," among other labels.[65] He suggested to his superiors in the Dutch West India Company that these new arrivals be required to depart in a "friendly way."

The company, however, was implored by Dutch Jews to permit the refugees to stay, for reasons including that many share-

---

[64] Jonathan Sarna, *American Judaism: A History* (New Haven: Yale University Press, 2004), 375.

[65] Sarna, 2; Morris Schappes, ed., *A Documentary History of the Jews in the United States 1654–1875* (New York: Citadel Press, 1950), 1.

holders of the company were members of the "Jewish nation."[66] Jews in New Amsterdam remained restricted in various ways, such as being forbidden to purchase a home or to open retail sales establishments,[67] but they eventually secured from the Dutch administrators civic rights nearly on par with other groups. The opposition of Stuyvesant eventually gave way to the persistence of the Jewish community of New Amsterdam.[68]

In 1793, the Commonwealth of Pennsylvania reported the first legal case relating to the free exercise of religion after ratification of the U.S. Constitution and the creation of the Bill of Rights. Note that those legal protections did not apply to the states, but the report offers a glimpse into the legal climate of the time. The tidy report from Pennsylvania reads as follows:

> In this cause (which was tried on Saturday, the 5th of April) the defendant offered Jonas Phillips, a Jew, as a witness; but he refused to be sworn, because it was his Sabbath. The Court, therefore, fined him £10; but the defendant, afterwards, waiving the benefit of his testimony, he was discharged from the fine.[69]

Phillips refused to testify on the sabbath, meaning Saturday as consistent with Jewish practice. The courts were open for business on Saturdays yet closed on Sundays, the Christian

---

[66] Schappes, 3.

[67] Wholesalers were apparently acceptable, a carryover indulgence from practices in the Netherlands as the nation fought for economic prominence in Europe.

[68] Schappes, *A Documentary History*, 4–13.

[69] Stansbury v. Marks, 2 Dall. 213 (Pa. 1793).

sabbath. Testimony in court may be compelled by means of a subpoena, which serves as an order of the court to appear. The Jewish religious requirement to keep the sabbath holy did not serve as an exemption from the public duty to testify in court. Phillips ultimately did not have to pay the fine, but the next witness in a legal case may not have fared so well.

Was this unfair? Requiring a Jewish witness to appear in court on Saturday forces a choice between following a civic requirement over a religious obligation. And yet the ability of a non-religious civic mechanism, that is, the courts, to function would be difficult if it had to accommodate the varied requirements of religious communities, a concern that only grows in a religiously diverse society. The unfair aspect of the situation may not be that Phillips was required to testify on a Saturday, but that the courts were closed on Sundays in deference to Christian sensibilities. Fairness takes a certain rough form when everyone is equally disgruntled. Public offices are now generally closed on Saturdays and Sundays, avoiding the conflict of at least these two dueling sabbaths. Making religious exceptions to otherwise neutral laws, however, would come to plague courts in the late twentieth century.

Preferential treatment of certain religious groups, and the singling out of others, remained an issue long after the Congress prohibited such actions by the federal government. For example, Jewish citizens were effectively banned from public office in Maryland, where officeholders were required to swear an oath of office including a "a declaration of a belief in the Christian religion."[70]

---

[70] Maryland Constitution of 1776, XXXV.

Lawyers were technically officers of the courts, making the practice of a law another prohibited occupation for Jews.

Accommodations were made in the requirement for those who would not make oaths on any occasion, including Quakers, Dunkers,[71] and "Menonists," (i.e., Mennonites) all of which are Christian groups.[72] Jews petitioned for many years to have the provision changed, either by omitting the requirement for such an oath or allowing them to make an oath using the "five books of Moses."[73] Proposed curative legislation was defeated in 1818, but eventually was passed in 1825, requiring however that those professing the "Jewish Religion . . . make and subscribe a declaration of his belief in a future state of rewards and punishments, in the stead of the declaration now required."[74] The oath taking party, by this logic, needs the fear of eventual divine punishment to make truthful testimony more likely.

Notably, Article VI of the federal constitution had decades before prohibited any religious test for federal office. Again, the U.S. Constitution was not about protecting the people from the powers of the government but about protecting the states from the powers of Congress. Jews and other religious groups would be subject to the vagaries of state laws until the religious protections of the First Amendment were applied against the states in the 1940s using the Equal Protection aspects of the Fourteenth Amendment.

---

[71] Dunkers is a colloquial name for German Baptists of the Church of the Brethren, also known as the Swarzenau Brethren.

[72] Maryland Constitution of 1776, XXXVI.

[73] Schappes, *A Documentary History*, 139–140.

[74] *Laws Made and Passed by the General Assembly of the State of Maryland*, 1824 Sess., 154.

Catholics in the United States

While Jews faced many widespread cultural biases and legal restrictions in colonial America, a relatively genial environment compared to Europe, Catholics endured open hostility and outright bans. Catholics and Protestants had fought for control of Europe for centuries after the start of the Protestant Reformation in 1517. The Eighty Years War, the Thirty Years War, the Treaty of Westphalia: the history of the continent and the modern borders of its countries were shaped by such religious struggles. English settlers, such as the Puritans of New England, were fleeing to the colonies to escape religious conflict, actual or perceived. But as the Reformed and Anglican subgroups of Protestantism wrangled over the shape of the Church of England, English Catholics were subjected to severe limitations as to work, education, and other liberties. Those anti-Catholic sentiments did not remain in Europe.

In 1700, for example, Earl Richard Coote, newly appointed governor of the colonies of Massachusetts, New York, and New Hampshire, enacted a law against "Jesuits and Popish Priests."[75] Coote's act as governor banished all Jesuits or other Roman Catholic clergy from these three colonial areas. It also prohibited the practicing or teaching "popish prayers," celebrating Masses, granting absolution, or using any other "Romish ceremonies of rites of worship" on pain of perpetual imprisonment and, upon

---

[75] Reprinted in Mark Massa, ed. *American Catholic History: A Documentary History* (New York: NYU Press, 2017), 20. See also "An Act Against Jesuits And Popish Priests," Massachusetts State Library, archives.lib.state.ma.us/handle/2452/118907.

escape and return, penalty of death. Such offenders could be seized without warrant and those helping or concealing such a person would be fined £200 and serve three days in the pillory. Catholic priests were not welcome.

This bias against Catholics may seem out of step with the image of Puritan settlers seeking religious freedom. But the Puritans sought their own religious liberty and judiciously ensured it against the dissent of others. Quakers and Baptists, such as Mary Dyer and Roger Williams, respectively, were driven from Massachusetts—Dyer was executed in 1659 for returning and refusing to leave.[76]

During the Glorious Revolution of 1688, English Protestants rallied around Parliament to overthrow King James II. The king was a Catholic and was moving to remove or to lessen religious restrictions against his tradition. He also sought to discipline anti-Catholic religious leaders, who in speaking or acting against Catholicism could be seen as speaking or acting against the king. For example, King James formed the Ecclesiastical Commission, which served to oversee the running of the Church of England. Its efforts to sanction several bishops for seditious libel, known as the Trial of the Seven Bishops, ended in their acquittal and the suspension of the commission. The ability of the government, in the form of the king, to control the running of religious institutions was effectively limited.

The Parliament then adopted a Bill of Rights, a list of further limitations upon the powers of the king versus Parliament and

---

[76] Maura Jane Farrelly, *Anti-Catholicism in America, 1620–1860,* (Cambridge University Press, 2018), 2. Roger Williams was not yet a Baptist, falling away from the Congregational fold within a few years of his exile.

the people.[77] These included having no power to suspend laws, allowing citizens the right to petition the king, giving Protestants the right to bear arms for their defense, protecting freedom of speech, and securing rights to a jury and against cruel and unusual punishments. The phrasing of these rights may ring familiar, as the language would in several key instances be adopted into the American Bill of Rights of 1789.

The language of "liberty" would become an important theme among Calvinist Protestants. It can be seen as a counterpoint to the rigid control imputed as the cornerstone of the Roman Catholic Church. Calvinists were encouraged to read the Bible without the intermediaries of a Church or priests. This focus on liberty became a keystone in the origin story of Puritan New Englanders.[78] And yet it stands starkly contradicted by the persecution of other religious groups, Protestant, Catholic, or otherwise. In essence, you had the freedom to choose not to be Catholic and to embrace the perceived freedoms inherent to Calvinism. If that does not sound entirely free, I would not argue the point.

But even this loose language of liberty was troublesome to certain contemporary critics. Thomas Case, an English clergyman of Presbyterian leanings, cautioned against the language of rights and liberty. If people could make up their own mind about their religious beliefs, it could open the way for the loss of traditions and the acceptance of sundry blasphemies: freedom from social class, liberty for women, and, in Case's estimation, the right to go to hell.[79]

---

[77] English Bill of Rights, 1689.

[78] English Bill of Rights, 19–20.

[79] English Bill of Rights, 20.

The identities of "English" and "Protestant" were becoming conflated.[80] As English Protestants reinforced their resistance to Catholic inroads into their society in the seventeenth century, English-American Protestants sought to do the same. Although Anglican and Reformed Protestants remained at odds regarding church structures, ecclesial hierarchies, religious rituals, and the like, an alliance of sorts was developing in opposition to the common threat of Catholicism.

Which brings us to "Pope Day." Pope Day was the American version of Guy Fawkes Night, commemorating the 1605 Gunpowder Plot by dissident Catholics to blow up the House of Lords with King James I inside.[81] The scheme failed, the plotters were tortured and executed, and English Catholics fell under wide and enduring suspicion even before the Glorious Revolution. Guy Fawkes Night celebrations, besides being raucous, involved burning effigies, particularly of Guy Fawkes and the Pope. It became a rally against Catholics and often for Puritan efforts within the Church of England.

A relative degree of common cause would ultimately be made among diverse Protestants across the various American colonies, a cause waged against this more salient enemy of Catholicism. In particular, the English Protestant colonists had some reason to fear incursions by Catholic forces that surrounded them, with the French to the north in Canada and to the west in what would become the territories of the Louisiana Purchase.[82]

---

[80] English Bill of Rights, 9.

[81] English Bill of Rights, 48.

[82] Ibid.

One of the few spots of Catholic tolerance was Maryland, which had from its beginnings encouraged Catholic emigration and integration—to a point. Maryland was founded as a proprietary colony, essentially land owned and directed by Cecilius Calvert, an English Catholic. It was given by King Charles I, who was sympathetic to Catholic concerns—perhaps owing to his marriage to a French Catholic, Queen Henrietta Maria. Maryland is named after the Queen. Charles would later be overthrown, tried, and executed by the English Parliament in 1649. The Commonwealth of England survived as a Protestant republic for a scant eleven years, during which time Calvert somehow managed to prevent anyone taking back Maryland.

In 1649, the same year as King Charles' execution, the colonial assembly of Maryland passed an *Act Concerning Religion* mandating tolerance for Trinitarian Christians. Those Christians who accept the Trinity, the formulation of God as the Father, Son, and Holy Ghost, were protected. This included Catholics and most Protestants. There were, however, limitations on such tolerance:

> That whatsoever person or persons within this Province and the Islands thereunto belonging shall from henceforth blaspheme God, that is Curse him, or deny our Savior Jesus Christ to be the son of God, or shall deny the holy Trinity the father son and holy Ghost, or the Godhead of any of the said Three persons of the Trinity or the Unity of the Godhead, or shall use or utter any reproachful Speeches, words or language concerning the said Holy Trinity, or any of the said three persons thereof, shall be punished with death and confiscation or forfei-

ture of all his or her lands and goods to the Lord Proprietary and his heirs.[83]

Lesser punishments were spelled out for disparaging the Virgin Mary, the Apostles, and the Evangelists. Using disparaging names was also a punishable offense, but the listed epithets include even seemingly commonplace terms and modern denominational names: "heritick, Scismatick, Idolator, puritan, Independant, Prespiterian popish prest [sic], Jesuite, Jesuited papist, Lutheran, Calvenist, Anabaptist, Brownist, Antinomian, Barrowist, Roundhead, Separatist, or any other name or terme in a reproachfull manner."[84] The Sabbath, meaning Sunday, was to be respected. And "no person or persons whatsoever . . . professing to believe in Jesus Christ, shall from henceforth be any ways troubled, molested or discountenanced for or in respect of his or her religion nor in the free exercise thereof. . . ."

This might be considered Mutually Assured Tolerance.

Eventually, the special status of Maryland as a Catholic haven ended. During the Glorious Revolution, a group of Protestants rose up and seized control of the colony from Charles Calvert, Cecilius' far less capable offspring. Catholicism was outlawed, forcing Catholics to retreat from public worship into home chapels. A Catholic would not again serve in Maryland's government until after the American Revolution. Maryland Catholics, nonetheless, fared better than others in the colonies due to their

---

[83] Maryland Toleration Act of 1649; text conformed to modern spelling for ease of reading.

[84] These names were not conformed to modern spellings, as I find them entertaining.

relative wealth and numbers as well as the long tradition of Catholicism in the area.

The revolution served as a critical moment in the shifting fortunes of American Catholics. Anti-Catholic sentiments were high before the conflict. One of the so-called Intolerable Acts of King George III, spurring the call for revolution, was the Quebec Act of 1774. This legislation expanded religious freedom to French Catholics in the English province of Quebec.

However, the outrage against the expansion of rights for the Catholic Quebecois to the north was tempered by the practicalities of waging a war against England. For example, General George Washington ordered the halt of celebrations of Pope Day. The Continental Army needed help, which was to be found from England's enemies in Europe, notably Catholic France. Apparently, it was deemed uncouth to be burning effigies of the Pope while Catholic soldiers and sailors from France came to the aid of colonial forces.

The increase of tolerance toward Catholics would ebb and flow for decades, but it would be sorely challenged by the massive influx of Irish Catholic immigrants in the 1840s and the tumultuous events of the American Civil War.

Latter-day Saints in the United States

The Church of Jesus Christ of Latter-day Saints, more colloquially known as Mormons,[85] has endured a uniquely challenging legal

---

[85] The name "Mormon" is in common usage but is not the preferred term as expressed by leaders of that faith tradition, who instead encourage the designation "members of the Church of Jesus Christ of Latter-day Saints" or "Latter-day

history in the United States. In the nineteenth century, the federal government sought to control, to curtail, and finally to eliminate the spread of Mormonism in the United States and its territories. These efforts forced a significant change in the religious practices of Latter-day Saints and their expression of beliefs.

Mormonism is an American-born faith tradition, founded by Joseph Smith in New York in 1830, when the Book of Mormon was published, giving an account of the lives of prophets who it said had lived in the Americas from ancient times. Smith describes receiving these texts on golden plates delivered by the Angel Moroni.

The Church of Jesus Christ of Latter-day Saints could simply have been another new denomination, one of many that proliferated during the religious fervor of the nineteenth-century United States. There were differences, of course, from other Christian traditions. There were the obvious additions, such as the new prophets and religious scriptures, which offered a supersessionist challenge to other Christian groups—an irony perhaps not lost on American Jews. There were collectivist religious communities that could be described as having proto-socialist characteristics and little boundary between church-and-state matters, at odds with more capitalist-minded and religious-liberty-oriented American Protestants.

In 1838, Governor Lilburn Boggs of Missouri went so far as to issue what has become known by Latter-day Saints as the

---

Saints." This is perhaps to avoid highlighting the Book of Mormon as a point of difference between this one group of Christians from others. The term "Mormon" will be used when quoting from court cases and historical accounts. "Latter-day Saints" will be used otherwise. Apologies for any confusion.

"Extermination Order." Boggs wrote to his militia leaders: "The Mormons must be treated as enemies and must be exterminated or driven from the State if necessary for the public peace—their outrages are beyond description. . . ."[86] And, needless to say, Boggs therefore did not see fit to describe their "outrages." The Missouri militia moved against the Latter-day Saints, who later fled the state to found the city of Nauvoo, Illinois.

The early Latter-day Saints repeatedly fled from various jurisdictions, owing to sharp disputes over what might be described as differing cultural outlooks—clannish business practices, bloc voting in elections, etc. But the greatest conflict was yet to manifest, an issue that nearly led to the destruction of the Church of Jesus Christ of Latter-day Saints: the question of polygamy.

In 1843, Joseph Smith recorded a revelation about marriage. It was revealed to him that, like the Biblical patriarchs Abraham and Jacob, religious leaders of his faith were expected to take additional wives. Here are selections from that text:

> Verily thus Saith the Lord, unto you my Servant Joseph, that inasmuch as you have enquired of my hand to know and understand wherein I the Lord justified my Servants Abraham, Isaac and Jacob; as also Moses, David and Solomon my Servants as touching the principle and doctrine of their having many wives, and concubines . . .

> I reveal it unto you my Servant Joseph then Shall you have power by the power of my Holy priesthood to take her and give

---

[86] "Boggs Extermination Order 44," Internet Archive, archive.org/details/BoggsExterminationOrder44/page/n1.

her unto him that hath not Committed adultery but hath been faithful for he Shall be made ruler over many for I have conferred upon you the keys and power of the priesthood. . . .

And again Verily I Say unto you my Servant Joseph that whatsoever you give on earth and to whomsoever you give any one on earth by my word, and according to my law, it Shall be visited with blessings and not cursings. . . .[87]

This revelation was not widely publicized for years, outside the inner circles of the church leadership. Smith and his followers had moved, or rather been driven, from New York, Ohio, and Missouri. They then founded Nauvoo, Illinois, to escape local conflicts. But conflicts did not merely arise from outside the fold.

In Nauvoo, several dissident members were excommunicated. By some accounts, this occurred because they took issue with the prospect of polygamy, specifically the awkward allegations that Smith had proposed marriage to their wives.[88] These were *polyandrous* proposals, the having of more than one husband, a marital institution without Biblical correlates. The aggrieved husbands banded together with others and published a newspaper, the *Nauvoo Expositor*, that criticized Smith and made allegations that he had more than one wife. The paper had only the one issue, as Smith and the Nauvoo City Council quickly held a

---

[87] Joseph Smith, "Revelation, 12 July 1843," from *Doctrine and Covenants*, josephsmithpapers.org/paper-summary/revelation-12-july-1843-dc-132/8.

[88] Ann Eliza Young, *Wife No. 19: Or, The Story of a Life in Bondage, Being a Complete Exposé of Mormonism and Revealing the Sorrows, Sacrifices and Sufferings of Women in Polygamy* (1875), 61.

hearing, found the printing press to be a public nuisance, and had it destroyed.

The publishers sought redress from the county government and a charge of inciting a riot was brought against Smith. Eventually, after some complex wrangling, raising the militia, and fleeing into Iowa for a time, Smith gave himself up to the authorities. A charge of treason was added to his alleged crimes, to little judicial effect. Smith, while waiting in jail, was seized and killed by a mob in 1844.

Under the new leadership of Brigham Young, the Latter-day Saints decided it was time to leave. They migrated *en masse* out of the United States. In 1847, they arrived in the valley of the Great Salt Lake, which then was within Mexican territory. However, the American Southwest came under U.S. control after the Mexican-American War. The Latter-day Saints sought to become the State of Deseret, an area encompassing most of current-day Utah, Nevada, and Arizona and sections of Colorado, Oregon, New Mexico, California, Idaho, and Wyoming. Congress approved a smaller area to be known as the Territory of Utah, primarily comprising the bulk of Utah and Nevada.

Statehood might seem an odd choice for a group that had recently fled the United States. But there was some basis to hope that a state within the United States founded by a religious group might have greater latitude in religious matters. This had been the case in Puritan-rich Massachusetts and, initially, in the Catholic haven of Maryland. The federal government was restrained by the Constitution from interfering in the establishment matters of the states or the free religious exercise of believers.

Legal Misfits in the United States

Being a territory is legally somewhat different from being a state; I will spare the reader a tedious primer on the subject. The specifics vary across situations, and history, but a territory is generally under the control of the federal government. Domestic matters, such as marriage, were typically left to local control, which may have been the hope of the Latter-day Saints. But, as will be seen, overriding federal interests could also come to bear in that balancing act. And the federal government was not terribly keen on the notion of polygamy. Havoc ensued.

For a time, the issue became embroiled in national politics. In 1856, the Republican Party platform included a condemnation of polygamy as well as a denouncement of slavery, calling these the "twin relics of barbarism."[89] Interestingly, this was couched as an argument against religious patriarchy, a modern refrain in a historic and divergent context. Linking slavery and polygamy lent a weight of moral authority to abolitionists and, conceivably, traded upon the perception that slaveholders' ownership of fellow human beings entailed more than merely manual labors (yes, that means systematic rape). And it was politically easier to attack the polygamous patriarchs in the far-flung Utah Territory rather than the slave-owning patriarchs of the South who were represented in Congress.

The Latter-day Saints responded to this external criticism with a Reformation, an intense period of soul-searching and

---

[89] Sarah Barringer Gordon, *The Mormon Question: Polygamy and Constitutional Conflict in Nineteenth-Century America* (Chapel Hill: University of North Carolina Press, 2002), 53. Author's note: this book is decidedly supportive of the Latter-day Saints' position, occasionally omitting less charitable materials, such as the backstory behind the *Nauvoo Expositor* controversy that led to the killing of Joseph Smith.

recommitment to the precepts of their community. This re-centering of values was paired with inflammatory language, predicting victory over Babylon (including the rest of the U.S.) and the prospect of violence against "Gentiles" or non-Latter-day Saints.[90] Federal officials were occasionally harassed, their offices ransacked, their quiet exit from the territory deemed the better part of valor.

There was also the Mountain Meadows Massacre of 1857. A group of settlers heading west were intercepted by the Nauvoo Legion, an LDS militia in the Utah Territory. Bound from Arkansas to California, the settlers were caught up in a declaration of martial law by Governor Brigham Young, owing to the growing hostilities with the federal government. Reports suggest that LDS dressed like Paiutes, a local Indigenous tribe, who were also solicited to participate in the raid.

While the specific orders and underlying motivations of the militia members and government officials are difficult to parse some 150 years on, it is clear that 120 settlers were massacred by the militia members, with only 17 children thought too young to report what happened left alive.[91] One man, John D. Lee, was convicted of the crime 20 years later. He was executed by firing squad in 1877, a result and a gap in time that would underscore a perception by anti-Mormon critics of extra-legal protection offered within the Latter-day Saints' government.

---

[90] Barringer Gordon, 59.

[91] See Richard E. Turley, Jr., "The Mountain Meadows Massacre," *Ensign* 37, no. 9 (September 2007), churchofjesuschrist.org/study/ensign/2007/09/the-mountain-meadows-massacre.

At that same time as the tensions in pre-Civil War Utah, there were violent clashes in Kansas over the prospect of the then-territory entering the Union as either a slave or free state. During this politically fraught period, the temptation for a distraction likely loomed large. The prospect of wading into the Kansas slavery conflict with federal troops was probably unattractive. Taking action against polygamy, however, would have been a more palatable option with far wider public appeal.

In 1857, the Utah War began. If that war slipped from your school's curriculum, here is a short recap. President James Buchanan ordered that a large contingent of federal troops be sent into the Territory of Utah. It was late 1857, however, and the weather in the Rocky Mountains was not cooperative. Congress did not support the continued expedition in the new year and Brigham Young toned down the Mormon Reformation rhetoric against "Babylon" in favor of states' rights arguments. The larger conflict came to nothing, and the Mountain Meadows Massacre became a historical footnote.

The American Civil War broke out in 1861, giving the Latter-day Saints of the Utah Territory a brief respite from federal intrusion. The question of polygamy, however, remained a public concern. The war concluded in 1865, but many of the background conflicts remained. Latter-day Saints would once again be faced with federal scrutiny. And they would be subject to the United States Supreme Court's first major foray into the First Amendment's jurisdiction over the free exercise of religion.

CHAPTER 7

Two's Company, Three's a Crime

IN 1862, THE UNITED STATES CONGRESS passed a law against bigamy, commonly known as the Morrill Anti-Bigamy Act, but perhaps more aptly read as the Anti-Mormon Act.[92] The law contained three sections. The first declared, "That every person having a husband or wife living, who shall marry any other person . . . shall . . . be adjudged guilty of bigamy. . . ." The second annulled the laws of the Territory of Utah that might be construed as establishing or supporting the institution of polygamy, "evasively called spiritual marriage, however disguised by legal or ecclesiastical solemnities, sacraments, ceremonies, consecrations, or other contrivances." Bonus points for alliteration.

Furthermore, the law made it unlawful for a corporation or association for religious or charitable purposes in a Territory to

---

[92] Laws of the Thirty Seventh Congress, Session II, Ch. 126 (1862).

hold real estate of greater than $50,000 in value, subject to for-
feiture and escheat[93] to the United States. This seemingly stray
financial matter was an attack on a pillar of Latter-day Saints
communal life and the centralized church. Real estate was
granted to the church by members, which was in turn returned
as a stewardship, that is, the land, farms, and buildings were to
be managed and controlled by the members but not directly
owned. Net profits from the properties, after the upkeep of one's
family, was to be given over to the church for its support and the
support of other Latter-day Saints.[94]

This socialist-seeming financial aspect of the Church of Jesus
Christ of Latter-day Saints was perhaps an import. Joseph Smith
had lived in western New York, an area so prone to religious
revivals that it came to be known as the "burnt over district" of
the Second Great Awakening, a period of religious revival during the early nineteenth century in the United States. In that area
of New York, there were numerous and varied religious groups,
utopian colonies and the like, some with churchly practices at
stark variance with other more established traditions. One such
group was the United Society of True Believers in Christ's Second Appearing, more commonly known as the Shakers of well-
wrought furniture fame. Craftsmanship aside, the Shakers were
religiously distinctive in many ways, espousing views of complete

---

[93] "Escheat" typically means the reversion of property to the government in
the event a person dies without heirs.

[94] Richard S. Van Wagoner, "Mormon Polyandry in Nauvoo," *Dialogue: A Journal of Mormon Thought* 18, no. 3 (Fall 1985), 68. Van Wagoner was an amateur
historian of Mormonism and a member of its church. He is also an entertaining
read.

egalitarianism between men and women, strict celibacy among all members, and communal ownership in all things. Smith may have gravitated toward the Shakers' latter religious innovation[95]—the others, not as much.

Into the brave new legal world of the Territory of Utah, growing ever more perilous for the Latter-day Saints through the work of Congress, came George Reynolds.[96] He was an English convert to the LDS church, active in European mission work and organizing. In 1865, he was invited to emigrate to Utah, after having coordinated the travel of many others to the territory. There he married his English sweetheart, Mary Ann Tuddenham. He became a secretary to President Brigham Young, which position likely led to his brush with legal fame.

Reynolds had in 1874 married his second wife, Amelia Jane Schofield, entering into a situation of plural marriage. President Young then asked Reynolds if he would be willing to serve as a test case against the Morrill Anti-Bigamy Act of 1862. The hope was that the First Amendment restrictions on the federal government would be applied to the Utah Territory. Reynolds agreed to the proposition.

The Church of Jesus Christ of Latter-day Saints hired George Washington Biddle of Philadelphia to defend Reynolds. Biddle was a Democrat, which political party would be the standard bearer for states' rights and local control for decades to come.

---

[95] Ibid.

[96] A Latter-day Saints biography of Reynolds appears in the August 1986 issue of *Ensign*. See Bruce A. Van Orden, "George Reynolds: Loyal Friend of the Book of Mormon," Ensign (August 1986). churchofjesuschrist.org/study/ensign/1986/08/george-reynolds-loyal-friend-of-the-book-of-mormon.

Democrats had also opposed the Reconstruction efforts in the South, advocating for a return of local control to the former Confederate states who would also oversee the rights and well-being of formerly enslaved people. Unsurprisingly, that line of logic would not turn out well for those who had been freed.

The U.S. government was represented directly by its Attorney General, Charles Devens, a Massachusetts Republican. Negative feelings toward the Latter-day Saints generally, and polygamy in particular, had not abated in the intervening years after the 1857 Utah War. While Reynolds' counsel sought to invoke the First Amendment limitations against federal interference with religion, the government's arguments focused on the nature of the crime of polygamy.

A cursory read over the First Amendment might give one the impression that "Congress shall make no law respecting an establishment of religion, or prohibiting the free exercise thereof. . . ." The Morrill Anti-Bigamy Act seemed to be just such a preferential law, singling out the religious practices of the Latter-day Saints and inserting the federal government into the local concerns of a territory. It was with some confidence that the Latter-day Saints agreed to this test of federal power.

Biddle also sought to use a rather subtle argument about the powers of the federal government regarding territories. Article 4, Section 3 of the U.S. Constitution authorized the Congress to make "needful" rules and regulations regarding a U.S. territory.[97] The Supreme Court had limited the extent of such federal pow-

---

[97] Barringer Gordon, *The Mormon Question*, 123.

ers two decades before in *Scott v. Sandford*.[98] This may have been an unwise tactical use of legal precedent by Biddle, as the "Scott" in that case was the Virginia-born Dred Scott, who the Supreme Court's decision had condemned to slavery.

Regardless of the applicability of the *Dred Scott* decision, the use of that particular precedent was culturally and politically insensitive, to put it mildly, so soon after the conclusion of the bloodiest conflict in U.S. history. The *Dred Scott* decision had tested the legal boundaries of the Missouri Compromise, the political decision to admit Maine into the Union as a free state and Missouri as a slave state to maintain a political equilibrium. Scott had argued that when he was brought by his owners into free territory, Wisconsin, he was automatically freed under the law. The Supreme Court decided against Scott, who was returned to slavery, though later manumitted, that is, freed by his owners. The case served as a political flashpoint leading up to the Civil War. The *Dred Scott* decision arguably also undermined perceptions of the authority of the Supreme Court and its political independence.[99] As the saying goes, way to read the room, Biddle.

Back to bigamy. The *Reynolds* case also turned on the nature of polygamy as an institution. The Bible contains numerous references to key figures engaged in plural marriages—Abraham, Jacob, Solomon, etc. With these Biblical supports in mind, Biddle argued that polygamy could not be deemed "malum in se," a legal term meaning "evil in itself." Congress might have the power to restrict or to prohibit an inherently evil activity, such as murder,

---

[98] 60 U.S. 393 (1856).

[99] See e.g., Barringer Gordon, *The Mormon Question*, 124.

but polygamy was outside that category of practices because of these scriptural supports.

And yet, one could also have argued *before* the Civil War, with similar Biblical support, that slavery in the United States was neither morally suspect nor culturally unusual, compared with the far less prevalent practice of polygamy. There are numerous references to enslaved people in the Bible, including their treatment, their need to obey, and even their availability for purposes of procreation in the context of polygamous relationships (i.e., Abraham and Hagar). Congress had recently passed three Amendments to the Constitution, and the states had ratified them, in an effort to extinguish slavery as an immoral practice. The Supreme Court would not invoke these Amendments in its decision in *Reynolds*. But the new political and legal reality of Congress being able to intervene in the local control of states was now firmly envisioned, if not always consistently applied. Having failed to protect the formerly enslaved people in the South, Congress could still go after the Church of Jesus Christ of Latter-day Saints.

The *Reynolds* court looked back into history to coin its arguments, which remain relevant and applicable well over a century later. In particular, it brought forth the writings of James Madison and Thomas Jefferson to backstop its efforts. In one key instance, quoting Jefferson's preamble to the Virginia Statute for Religious Freedom of 1786, the Court wrote:

> In the preamble of this act . . . religious freedom is defined; and after a recital 'that to suffer the civil magistrate to intrude his powers into the field of *opinion*, and to restrain the profession or

propagation of principles on supposition of their ill tendency, is a dangerous fallacy which at once destroys all religious liberty,' it is declared 'that it is time enough for the rightful purposes of civil government for its officers to interfere when principles break out into *overt acts against peace and good order*.' In these two sentences is found the true distinction between what properly belongs to the church and what to the State.[100]

The distinction was between opinion and action. A belief can be held, and even be shared, but the moment it is *acted upon* to the detriment of peace and good order, the resulting action becomes a matter for governmental scrutiny and potential control. One might argue that the right to free exercise is much diminished if it is restricted to mere thought and expression, excluding action based on belief. "Exercise" becomes a hollow shell.

But the century-old language of Thomas Jefferson intersected well with the needs of the post-slavery Supreme Court. Congress did not have the power to interfere with the states before the Civil War, but after the war it suddenly did. This shift in powers adopted by the Court was not enough to rescue Reconstruction, or to shield newly freed people from the burgeoning evils of Jim Crow laws.[101] But it was enough to go after the Latter-day Saints and would in time strengthen federal reach into state matters.

---

[100] *Reynolds*, 163.

[101] One reason the Jim Crow laws were sustained, or in truth ignored, was that they often were built upon personal racism rather than state racism. The Supreme Court overruled a series of nineteenth-century federal laws that sought to protect formerly enslaved people from aspects of personal prejudice, such as

Attorney General Devens also deployed fervent rhetoric regarding the evils of polygamy and the prospect of religious exemptions to criminal laws. Devens literally suggested that gangs of "Thugs" from India, or more specifically Thuggee bandits, might settle in the territories, roving the land and strangling with religious impunity.[102] This was a tabloid approach to argument, relying upon well-known if geographically remote fears, quite similar to the modern practices of 24-hour news that rely upon such anxiety farming to ensure viewership.

The Court picked up this line of thinking, asking whether human sacrifice could be allowed based upon religious belief. The Court answered this question, understandably in the negative, finding against Reynolds:

> Can a man excuse his practices to the contrary because of his religious belief? To permit this would be to make the professed doctrines of religious belief superior to the law of the land, and, in effect, to permit every citizen to become a law unto himself. Government could exist only in name under such circumstances.[103]

---

being barred from inns or shops. The Court found that the post-Civil War amendments did not give the federal government such power. This changed in the 1960s, a circumstance to bear in mind when answering the question of whether someone has the personal right to discriminate on the basis of their religion.

[102] "Is Polygamy a Crime?" *New York Times*, November 15, 1878, 4. Thugs or *Thuggees* were said to be a group of bandits that travelled about India robbing and killing travelers. They allegedly had murky religious connections to the goddess Kali. In the nineteenth century, British colonial authorities sought to wipe out banditry in general, and the Thugs specifically.

[103] *Reynolds*, 166–167. See also, *Late Corp. of the Church of Jesus Christ of Latter-day Saints v. United States*, 136 U.S. 1, 49 (1890). "No doubt the Thugs of India imagined that their belief in the right of assassination was a religious belief."

The allusion to human sacrifice may seem hyperbolic, but Devens had included in his arguments some red meat appeal: an invocation of the Mountain Meadows Massacre. That was not a theoretical offense committed in South Asia, but a historic American tragedy that would have been quite familiar to the public audience of the proceedings. John D. Lee, the sole member of the Nauvoo Legion to be tried for the Mountain Meadows Massacre, was executed for his crimes on March 23, 1877. At least one extended account of his confession and the events involved appeared in the *New York Times*.[104] *Reynolds* was decided in 1878, one year later.

In reaching its conclusion against Reynolds and in support of the statute, the Court found that polygamy was akin to being *malum in se*, inherently evil, at least for Americans and Europeans: "Polygamy has always been odious among the northern and western nations of Europe, and, until the establishment of the Mormon Church, was almost exclusively a feature of the life of Asiatic and of African people."[105] English courts had always held a second marriage to be void, and the act was subject to criminal penalties including death.

In addition to relying upon such precedents, the *Reynolds* decision seems to have embodied a less obvious justification: there is something not quite right about the Latter-day Saints, the "weirdness" argument implicitly seen in the 1970s Tennessee

---

[104] "The Great Mormon Crime," *New York Times*, March 24, 1877, 4. Lee was killed by firing squad. The presiding pastor ministering to the prisoner at the execution was a Methodist, which could be described as either bad planning or petty cruelty.

[105] *Reynolds*, 164.

snake-handling case. They had multiple wives, they owned property in common, they were culturally insular: to hazard some
historical speculation, the Latter-day Saints did not fit into U.S.
society like other more familiar strains of American and European Protestants. Or, to make some time-remote social observations, the Latter-day Saints were deemed by the Court to be
more "Asiatic" or "African," and arguably less Anglo-Saxon, less
white, and therefore less acceptable. The religious practices of
the Latter-day Saints fell out of step with the Northern and Western European mode, instead modeling the polygamous practices
of African and Middle Eastern cultures, and therefore their practices were seen as less worthy of legal protection.

And those differences may trade upon other indwelling prejudices. Jews and Catholics were often eyed suspiciously for being
tight-knit, exclusionary communities. The Church of Jesus Christ
of Latter-day Saints was centralized and authoritative in the
lives of its members, dictating aspects of personal behavior and
intimate family matters. Long before the struggles over polygamy, the Latter-day Saints faced persistent hostility under the
leadership of Joseph Smith. The fertile environment of the Second Great Awakening birthed many small "oddball" religious
communities with alternate lifestyles and utopian aspirations.

The key difference? The Latter-day Saints were successful at
it, aggressively expanding in territory and members. They built
towns, like Nauvoo, and even a whole society in the deserts of
the Southwest. And they were accumulating wealth along with
the power of numbers, which was clearly a worry of Congress as
it sought to strip territorial charities of real estate exceeding
$50,000. The Church of Jesus Christ of Latter-day Saints was

becoming unnerving, like the other great specter of American Protestantism: the Roman Catholic Church.

Additionally, communal ownership by groups was and would be problematic for the federal government. For example, in 1890, Congress passed the Dawes Act, an effort to break up large land tracts held communally by tribes of Indigenous people. Private property was a cherished right, one that the federal government seemed determined to spread among those less smitten with its attractions. It may not have been a coincidence that smaller tracts of land split among many impoverished Indigenous people would be easier to purchase than from centralized tribal authorities with fiduciary obligations to members.

What happened after *Reynolds*?

Reynolds received a sentence of two years in prison at hard labor and a fine of $500, with the hard labor requirement being later dropped and the sentence reduced to 18 months. He served his time in a Utah prison, where the weather was harsh. He was able to write and helped to develop the first concordance of the Book of Mormon, a reference guide used to find words and passages in the religious text. He returned to work for the LDS presidency, now occupied by John Taylor. He married a third wife, Mary Gould—and, yes, there were still the other two women in the marital picture. Reynolds had 32 children among his three wives.

Congress kept passing anti-Mormon laws, including the Edmunds-Tucker Anti-Polygamy Act of 1887.[106] It allowed the testimony of husbands or wives against their spouses, annulled

---

[106] Forty-Ninth Congress, Sess. II, c. 397, 1887.

territorial laws allowing illegitimate children to inherit (that is, children of plural marriages), disincorporated the Church of Jesus Christ of Latter-day Saints and related entities, seized real estate and funds from such entities to support public schools in the Utah Territory, took away the right of women to vote granted in 1870, replaced local judges and school administrators, and prohibited the use of "any book of sectarian character or otherwise unsuitable." The later Supreme Court case of *Davis v. Beason*[107] would uphold a requirement that voters take an oath that they were not members of any organization that teaches its members to commit the crime of bigamy or which practices "celestial marriage." And the Supreme Court, comparing the Latter-day Saints to murderous Thugs, refused to overturn the dissolution of the Church of Jesus Christ of Latter-Day Saints or the seizure of its assets.[108]

After this onslaught, the LDS church had had enough. In 1890, the president of the Church, Wilford Woodruff, issued an official declaration. He announced that the Church of Jesus Christ of Latter-day Saints was not teaching polygamy or plural marriage and that ceremonies to such effect were not being performed at LDS temples, as worship-related properties were among the few

---

[107] 133 U.S. 333 (1890).

[108] "One pretense for this obstinate course is that their belief in the practice of polygamy, or in the right to indulge in it, is a religious belief, and therefore under the protection of the constitutional guaranty of religious freedom. This is altogether a sophistical plea. No doubt the Thugs of India imagined that their belief in the right of assassination was a religious belief; but their thinking so did not make it so. The practice of suttee by the Hindu widows may have sprung from a supposed religious conviction." Late Corp. of the Church of Jesus Christ of Latter-Day Saints v. United States, 136 U.S. 1, 49 (1890).

not seized by the federal government. Woodruff noted that Congress had passed laws against such practices and that he was submitting to those laws on behalf of the Church, advising the "Latter-day Saints to refrain from contracting any marriage forbidden by the law of the land."[109]

Perhaps understandably, the Latter-day Saints capitulated to the federal authorities. President Benjamin Harrison issued an amnesty, pardoning all those who might have been found in violation of the Edmonds and Edmunds-Tucker Acts who had abstained from unlawful cohabitation since November 1, 1890. Remaining LDS funds were returned. Many plural marriages dissolved and cohabitation ceased, but not always. Mexico also prohibited polygamy but was less arduous in enforcement, inviting an influx of Latter-day Saint religious refugees.[110]

The Supreme Court would not directly apply the First Amendment's religious protections to the states until the 1940s. But the *Reynolds* decision marked a subtle shift into "state" intervention, albeit from a case involving an U.S. territory. The Fourteenth Amendment and the abandoned blueprints for Reconstruction would be the kernels of the idea. The push would be stymied for years, but federal influence into religious questions would begin to make inroads along with the economic innovations of the Great Depression.

---

[109] Official Declaration 1, The Church of Jesus Christ of Latter-day Saints, October 6, 1890.

[110] "The Manifesto and the End of Plural Marriage," The Church of Jesus Christ of Latter-day Saints, churchofjesuschrist.org/topics/the-manifesto-and-the-end-of-plural-marriage.

And the trend toward separating church from state would take on new urgency with the massive influx of immigrants from around the world during the late nineteenth and early twentieth century. People of different cultures and religions would dramatically alter the ecosystem of religion in the United States. But before any of that happened, before even the Civil War began, there was a challenge to the hegemony of American Protestantism unlike any before in U.S. history. It was the result of a great tragedy and, one might say, a particular problem with potatoes.

CHAPTER 8

Historical Interlude: The Irish and the Know-Nothings

IN ORDER TO UNDERSTAND the outsized influence of anti-Catholicism in the nineteenth-century United States, it would be useful to examine some history of Irish Catholic immigration and the events leading up to a mass exodus of these refugees to the United States. The resulting religious conflicts between Catholics and Protestants would overlap with racial tensions after the Civil War, leading to enduring racial, political, and religious tensions that remain recognizable to this day.

In 1845, major signs of a blight appeared on the potato crops of Ireland, a lush land that produced a steady surplus of food.[111]

---

[111] Enda Delaney, *The Curse of Reason: The Great Irish Famine* (Dublin: Gill Books, 2012), 76. For an extensive resource on the Great Famine and the politics

That bounty of food, however, did not belong to the people of Ireland, meaning the farm workers. It generally took the form of either cash crops intended for export by often absentee landlords or grains used for distilling alcoholic spirits rather than food for the local population. Many a firkin[112] of butter was shipped overseas.[113]

And so began the Great Famine. In 1845, between a third and one half of the Irish potato crop failed. In the following year, three quarters was lost. In those same years, large amounts of grain, butter, and livestock were exported, a testament to the laissez-faire economic policies of the English government. The invisible hand of the free market would provide, eventually. Just not speedily or, perish the thought, charitably.

Irish landlords were expected to fund famine relief for those on their lands, which depressingly prompted the eviction of tenants to reduce potential costs.[114] Tenants were ushered out of their homes, which were then promptly destroyed by mercenary gangs, allowing no possibility of return. Conversely, anyone holding land, even as low as an acre, was ineligible for relief. This led to even small landholders being forced to relinquish their farms rather than starve.[115] Eventually, to "assist" matters with recalcitrant owners, land encumbered by debt was subject

---

of the time, see Christine Kinealy, Gerard Moran, and Jason King, *The History of the Irish Famine Vols. 1–4* (Routledge, 2019).

[112] A "firkin" may be defined as a small cask or barrel, containing 9 imperial gallons or 41 liters.

[113] Delaney, *The Curse of Reason,* 107.

[114] Delaney, 171–172.

[115] Delaney, 173.

to seizure and auction. This encouraged English speculators to buy Irish land cheaply, often to establish large cattle ranches requiring far fewer tenants to support the export of many more buttery firkins.

The Irish people were left with few choices for survival. Relief efforts were stingy and even intentionally cruel to avoid dependency, to proffer a pair of armchair historical opinions. One program involved importing maize, what Americans call corn. Maize was an unfamiliar grain. Most Irish found it unpalatable and it requires a degree of care in preparation, such as with lime (as in the chemical, not the fruit), to make it nutritionally accessible. This importing of food was done in secret by Prime Minister Peel in the early years of the famine. The yellow maize meal came to be known as "Peel's brimstone."[116]

This was not a coincidental choice of emergency foods. It was a conscious decision made in a wider culture strongly averse to providing "outdoor relief," meaning direct monetary or physical aid to the poor outside a dreary "workhouse" setting. Workhouse residents were not allowed to live with family members. Men were separated from women, including spouses, and often older children were removed from their parents' care. Some workhouse tasks literally included bone-crushing, the grinding of bones to make fertilizer, or the breaking up of rocks, an activity more readily associated with prison life.

Many instead opted to risk their lives on dangerous voyages to the English colonies, or to one former colony, the United States. Hundreds of thousands of Irish Catholic immigrants fled

---

[116] Delaney, 102.

to the United States, congregating in major northern cities such as New York, Boston, and Chicago. Those fleeing the famine were often unskilled, particularly for their new urban settings, and had few resources available other than their own labor.

Pre-famine Irish immigrants to the United States typically had been from Ulster, a majority Protestant county in the north of Ireland.[117] Many were skilled in trades, such as weaving. Other less-skilled emigrants were often indentured servants, paying for passage to the U.S. with a term of servitude. They were not enslaved, subject to chattel ownership and complete elimination of legal rights, though it would have been a harsh existence planting and harvesting crops like tobacco in the American South. Indentured servants could not be held indefinitely and mostly were volunteers for the Atlantic passage, though there were frequent and tragic exceptions to that rule.

Distinct laws, rules, and procedures were eventually imposed, violations of which were subject to the penalty of death "without the benefit of clergy":

> British law required that all British subjects emigrating as servants should, before sailing, execute indentures stipulating the number of years of service entered into, and whether the labor to be performed was a definite trade or any kind of work required by the other party to the contract. The master, in consideration of his right to the servant's labor, agreed to provide food, clothing, and lodging for the stated period of time, and generally to

---

[117] See e.g., James Kelly, "The Resumption of Emigration from Ireland after the American War of Independence: 1783–1787," *Studia Hibernica* No. 24 (1988), 61–88.

allow additional compensation in the nature of provisions, clothing, and equipment upon the expiration of the term. This allowance came to be known as "freedom dues" and sometimes, particularly in the beginning, included land.[118]

The use of "servants" to farm the land was envisioned as the only possible means to develop the lands of the South and the mid-Atlantic states. If free workers were hired, the logic goes, their wages would exceed the net value of the crops produced. Indentured servants filled this gap, to an extent, until widespread use of enslaved Africans made indentured servants less economically attractive for plantation farming. "No system of free labor could have been maintained in the colonies until a comparatively late date."[119] In an editorial aside, this was a remarkably bloodless way of describing the strip mining of human misery.

Again, both forms of bondage were tragic, but they were not equally so. Indentures by definition ended. One's children were not included in bondage or sold from their parents. Servants were expected to be paid some amount at the end of the term. Both conditions were bad but one was far worse, just as there is a difference between being flogged and being beheaded.

This was not merely a semantic difference without real-world effect. The equating of those two legal states—time-limited indentured servitude and time-indefinite chattel slavery— arguably fed into post-war tensions between Irish immigrants and newly free Africans and remains a point of conflict between

---

[118] *History of Wages in the United States from Colonial Times to 1928*, Bureau of Labor Statistics, U.S. Dept. of Labor, 1934, 27.

[119] Bureau of Labor Statistics, 28 (citation omitted).

Irish Americans and African Americans.[120] Comparing these two forms of bondage was a tactic used to create political divisions in the nineteenth century. Creating false equivalencies of suffering and stoking racial distrust, leading to animosity encouraged by political manipulators: this is also not a tactic resigned to the pages of history.

During the American Civil War, as the conflict dragged on far longer than anticipated, the Union eventually established conscription for the war effort. This led to the 1863 Enrollment Act, which provided:

> That all able-bodied male citizens of the United States, and persons of foreign birth who shall have declared on oath their intention to become citizens under and in pursuance of the laws thereof, between the ages of twenty and forty-five years, except as hereinafter excepted, are hereby declared to constitute the national forces, and shall be liable to perform military duty in the service of the United States, when called out by the President for that purpose.

There were explicit exceptions to the draft, often sensible matters such as an only son remaining at home to support a widowed mother. The less explicit exceptions, applied in practice rather than in the text of the Act, were substitutions. Someone could be hired to take one's place or a substitution fee of $300 could be paid. Given that a day laborer in New York earned

---

[120] Liam Stack, "Debunking a Myth: The Irish Were Not Slaves, Too," *New York Times*, March 17, 2017, nytimes.com/2017/03/17/us/irish-slaves-myth.html.

approximately $1.00 for a day's work in 1860, the buyout option was unattainable for the typical worker. But the fees for taking someone's place, even at the risk of one's life, would have been attractive for the destitute.

On July 13, 1863, the draft officially came to New York City. The rollout of the government program was met with widespread violence, looting, and loss of life.[121] Officials and police were attacked and some were killed. A Black man, merely a bystander, was lynched by a white mob while other Black people were harassed in the streets. The "Orphan Asylum for Colored Children" was ransacked, looted, and set ablaze, though at least the children were able to flee. The rioting lasted for days.

The press, or at least the Republican/pro-Union leaning papers, concluded that the core of the mob was from elsewhere. The perpetrators were giving "vent to their thoughts with an accentation which was never acquired on this side of the Atlantic."[122] The implication of this chewy description and other jaundiced references is that the violence was committed by Irish immigrants.

One witness to the 1863 draft riots was Thomas Nast, a German immigrant and young artist. He was best known for his political cartoons in *Harper's Weekly*, a popular New York periodical with a Republican editorial bent. His experiences during the Draft Riots would inform his drawings for years to come, including the burned-out hulk of the orphanage. His cartoons also relied upon stereotypical representations of the Irish: brutish and thug-like, often drunk, and prone to violence. These images

---

[121] *New York Times*, July 14, 1863, 1.

[122] Ibid., col. 4.

were also in stock usage to represent the Democratic Party, which was the political party associated with Irish immigrants for many decades after their mass migration.

For years, distrust toward the objectives of the Civil War had been incited by the rhetoric of pro-slavery, anti-war forces in the Northern states. Immigrants, particularly Irish Catholics, were advised that freeing enslaved Africans would lead to fewer jobs and greater competition for work. The Emancipation Proclamation of 1863 seemed to confirm that prediction. And the Enrollment Act, also in 1863, may have had the unintended effect of confirming the working class worry that it was a "rich man's war but a poor man's fight." The perception was that a wealthy man could buy his way out of fighting, a not entirely unfounded concern at least in the early years of the draft. This series of worries and events culminated in the outbreak of deadly racial violence. And it cemented an enduring political divide, with Republicans and Black people on one side and Democrats and Irish Catholics on the other.

Before proceeding further, it is important to note that "Republican" and "Democrat" in this context have no simple correlation to the modern parties, which would experience a dramatic inversion of alliances in the twentieth century. It is easy to lose sight of shifting coalitions over a century later. Post-Civil War Democrats would come to absorb the political remnants of the Confederacy, those for whom the war had been transmogrified after the fact into an economic battle about free enterprise and self-determination, a questionable claim in a conflict about owning others. Republicans had embraced abolitionism to varying degrees before and even during the war—but winning can adjust one's memory right quickly. Tepid support became hearty endorsement after the dice had fallen the right way.

Along the path to victory, however, the Republicans embraced a surprising political bedfellow, a populist group which had mixed feelings about slavery but a strong opinion about the problems of immigration. This was the Native American Party, absolutely no relation to Indigenous people. It was a nativist, anti-immigrant, and notably anti-Catholic political group, incited by the influx of European Catholics from Germany and Ireland. This political group grew in strength and prominence in the 1850s. The name "Know Nothing" was endurably attributed to the group because the alleged advice members were given about its doings and origins: when asked, simply say "I know nothing."

Know Nothing candidates performed well in the elections of 1854, particularly in places like Massachusetts where Know Nothings swept the state legislature. This electoral success led to a formalization of the group as the American Party. This political prominence was short-lived, as the new party split and soon dissolved over infighting about slavery. Nathaniel Banks, a Know Nothing from Massachusetts who became a member of Congress under their banner, left the group for the Republicans when he could not support the group's anti-immigrant policies. His switch led to the defection of about two thirds of other Know Nothing members to the Republican Party.

And yet such party defections did not entirely track with Banks' reticence about an anti-immigrant platform. This shift may have spurred the Republican Party, along with its new members, to adopt political opposition to immigration generally, and Irish Catholics implicitly, as a core Republican principle in the late nineteenth century. The American/Know Nothing Party collapsed, but it would live on in spirit.

Conversely, Irish Catholics became involved in Democratic Party politics—a two-party system leaves little room for maneuvering. In New York, newly arrived immigrants faced various difficulties, but the infamous Tammany Hall political machine of the Democratic Party responded to those needs with sponsorship and support in exchange for votes. Such patronage was not always subtle, or exactly legal, but it secured Irish votes for generations.

Thus the Irish Catholics and the Democrats stood opposed to emancipated Black people and the Republicans. A tug of war over political control ensued for decades. And one critical, and bitter, area of dispute was over public schools and the role of religion.

CHAPTER 9

Bible Wars

GROWING UP CATHOLIC, the Bible did not directly play a prominent role in my religious education. Religion was taught within a framework of tradition, whether through catechism at church on weeknights for the "publics" or by daily religious classes held at a parochial school. And that framework did not include Bible study. Such an observation may be more anecdote than evidence of the religious pedagogy of the 1970s, but the role of the Bible in the education of children was a hotly disputed matter in the nineteenth century.

The term "parochial" derives from the word "parish." The parochial school therefore means the school of the parish, a term for the area surrounding and supporting a particular church. Parochial schools in the United States are generally thought of as Catholic schools, though the term "parish school" would have historically indicated one associated with the church of the parish, which could have been Congregationalist, Unitarian, or another "established" church.

Schools became important in the mindset of Reformed Protestants, those Protestant traditions that valued the reading of religious scripture above all else. In keeping with that emphasis, the General Court of Massachusetts (i.e., its legislature) passed the "Old Deluder Satan Law of 1647."[123]

It being one chief project of that old deluder, Satan, to keep men from the knowledge of the Scriptures, as in former times keeping them in an unknown tongue, so in these later times by perswading from the use of tongues, that so at least the true sense and meaning of the Originall might be clowded by false glosses of Saint-seeming deceivers and that Learning may not be buried in the graves of our fore-fathers in Church and Commonwealth. . . .

This is a not terribly subtle dig at Catholicism, in which tradition the Bible was used in Latin translation. The observation that the "true sense and meaning of the Originall" scriptures might unfold was presented with great solemnity in the statute, notwithstanding the original scriptures being set down in Ancient Hebrew, Greek, and Aramaic while the Puritans[124]

---

[123] "Old Deluder Satan Law of 1647" in *The Laws and Liberties of Massachusetts* (Cambridge: Harvard University Press, 1929), mass.gov/files/documents/2016/08/ob/deludersatan.pdf.

[124] For clarity, Puritans were Congregationalists associated with the Church of England who sought to "purify" from within. Pilgrims were religious Separatists who found the Church to be irredeemably corrupt, prompting the initial voyage to the colonies. Eventually, as migration across the Atlantic increased, the Pilgrims would come to be subsumed into the wider Puritan community. And, notably, neither colonial group likely had buckles on their hats.

of the Massachusetts Bay Colony likely studied the Bible in English.[125]

> [I]t is therefore ordered by this Court and Authoritie therof;
> That every Township in this Jurisdiction, after the Lord hath
> increased them to the number of fifty Housholders, shall then
> forthwith appoint one within their town to teach all such chil-
> dren as shall resort to him to write and read, whose wages shall
> be paid either by the Parents or Masters of such children, or
> by the Inhabitants in general, by way of supply . . . and it is fur-
> ther ordered, that where any town shall increase to the num-
> ber of one hundred Families or Housholders, they shall set up a
> Grammar-School, the Masters thereof being able to instruct
> youth so far as they may be fitted for the Universitie. And if any
> town neglect the performance hereof above one year then
> everie such town shall pay five pounds per annum to the next
> such School, till they shall perform this Order.[126]

Towns were required to hire teachers, who were often ministers working, teaching, and preaching in the local meetinghouse.
They were to be supported through taxation, although public
education was not yet entirely subsidized. Tuition, known as
"rates," could be and was charged, a hybrid form of public and

---

[125] The Pilgrims most likely used the Geneva Bible, an English translation published in 1560. That version contained notations consistent with Calvinist interpretations of the scriptures, which were presumably free of "clowd[ing] false glosses" of any kind. The later Authorized Version, or King James edition, of the Bible was published in 1611 with almost no notations, in part to avoid doctrinal controversies.

[126] Old Deluder Satan Law of 1647.

private schooling. Not everyone could attend due to the cost. And not everyone would attend due to the preferences of parents and the reliance upon children for labor. Contemporaneously, other states such as New York and Pennsylvania had charity schools which were free regardless of class, though limited in enrollment. These schools were sponsored by religious groups such as the Quakers, Episcopalians, and others. As one author opined, "Under these early arrangements, no schooling was entirely tax-supported, universally available to all children, or secular in content."[127]

The school texts taught were generally religious in nature, whether passages from the Bible or specialized children's books based upon religious language and stories. One example was the *New England Primer*, first published between 1687 and 1690. The *Primer* contained standard material for teaching reading, plus a varying selection of overtly religious materials such as the Westminster Shorter Catechism, or "Spiritual Milk for Boston Babes." The latter was a children's catechism written by Rev. John Cotton, an influential Puritan minister.[128] An eighteenth-century edition of the *Primer* also introduced a well-known prayer: "Now I lay me down to sleep, I pray thee, Lord, my soul to keep. If I should die before I wake, I pray thee, Lord, my soul to take."

---

[127] Steven K. Green, *The Bible, the School, and the Constitution: The Clash That Shaped Modern Church-State Doctrine* (Oxford: Oxford University Press, 2012), 13.

[128] The full title of the 1656 New England version was "Spiritual Milk for Boston Babes in Either England. Drawn out of the Breasts of Both Testaments for Their Souls Nourishment but May Be of Like Use to Any Children." The title in common use was, understandably, shortened.

Under the Massachusetts "Old Deluder" statute, a grammar school was a higher threshold for larger towns, with a greater expectation as to the level of education offered. Education was again a cornerstone of religious observance because Biblical fluency equated to religious understanding for the Bible-centric Reformed tradition. The school curriculum was therefore notably focused on attaining the capacity "to write and read" as set out in the statute. Not expressly mathematics, though that may have been a practical addition. Not U.S. history or science, geography or civics, topics perhaps no more than nascent glimmers in a colonial-era mindset.

While the subject matter was limited, the expectation of common literacy was an innovation. Most children would have been educated in the home to varying degrees by their families. The "Old Deluder" law was in a sense government intervention, forcing families to pay for schooling for children. That requirement might even result in a boy—yes, sadly just boys—being found suited for university, which at the time could have likely led to a life in religious ministry. Also sadly just boys.

Taxing non-Congregationalists to support a Congregational church led to protests and agitation, culminating in the disestablishment of all state-sponsored churches by 1833. In the same way, the founding of public education on a religious platform would in time prompt fierce sectarian conflict and simmering social tensions. And yet most actors in this historical drama had a sense that moral education was necessary for children alongside teaching them to read and to write. How, or whether, that education could be provided in a nonsectarian fashion was the crux of their disagreement.

Schools would become a religious battleground in the nineteenth century as the prevalence of publicly funded education expanded. One advocate for wider access to education was Horace Mann, who sought to ensure the place of public schools in Massachusetts and their specific purpose as places to teach ethics and morals. Mann was a politician from the now defunct Whig Party and he served in various capacities, including as a congressional representative. But he is best known for his involvement in the early development of public education; schools around the nation bear his name as a testament to that legacy.

Mann sought to balance the need for the education of children with the religious expectations of the adults in the wider society. It was not always an easy dance. Mann was a progressive figure for his time, though the incremental progress of the early nineteenth century may not bear up to the impatient scrutiny of later points in time.

The Massachusetts schools relied upon religious texts to teach reading. And yet Mann, in his own way, sought to prevent sectarianism, as he once reported to the Massachusetts legislature: "Our Public Schools are not Theological Seminaries. . . ."[129] The school system does not teach the "distinctive doctrines" of specific denominations, but it "earnestly inculcates all Christian morals; it founds its morals on the basis of religion; it welcomes the religion of the Bible; and, in receiving the Bible, it allows it to do what is allowed to do in no other system,—*to speak for itself.*"[130]

---

[129] Annual Report of the Board of Education, Twelfth Annual Report of the Secretary of the Board, 1849, 116.

[130] Board of Education, 117 (emphasis in original).

The argument over the content of "Christian morals" occurred at a time in U.S. history in which there were few citizens who did not identify as Christians—or male, white, and relatively rich. Jews and Indigenous people were typically ignored, Muslims were almost exclusively enslaved, and other dissenting religions were few and far between.

Massachusetts is not called a state, but a commonwealth. This currently amounts to persnickety grammarians correcting referrals to the "State of Massachusetts." But the idea of a commonwealth versus a state had historical significance.[131] In a commonwealth, at least in philosophical theory, society exists to promote the common good, the needs of the whole being ultimately more important than the needs, or desires, of the parts. It is a shared enterprise, not something parceled out as a bundle of rights to be hoarded by its citizens.

Imagine the distinction between forming a militia for the common defense and the right to bear arms personally (and no, I am not trying to pick a fight). Defending society is not the same as defending a household. These are different ways of approaching similar problems, centering either on the group or the individual. The path one takes changes if the goal is protecting society's well-being versus enshrining one's personal rights or privileges. Different objectives are being protected and different ways of thinking are being emphasized.

The commonwealth was responsible for the whole, including the moral wholeness of society. The establishment of local

---

[131] See, e.g., Johann N. Neem, "The Elusive Common Good: Religion and Civil Society in Massachusetts, 1780–1833," *Journal of the Early Republic* 24, no. 3 (Autumn 2004), 386.

churches, the so-called Standing Order, was premised on this responsibility. Conversely, independent or dissenting churches seeking to organize were viewed from within the Standing Order as contrary to that collective sense of the good. The states (and commonwealths) retained the right to establish churches and in doing so retained the right to determine the best way forward for the moral education of local society. The debate, politically and historically, would then turn on whether the educational system was teaching religious doctrines or instilling moral values. And, perhaps, whether there is any difference.[132]

Leaving aside the educational efficacy of handing out selections from the Bible to children just learning to read (with or without footnotes), does using the Bible in public schools in this way avoid a problem of establishment of state-sponsored religion? The First Amendment would not apply to Massachusetts for another century when the amendment was incorporated in the 1940s. The 1780 Massachusetts constitution addressed the issue of education squarely:

As the happiness of a people, and the good order and preservation of civil government, essentially depend upon piety, religion and morality; and as these cannot be generally diffused through a community, but by the institution of the public worship of God, and of public instructions in piety, religion and morality: Therefore, to promote their happiness and to secure the good order and preservation of their government, the people of this commonwealth have a right to invest their legislature with

---

[132] Neem, 388.

power to authorize and require, and the legislature shall, from time to time, authorize and require, the several towns, parishes, precincts, and other bodies politic, or religious societies, to make suitable provision, at their own expense, for the institution of the public worship of God, and for the support and maintenance of public Protestant teachers of piety, religion and morality, in all cases where such provision shall not be made voluntarily.[133]

This portion of the Massachusetts constitution was amended in 1833 at the time of disestablishment and the reference to teachers was dropped. But that deletion did not necessarily change the *content* of the lesson plans or the desires of religious advocates, in Massachusetts or in other jurisdictions.

After the American Revolution, the call for public education grew. But what were the goals of that initiative? The Massachusetts model had clear religious aims, linking the Bible with the moral education of the children of the Commonwealth. Another purpose for requiring public education was assimilation. As diverse groups emigrated to the United States, the need to instill "American" cultural values would have been of paramount importance, at least to some, who sought to reduce social friction and to foster moral behavior.[134] Whether that was a naïve expectation when it came to the subject of religion remained to be seen. But as Horace Mann wrote, "In no school should the Bible have been opened to reveal the sword of the polemic, but to unloose

---

[133] Excerpt from the Massachusetts Constitution, Art. III.

[134] Green, *The Bible, the School, and the Constitution*, 11.

the dove of peace."[135] Sadly, something else was occasionally unloosed: violence.

In 1844, a year before the Great Famine in Ireland began, there were anti-Catholic riots in and around Philadelphia. What spawned the riots? The suggestion that Catholics were seeking to have the Bible removed from public schools. And the "Bible" in question was the King James Version, which notably does not contain explanatory notations. This omission had been a conscious choice by its patron, King James I of England. He commissioned a translation to be free from competing doctrines thereby, in theory, silencing the disputing factions within and around the Church of England. The debates did not end, but an editorial balance was struck by the translators at the unyielding direction of the king.

In the 1840s, reading from the King James Version was a standard part of the school curriculum in Philadelphia. But the local Roman Catholic bishop, Francis Kenrick, had requested that Catholic school children be permitted to read from a different version, the Douay-Rheims Bible.[136] In May 1844, this request led

---

[135] Green, 22.

[136] This English translation of the Bible was published in 1582, decades before the KJV. It was the preferred English translation for Catholics. One point of preference for the translation was that it had been found to be free from "doctrinal and moral error," obviously by Catholic authorities. One Catholic source wryly noted that being free from such errors is not the same as being a good translation: "If someone utters the Spanish sentence '*La manzana es verde*' and I translate that as 'The apple is red,' then I have not committed a moral or theological error, but I *have* committed a translation error (*verde* means green, not red)." See Jimmy Akin, "Uncomfortable Facts about the Douay-Rheims," *Catholic Answers,* February 1, 2002, catholic.com/magazine/print-edition/uncomfortable-facts -about-the-douay-rheims.

to a directive from the Board of Controllers of the public school that children could read from alternative Bible versions, such as the Douay-Rheims. This sparked protests by nativist groups, including by the American Republican Party. This was a precursor group to the Know Nothing Party rather than an incarnation of the modern Republican Party, which would not be formed for another decade.

The proto-Know Nothings held a rally in a predominantly Irish Catholic neighborhood outside the city in the then suburb of Kensington, since annexed into Philadelphia. The group sought refuge from bad weather in a local marketplace, but the rhetoric grew heated in these closed quarters and local Irish Catholics clashed with the interlopers. When the latter fled to the streets, some assailants fired guns upon them from surrounding buildings. One man among the nativists, George Schiffer, was killed. The violence spread with attacks on the Seminary of the Sisters of Charity and surrounding houses.

A subsequent mob returned to Kensington, set fire to the marketplace where the riots had begun as well as many houses and even the Hibernia fire station. Later violence destroyed a Catholic church, its rectory, and the previously attacked Seminary of the Sisters of Charity. Another Catholic church and a school were set ablaze in Philadelphia. Violence periodically erupted over the coming months, with dueling militias being called forth and armed groups guarding neighborhoods and religious buildings. Overall, fourteen people died in the violence and dozens more were injured.

Violence over the choice of Bibles also found its way into the classroom. March 14, 1859, was a school day in Boston, Massachusetts. McLaurin F. Cooke, a schoolteacher, was leading his class at the Eliot School. Once per week, the children were required to recite the Ten Commandments, and this was such a day. Thomas J. Wall, an eleven-year-old boy, refused to do so. A local Catholic priest had implored Thomas and other students at the school not to comply with the recitation because these commandments were presented from a translation unacceptable to Catholic authorities. The children were promised a religious medal if they held firm, rather than be "cowards to their religion."[137] They were further warned that their names would be read before the Sunday congregation if they failed to comply. Thomas refused to recite.

The teacher called Thomas before the class. Thomas was warned that if he did not recite the Ten Commandments, he would be punished until he did. The teacher took a rattan stick, three-eighths of an inch in diameter. With the stick, he whipped Thomas on his hands. He would do so for a span of time and then instruct Thomas to comply with the assignment. This cycle of whipping and instruction continued on for thirty minutes. There were occasional breaks when the teacher would leave the room, and Thomas' fellow Catholics would encourage him to hold out against the punishment. Eventually, however, Thomas submitted to the requirements of the day and the whipping ceased.

Thomas' father swore out a criminal complaint against the teacher for the whipping. The teacher was arrested and charged. The legal case was eventually considered by a court, which found that the teacher had not committed any wrongdoing. Corporal

---

[137] Wall v. Cooke, 7 Amer. L. Register 417, 419 (1859).

punishment was not itself deemed a problem in the schools of 1859. This degree and method of punishment was also not of concern, regardless of modern feelings on the matter. The teacher was declared to be following the directives of the school authorities who in turn were complying with the Massachusetts statute for public schools. With all this decided, the teacher was found not guilty.

The enabling statute for the public schools required that pupils read daily some portion of the Bible from the "common English version."[138] The Boston School Committee further directed that "The morning exercises of all schools will commence with reading a portion of the Scriptures . . . followed with the Lord's Prayer repeated by the teacher alone, or chanted by the teacher and the children in concert . . . and also that the pupils will learn the Ten Commandments, and repeat them once a week." The Ten Commandments are, of course, set forth in the Bible, and the Lord's Prayer is drawn from the Gospels of Matthew and Luke.

The teacher complied with the law, but did the law itself violate the rights of the child? According to the *Cooke* court, no. The legislature had also directed the schools and their teachers:

> to exert their best endeavors to impress upon the minds of children and youth . . . the principles of piety, justice, and a sacred regard to truth, love to their country, humanity and universal benevolence, sobriety, industry, and frugality, chastity moderation, and temperance, and those other virtues which are the

---

[138] *Cooke*, 421.

ornaments of human society, and basis upon which a republican constitution is founded.[139]

The Bible was offered as the lynchpin of this effort, the vehicle for instilling this long list of virtues into the budding minds of students. As described in *Cooke*, public schools were "the granite foundation on which our republican form of government rests." Recall that public schools had been a feature of Massachusetts, and Boston specifically, since the seventeenth century. Boston schools as an institute had long preceded the United States as a republic. And the Bible had been at the center of this educational effort for over two centuries. That historical longevity does not necessarily make what happened acceptable, given the shifting legal protections of religious rights, but use of the Bible was a long-standing tradition.

Why not allow a child of a differing faith to be excused from the exercise? To prevent the tyranny of the *minority*. "[W]hen one pupil can be found in each public school of the Commonwealth with conscientious scruples against reading the Bible . . . the Bible may be banished from them, and so the matter of education may be taken from the State government and placed in the hands of a few children."[140] If the Bible verse being read one day treads upon a sectarian belief, or the version used does not comport with a particular denomination, the Bible could be banned.

And so, every denomination may object for conscience sake, and war upon the Bible and its use in common schools. . . . If

---

[139] *Cooke*, 420–421.

[140] *Cooke*, 422.

tender conscience may rightfully claim such unlimited power, what constitutional injustice is daily done in our courts of law, by swearing by the Protestant by the uplifted hand, the Roman Catholic upon the Evangelists, the Jew upon the Pentateuch, while facing East, with his head covered, and refusing to admit the Infidel as a witness at all!

The *Cooke* judge gets quite worked up over this notion, inciting the reader with a rare and incredulous exclamation point.

The Massachusetts constitution protected religious liberties, but that protection rather precisely extended to worship and belief and not to the curriculum of schools. It was to protect "the Buddhist and the Brahmin, the Pagan and the Jew, the Christian and the Turk" from being "subjected to fines, cast into prisons, starved in dungeons, burned at the stake, or made to feel the power of the inquisition." Furthermore, the Bible had been long used in the schools and the student is not requested to believe it, "to receive it as the only true version of the laws of God." As this logic goes, the schoolchildren of Boston were not being required to believe what they were reading or mean what they were praying, either a saving grace or a disheartening reality of the process.

The *Cooke* case followed a similar dispute in Maine, without the whipping or exclamation points. In *Donahoe v. Richards*, a "scholar" (i.e., student) was expelled for refusing to read from the King James Version of the Bible. The case was a struggle over definitions, with the expelled student seeking not to be forced to read a version of the Bible inconsistent with her religious tradition and the school authorities decrying an effort to remove the Bible from schools. "Can anyone doubt that the real question is not whether each child shall choose its version [of the Bible], but whether the Bible shall be read at all?"[141]

Actually, one could credibly doubt that conclusion because the student had expressly requested the option of using a different version of the Bible. The school authorities, through their counsel, transformed that request for an option into the imposition of a ban. These advocates for the school further raised the rhetorical stakes of the debate: "The entire book [the Bible] is the noblest monument of style, of thought, of beauty, of sublimity, of moral teaching, of pathetic narrative [i.e., emotion arousing], the richest treasury of household words, of familiar phrases, of popular illustrations and associations, that any language has ever possessed."

Subtle, this was not.

The court eschewed such heightened language but came to an effectively similar result. The school authority had a right to choose the Bible as a school text. The Bible could be used, but the tenets of any particular sect could not be taught. And it was found that "No theological doctrines were taught. The creed of no sect was confirmed or denied. The truth or falsehood of the book in which the scholars were required to read was not asserted . . . the Bible was used merely as a book in which instruction of reading was given."[142] Reading the Greek myths or the Qur'an would similarly not interfere with the religious beliefs of students or affirm the truth of those texts, assuming those had

---

[141] Donahoe v. Richards et al., 38 Maine 379, 383 (1854).

[142] *Donahoe*, 399.

been grammar school textbook options offered in the State of Maine in 1859.

The choice of one translation of the Bible over another was not sufficient cause rising to the level of an infringement of the student's civil rights. A preference for one version could be expressed by the schools without establishing a religious preference. And in a remarkable bit of legal jiu jitsu, the *Donahoe* court turned the argument about selecting Bibles around: "The right of one sect to interdict or expurgate [such a choice], would place the schools in subordination to the sect interdicting or expurgating . . . surrender[ing] the power of the State to a government not emanating from the people, nor recognized by the Constitution."[143]

In summation, the *Donahoe* court invoked the grand purpose of assimilation, which would become an enduring theme in the struggle over religion in the schools: "In no other way can the process of assimilation be so readily and thoroughly accomplished as through the medium of public schools, which are alike open to the children of the rich and poor, of the stranger and the citizen. It is the duty of those to whom this sacred trust is confided to discharge it with magnanimous liberality and *Christian kindness*."[144]

Christian kindness, a term used as a generic virtue rather than a doctrinal aspect of a religious tradition. The King James Version of the Bible is just a book, one offered up as a trove of cultural and linguistic treasures, the pinnacle of the English lan-

---

[143] *Donahoe,* 407.

[144] *Donahoe,* 413 (emphasis supplied).

guage, and not as a religious text. In *Donahoe* and *Cooke*, the courts assumed that a version of the Bible could be studied as literature without the inculcation of religious doctrine, much like the goal set forth by Horace Mann.

However, these bland pronouncements about the general utility of the Bible as morally ennobling literature ignored deep distrust over the issue. There are decidedly fewer street battles over reading Hamlet. Immediately before the earlier and deadly Philadelphia riots of 1844, the school board had voted to allow Catholics and other students to use their preferred Biblical translation. The Know Nothing protests came as a result of that decision, which would not have removed the Bible from the classrooms but would have displaced the preferred Protestant version of the Bible from exclusive use.

The culture of the United States in the 1840s, as well as its courts, assumed that a homogenized Protestantism was the philosophical basis for moral understanding and the necessary route toward social assimilation. As was seen a few decades later, a massive influx of European immigrants, including many Catholics, strained that cultural assumption. American Catholics in particular responded to rejections of their concerns about public education by trying to build an independent system of parochial schools. The late nineteenth-century fight over how to fund those schools caused an enduring political rift, one that has survived to the present day.

CHAPTER 10

Separation of Church and School

ON SEPTEMBER 29, 1875, President Ulysses S. Grant gave a speech before a veteran's group in Des Moines, Iowa.[145] This might seem an underwhelming political prelude to what will become a long-lived legal controversy. Indeed, President Grant's celebrity star may have dimmed over time, but an account of this seemingly minor event has been set down in glowing tones: "President Ulysses S. Grant, the most illustrious soldier of the century, whose name and fame were cherished with those of Washington and Lincoln, honored the reunion with his quiet and unostentatious presence."[146]

---

[145] This was a reunion of the Society of the Army of the Tennessee, a Union army that General Grant led during the Civil War, such as at the Battle of Shiloh. The text of the speech may be found at "President Grant's Des Moines Address," *The Annals of Iowa* 3, no. 2 (1897), 138–139.

[146] J.A. Swisher, "Grant's Des Moines Speech," *The Palimpsest* 6, no. 12 (1925) 409–410.

Grant's address was unostentatiously brief, sounding a note of solidarity with his former troops and commitment to the Union they had defended. He stated that he was not trying to be partisan in his remarks, but to encourage protection of "free republican institutions." He predicted that if the Union was to face a similar challenge, "the dividing line will not be the Mason and Dixon's, but between patriotism and intelligence on the one side and superstition, ambition and ignorance on the other." The last three qualities are broad but their target was likely singular: Catholic Democrats.

The timing of the speech was notable, one year before the United States centennial would be held. It would be a national celebration falling about a decade after the conclusion of the Civil War, Grant's claim to enduring fame, and the assassination of President Abraham Lincoln, Grant's staunch political patron during the war.

President Grant begins his speech in broad terms, but quickly gets specific:

> Let us all labor to add all needed guarantees for the more perfect security of Free Thought, Free Speech, a Free Press, Pure Morals, Unfettered Religious Sentiment and of Equal Right and Privileges to all men respective of Nationality, Color or Religion. Encourage free schools and resolve that not one dollar of money appropriated to their support no matter how raised, shall be appropriated to the support of any sectarian school. Resolve that either the state or the Nation, or both, combined shall support institutions of learning sufficient to afford to every child growing up in the land the opportunity of a good common

school education, unmixed with sectarian, pagan or atheistical tenets. Leave the matter of religion to the family circle[;] the church and the private school supported entirely by private contributions. Keep the church and state forever separate. With these safeguards I believe the battles which created us "the army of the Tennessee" will not have been fought in vain.

One might read this text and mistakenly surmise that the American Civil War was a dispute over religion. While oblique sounding over a century later, the address must be considered in its historical and, more importantly, political context. The political landscape had been reshaped by the war, and Grant's message about religion treads firmly upon that landscape's most unstable fault line, one continually erupting between Protestants and Catholics.

To his credit, President Grant had not abandoned the abolitionist cause, even though he may not have highlighted it in the speech. He was far more a champion for formerly enslaved people than his predecessor, Andrew Johnson, a pro-Union Democrat from Tennessee, an ardent opponent of Reconstruction, and the first president to face impeachment.

After the war, the leaders of the former Confederate states were passing laws that in essence recreated slavery. The Republican-controlled U.S. Congress began passing their own laws, restricting or annulling those efforts. Johnson in turn vetoed these federal laws, which vetoes were typically overridden. He was impeached and his trial was conducted before the U.S. Senate. Johnson's primary offense was illegally trying to get rid of his Secretary of War, Edwin Stanton, who staunchly opposed Johnson's anti-Reconstruction efforts. By one vote, Johnson was not removed from office. He served out his term and was later elected from Tennessee to the U.S. Senate, dying in office after five months.

A political split came to exist between, on the one hand, Republicans and emancipated Black people, and on the other, Democrats and Catholics. Black people had obvious reasons for supporting Republicans, who championed Reconstruction and worked against Southern efforts to re-entrench the trappings of slavery. Conversely, Catholics were often urban workers, who developed strongholds of influence in cities and labor unions. Irish immigrants in particular had been supported by Democratic political machines, notably Tammany Hall in New York City. These groups offered tangible support to city residents before welfare systems existed and helped immigrants with paperwork toward citizenship and efforts to assimilate.

These underlying religious and racial biases in politics would last for decades. And the expression of these differences would take many forms, shifting back and forth across that political divide as the two sides traded control. This moving pendulum of power resulted in wrangling over the Reconstruction of the South, the impeaching of President Johnson, ratifying the anti-slavery amendments to the Constitution, and creating restrictive immigration policies such as the Chinese Exclusion Act of 1882.

Immigration had been a relatively relaxed process since the Naturalization Act of 1790, allowing large numbers of immigrants into the country freely. This mostly open border would remain so well into the twentieth century, allowing millions of Irish refugees and later Eastern and Southern Europeans into the country after short waiting periods. By comparison, current practices and backlogs for some immigrants (e.g., Mexicans) applying to become U.S. citizens make the wait time for a "green card" more like 10 to 15 years.[147] Waiting in line could mean waiting for decades (which may be the point).

As for religion, political battles would be waged over school funding for religious schools as suggested by Grant's Des Moines address. The terms "religious" or "sectarian" are typically used, but many opponents to such school funding had one primary target in mind: parochial schools sponsored by the Roman Catholic church. Public schools were state-funded, but as previously described, the curricula often included "moral education" of some variety. Catholics were concerned by this subject matter because it was felt to be at odds with Catholic teachings and practices, while being more in keeping with broadly Protestant terms. Conversely, Protestants thought reading from the Bible, and specifically the King James Version of the Bible, was an essential facet of the moral education of civic-minded citizens.

There was at this time in history prayer in schools. Which prayer? Typically the Lord's Prayer. Which version? One likely similar to the Anglican Book of Common Prayer of 1662:

Our Father, which art in heaven, Hallowed be thy Name. Thy Kingdom come. Thy will be done in earth, As it is in heaven. Give us this day our daily bread. And forgive us our trespasses,

---

[147] Visa Bulletin, September 2019, U.S. Dept. of State, travel.state.gov/content/travel/en/legal/visa-law0/visa-bulletin/2019/visa-bulletin-for-september-2019.html.

As we forgive them that trespass against us. And lead us not into temptation, But deliver us from evil. For thine is the kingdom, the power, and the glory, For ever and ever. Amen.

The last line, about "the kingdom, the power, and the glory," is not typically included in Catholic versions of the prayer, while most Protestants add it. The line is not "original," if one credits its absence from the earliest written versions of the Gospel of Matthew. Later versions contain the line, which notably appears in the King James Version of Matthew 6:13. Conversely, the line does not appear, and has never appeared, in the form of the prayer set out in the Gospel of Luke. Why all the fuss over a few words? An entire war was once fought over who would receive bread and wine during Christian communion, as opposed to just receiving the bread.[148] Religious disputes are not always simple matters to "get over."

President Grant was picking up on the ongoing religious struggle between Protestants and Catholics. The earlier Bible

---

[148] The Hussite Wars, also known as the Hussite Crusades, were waged between 1419 and 1434 in Bohemia, a part of the Holy Roman Empire in the area now known as the Czech Republic. The conflict was about more than bread and wine, including papal corruption and local control of religious life. Plus, a key leader of the movement, Jan Hus, was seized and executed under a rather faulty promise of safe passage to negotiate peace with the papacy. But this demand for both "species" of communion, the bread and wine, was the most concrete symbol of the conflict. In an aside to the aside, the Hussites almost succeeded in defeating the combined papal forces, but a faction of the group changed sides in the dispute and the remaining rebels were put down. One key concession for the betrayal was the authorization for provision of bread and wine for communion to the common Bohemian people. For far more detail about the Hussites, see Steven Ozment, *The Age of Reform 1250–1550: An Intellectual and Religious History of Late Medieval and Reformation Europe* (New Haven: Yale University Press, 1980).

riots of the 1840s and 1850s occurred during an economic down-turn, perhaps stoking the tensions leading up to the riots and the not too far-off Civil War. Catholic bishops had sought to make the best of the public school option by obtaining the right for students to use Catholic translations of the Bible. But as those efforts faced opposition and lawsuits, the Catholic churches in the United States began to plan for a separate system of paro-chial schools without the overlay of Protestant teachings and texts. The question then became how to pay for these schools. And the answer was, Catholics hoped, to share public funds ded-icated to the then-existing system.

Into this debate steps Ulysses S. Grant. President Grant strikes a secular tone in his 1875 remarks, which through the lens of history could seem an even-handed effort; there are, after all, logical reasons for seeking to shield public coffers from the demands of particular religious groups. General Grant, however, was not always so high-minded in his religious sentiments. He issued a less than even-handed pronouncement in 1862, his infa-mous General Order No. 11. The order held in pertinent part that: "The Jews, as a class violating every regulation of trade established by the Treasury Department and also department orders, are hereby expelled from the department within twenty-four hours from the receipt of this order."[149] The "department" was the military district Grant oversaw comprising parts of Ken-tucky, Mississippi, and Tennessee.

---

[149] There are some suggestions that Grant did not mean *actual* Jews but dis-reputable traders in the area, who he for some reason then categorized as "Jews." Not the most stirring defense against anti-Semitism.

President Lincoln was immediately informed of the incident by Jewish representatives from the "department" and he promptly issued the following telegram to Grant: "A paper purporting to be General Orders, No. 11, issued by you December 17, has been presented here. By its terms, it expels all Jews from your department. If such an order has been issued, it will be immediately revoked." Interestingly, the General Order No. 11 affair galvanized Jewish citizens to petition the federal government for immediate redress of the problem. Their efforts were directly rewarded, bolstering a sense of the civic position of Jews in the United States. In spite of enduring prejudice, the episode offered a concrete example of fighting back against bigotry and winning.[150]

The religious intolerance reflected in that anti-Semitic order of 1862 may have manifested in the perceived religious intolerance and anti-Catholicism of the speech in 1875. Issues of religion were not far from the political calculus of the time. The Republican push for universal public education free from sectarian influence had a threefold attraction: offering up a social reform issue to a public weary of Reconstruction-era upheaval, undercutting the Democrats' Catholic supporters, and (hopefully) distracting the electorate from the sundry scandals plaguing the Grant administration.[151]

---

[150] Sarna, *American Judaism*, 121–122.

[151] Green, *The Bible, the School, and the Constitution*, 185–186. It is worth noting that the infamous "Whiskey Ring" bribery scandal during Grant's term in office came to light in May 1875. Grant's Des Moines speech on school funding was given in September 1875. The corruption trials started in October 1875. Barely a coincidence.

For example, the Republican Party platform before the Presidential election of 1876 provides:

> The public school system of the several states is the bulwark of the American republic; and, with a view to its security and permanence, we recommend an amendment to the constitution of the United States, forbidding the application of any public funds or property for the benefit of any school or institution under sectarian control.

The Democratic platform of the same year takes a different tack:

> The false issue with which they [the Republicans] would enkindle sectarian strife in respect to the public schools, of which the establishment and support belong exclusively to the several States, and which the Democratic party has cherished from their foundation, and is resolved to maintain without partiality or preference for any class, sect or creed, and without contributions from the treasury to any.

As the Democrats of the time suggested, education was not a federal issue. Schools were the purview of the states. But the passage of the Reconstruction Amendments after the Civil War had federalized many formerly local concerns—how could formerly enslaved people be protected if pre-war laws concerning their treatment simply snapped back into effect? The Republicans pushed for greater federal control over the Southern states, while calls to support states' rights often sounded most loudly in the former Confederacy. And, not coincidentally, the press for nonsectarian school funding by Republicans would undercut Catholics who were seen as pro-Democratic. There were undoubtedly people sincerely interested in the separation of church and school, but sincerity can often be allied with cynicism when it comes to achieving political results.

After the war, the Republicans had succeeded in amending the U.S. Constitution to protect free Black people and, as developed over the following decades, to expand the power of the federal government within state government matters. A new push to amend the Constitution concerning school funding was championed by James G. Blaine of Maine. He was the son of a Presbyterian father and a Roman Catholic mother, raised into his father's faith. He served in the House of Representatives and then in the Senate. He was a powerful orator, in a time when that mattered, and became a strong voice in the Republican Party. Blaine sought the Republican nomination for President in 1876 and 1880, which he lost. Finally, he was selected as the nominee in 1884, losing in the general election to Grover Cleveland.

Blaine's family background might imply a more neutral stance on church-state matters, but his efforts on behalf of the Republicans no doubt muddied that position for the public. In modern terminology, his push for the amendment regarding school funding served to rally the Protestant base of the Republican Party even as it may have energized (and angered) the Democratic Party and its Catholic supporters. He dropped his advocacy of the amendment after he lost the 1876 election, and the effort did not factor in his electioneering efforts for the presidency in 1884.[152]

---

[152] Green, 196.

Regardless of his inner motivations, the effort was dubbed the "Blaine Amendment," inextricably linking Blaine with what is often equated to an anti-Catholic measure. The proposed amendment read as follows:

> No State shall make any law respecting an establishment of religion, or prohibiting the free exercise thereof; and no money raised by taxation in any State for the support of public schools, or derived from any public fund therefor, nor any public lands devoted thereto, shall ever be under the control of any religious sect; nor shall any money so raised or lands so devoted be divided between religious sects or denominations.[153]

The proposal passed in the House of Representatives, 180–7, but failed by four votes in the Senate. The amendment never went into effect on the federal level but was far more popular on the state level. A majority of states at that time ratified versions of the "Blaine Amendment" into their constitutions, broadly limiting the public funding of sectarian schools.

Again, most such "sectarian" schools were Catholic. The pressure for and development of a separate Catholic school system arose around the time of the Bible Riots prior to the Civil War and intensified afterwards. In 1852, at the First Plenary Council of Baltimore, a gathering of American Catholic bishops called for the creation of schools in every parish, with the teachers to be paid out of parish funds. A later Baltimore council in 1866 called for the purging of school materials contrary to the faith. Another

---

[153] 4 Cong. Record 5453 (1876).

in 1884, notably after Grant's speech, instructed that: "Parents must send their children to such schools unless the bishop should judge the reason for sending them elsewhere to be sufficient. Ways and means are also considered for making the parochial schools more efficient. It is desirable that these schools be free."[154]

Financial support for such schools, if they were indeed to be free, would have been a great expense for a parish, particularly for working class immigrants. The desire to share public school funding was an obvious offshoot of that concern. Public funds were already flowing to Catholic organizations, most notably in eastern cities such as through the largesse of the Tammany Hall political system in New York City.[155] The argument that education funding should be made through a per-pupil calculation survives into modern times as a desire for school vouchers usable even at religious schools.

One argument brewing in the era of the Blaine Amendment was the perception that schools were becoming increasingly secular. This had been a concern during the Bible Riots, but the argument at that time was that Catholics were seeking to remove the "Bible" from the classroom with their objections against the King James Version. That argument transformed over time and found its way into Catholic concerns, such as from this magazine editorial in the *Catholic World* of 1869:

---

[154] William Fanning, "Plenary Councils of Baltimore," in *The Catholic Encyclopedia* (New York: Robert Appleton Company, 1907), newadvent.org/cathen/02235a.htm.

[155] Green, *The Bible, the School, and the Constitution*, 181.

[W]e favor secular learning and science; but we oppose separating secular training from religious training, and can never consent to the secularization of education. Here is where we and the present race of Protestants differ. It is because the common schools secularize, and are intended by their chief supporters to secularize, education and to make all life secular, that we oppose them, and refuse to send our children to them where we can possibly avoid it.[156]

Protestants would differ on the matter, with more liberal groups approving of the removal of Bible reading and religious exercises (e.g., school prayer) from the classroom. More Evangelical Protestants generally opposed both the "secularization" of the schools and the public funding of a parallel system of Catholic schools.[157] And yet even those who opposed sectarian schooling might still assert that Bible reading was not sectarian but merely "Christian," an argument offered with nary a tremor of cognitive dissonance.[158]

The federal Blaine Amendment failed and yet the "mini-Blaines" flourished across the states. The implicit intent of the Blaine Amendment and its progeny may have been to undermine support for Catholic schools. But if that was arguably the original objective, the broadness of the language permitted those same state amendments to be used generally to prevent the funding of religious schools or, critically, religion in schools. The

---

[156] "Our Established Church," *Catholic World* IX, no. 53, August 1869, 584.

[157] Green, *The Bible, the School, and the Constitution*, 185.

[158] See Green, 191–192.

historical root of so-called secularism in the public schools was partly a desire to keep public schools blandly Protestant. The language of those efforts was generic, to avoid sectarian claims, but the intention was somehow to keep the Bible readings and the morning prayers as moral instruction rather than denominational advocacy.

Once enacted, however, the Blaine Amendments could be used as worded to secularize the schools. The First Amendment was intended to avoid religious preferences by the federal government. It did not apply to the states, which were free to maintain or to establish churches. In a quirk of history and politics, it took these backhanded efforts against Catholics to exclude, in time, almost all religious aspects from a school curriculum. As the backroom political fights of the 1870s slipped away, the real-world consequences of prohibiting funding of sectarian education would endure and grow over the decades that followed.

CHAPTER 11

Making a Federal Case Out of It: The Jehovah's Witnesses

IT WAS 1940 IN THE UNITED STATES. Europe was at war; the U.S. was not.

In response to the Great Depression, President Franklin Delano Roosevelt had pressed on many legal and political fronts to drag the U.S. economy out of its doldrums. The national government began to intervene in widespread matters of employment, agriculture, culture, and economics. At the ends of the political spectrum, this was seen either as saving the nation from decades of mismanagement and inequality or FDR and his coterie sticking the government's proverbial nose into matters private and local. This expression of federal power in the various states was much like the Reconstruction period in the 1860s and 1870s and faced a range of opposition, including Supreme Court decisions striking down major programs. After decades of judicial opposition to FDR's economic policies, the Supreme Court finally moved to support the regulation of the economy, such as through state minimum wages.[159]

The Roosevelt Administration was not explicitly or implicitly concerned with religion in this economic context. But a widening footprint of federal interests began to shift a historic balancing act. The federal government's role in local religious issues slowly began to grow alongside other expanding influences. And an outsized portion of that growth in the 1940s is coincidentally the result of one religious group's particular mix of preoccupations and prohibitions: the Jehovah's Witnesses.

In 1870, Charles Taze Russell helped form a Bible study group in Pittsburgh, Pennsylvania. This would become known as the Bible Student movement, from which would eventually arise the religious tradition of the Jehovah's Witnesses. A haberdasher, Russell later became a preacher who was heavily influenced by chiliastic thinking, meaning millenialist or millenarian notions that the world will be shortly transformed or destroyed by apocalyptic events. In particular, Russell looked to the Adventist movement in Christianity (e.g., the Seventh-Day Adventists), which movement had in various incarnations repeatedly, and from a laymen's perspective unsuccessfully predicted the end of the world through the Second Coming of Jesus Christ.[160]

In the years 1873–1874, according to Adventist authorities, Jesus was to return. Therefore, by their sense of unfolding religious

---

[159] West Coast Hotel Co. v. Parrish, 300 U.S. 379 (1937).

[160] See, e.g., Jonathan Butler, "From Millerism to Seventh-day Adventism: 'Boundlessness to Consolidation,'" *Church History* 55, no. 1 (March 1986), 50–64.

events, the world was to come to an end in one form or another. And yet neither Jesus' return nor the end of times occurred in any demonstrable sense. This was not an isolated incident. Adventists and their precursor group, the Millerites, had been predicting the end of the world since the 1840s—one major buildup and climb down in 1844 came to be known as the "Great Disappointment."

Russell and others eventually diverged from this school of thinking, concluding that the Second Coming of Jesus had indeed occurred in a *spiritual* sense.[161] Russell in particular concluded that the appropriate remaining task for the faithful was to gather the flock in anticipation of the true end in 1878, when they would be spirited away before the upcoming travails of Armageddon. And yet 1878 came and went without relevant incident or the "rapturing" of the faithful. There was a series of these prophetic disappointments, dates offered by Russell and later by leaders of the Jehovah's Witnesses without the end being obviously nigh: 1878, 1914, 1918, 1925, and 1975.[162]

Any group that is anticipating the end of the world, perhaps understandably, would not spend much time or effort in the way of building durable institutional structures. Over time, however, the Jehovah's Witnesses began to organize and to redefine themselves in light of these events. These dates, in hindsight, held great meaning and importance. Like Russell's insight about a spiritual Second Coming, the Jehovah's Witnesses reinterpreted the prophesized dates. For example, the 1878 disappointment

---

[161] Joseph F. Zygmunt, "Prophetic Failure and Chiliastic Identity: The Case of Jehovah's Witnesses," *American Journal of Sociology* 75, no. 6 (May 1970), 931.

[162] Zygmunt, 933 and 941.

was said to mark the moment when "nominal Christian churches were cast from God's favor."[163] This is significant because it also marked a denominational moment at which Jehovah's Witnesses began to take a sharply critical view of other Protestants, entering a vigorous phase of evangelical outreach to save as many souls as possible from the clutches of Babylon, that is, every other religious group.

In the fertile period from 1914 to 1925, bookended by prophetic dates seemingly gone by, the "Time of the Gentiles" was said to have expired. Besides ushering in an aggressive era of evangelization, this conclusion about the nature of God's plan would lead to a period of rejection of worldly authority.[164] Jehovah's Witnesses had previously been more accommodating of government expectations and influences, but a new phase of open defiance of government authorities and related legal disputes began.

In 1940, Newton Cantwell and his sons, Jesse and Russell, were arrested in New Haven, Connecticut.[165] They were charged with breaching the peace. They had been going house to house with books, pamphlets, and a portable phonograph. They would ask the occupants if it would be permissible to play a record. One recording described a book entitled "Enemies" which included an attack on Catholicism. The particular neighborhood in which the arrest arose was predominantly Catholic, a circumstance likely leading to the complaint to the police and the Cantwells' subsequent troubles.

---

[163] Zygmunt, 935.

[164] Zygmunt, 936.

[165] Cantwell v. Connecticut, 310 U.S. 296 (1940).

They were charged under the following provisions of a local statute:

> No person shall solicit money, services, subscriptions or any valuable thing for any alleged religious, charitable, or philanthropic cause, from other than a member of the organization for whose benefit such person is soliciting or within the county in which such person or organization is located unless such cause shall have been approved by the secretary of the public welfare council. Upon application of any person in behalf of such cause, the secretary shall determine whether such cause is a religious one or is a bone fide object of charity or philanthropy and conforms to reasonable standards of efficiency and integrity, and, if he shall so find, shall approve the same and issue to the authority in charge a certificate to that effect. Such certificate may be revoked at any time. Any person violating any provision of this section shall be fined no more than one hundred dollars or imprisoned not more than thirty days or both.

The Cantwells argued that they were distributing books and pamphlets and were therefore not subject to this law. The trial court and ultimately the Connecticut Supreme Court found that they had been soliciting funds for a religious cause and therefore the statute and its registration requirements did apply. The courts both found that solicitation was being regulated rather than religious speech or religious publications. Jesse Cantwell was also convicted of an additional charge for having played the "Enemies" recording to a pair of Catholic men on the street, who were angered by the critical message about Catholicism and deemed it an insult and an assault.[166]

The U.S. Supreme Court overturned these convictions. The statute violated both the First and Fourteenth Amendments of the U.S. Constitution: "The First Amendment declares that Congress shall make no law respecting the establishment of religion or prohibiting the free exercise thereof. The Fourteenth Amendment has rendered the legislation of the states as incompetent as Congress to enact such laws." Critically for discussions about religious freedom, the Supreme Court had "incorporated" the First Amendment provision regarding the free exercise of religion, making it a legal restriction directly affecting the states of the Union. The significance of this process is both deep and broad, transforming the religious rights in the 1940s through the First Amendment. And that process arguably begins with *Cantwell*, for prior to this decision the Supreme Court would have left similar matters of religious regulation to the individual states.

The Court in *Cantwell* noted that there were two key aspects of the Free Exercise Clause: the freedom to believe and the freedom to act.[167] It opined that the freedom to believe is absolute but that the freedom to act is limited as necessitated by the protection of society. And yet that need for protection must not unduly infringe upon the underlying freedom in question. Connecticut authorities could regulate the time, place, and manner of religious solicitations and could by their efforts

---

[166] An "assault" is like a threat, as in "I will punch you." A "battery" is the threat carried out, as in "Oh my, I have been punched."

[167] *Cantwell*, 303.

appropriately seek to assure good order, peace, and comfort in the community.

However, requiring a certificate to authorize religious solicitation was too restrictive. It potentially allowed a total prohibition against the actions of a religious person or group. The official granting or denying the certificate had the power to determine if something was "religious" by nature. This broad power could allow for blanket censorship. "[T]o condition the solicitation of aid for the perpetuation of religious views or systems upon a license, the grant of which rests on the exercise of a determination by state authority as to what is a religious cause, is to lay a forbidden burden upon the exercise of liberty protected by the Constitution."[168]

A license is legally different from a right. A license is discretionary and may be rescinded, such as a driver's license denied for failing a test or rescinded for a bad driving history. A right is inherent to the person, though it may be subject to certain restrictions consistent with good social order as described by the Court. A restriction, however, is not a denial. The Cantwells' solicitation was upheld, and the certificate requirement was not.

Similarly, Jesse Cantwell's conviction for his street encounter with the two Catholic men was also reversed. There had been no assault, meaning no threat of bodily harm, in his actions. He sought to persuade his audience to buy a book, even if the expressed views were "misguided" in the eyes of those listening. In matters of both religious and political speech, "in spite of the probability of excesses and abuses, these liberties are, in the long

---

[168] *Cantwell*, 307.

view, essential to enlightened opinion and right conduct on the part of the citizens of a democracy."[169] Not liking what someone has said is not the same as experiencing legal harm.

A question: where does one draw the line between the protection of religious freedom and the protection of speech generally? These are not the same rights. The scope of religious behavior obviously may extend beyond the realm of speaking to passers-by on the street or even distributing books and pamphlets. Coincidentally, the U.S. Supreme Court was considering during the same 1940 court session another case about religious rights, one involving Jehovah's Witnesses again in a spot of trouble.

Two schoolchildren, Lillian and William Gobitas (misspelled in the Court's opinion), were expelled from the public schools of Minersville, Pennsylvania. The infraction that precipitated the expulsion was their refusal to salute the American flag and to recite the Pledge of Allegiance. The school-sanctioned ceremony involved rising and placing the right hand over one's heart and saying, "I pledge allegiance to the flag of the United States of America and to the republic for which its stands; one nation indivisible, with liberty and justice for all."[170] The children's family were Jehovah's Witnesses and the pledging allegiance to a worldly object was inconsistent with their religious sentiments: "such a gesture of respect for the flag was forbidden by command of scripture."[171]

---

[169] *Cantwell*, 310.

[170] For those familiar with a slightly different version, the additional phrase "under God" would not be in general use until the 1950s and would not be formally added to the Pledge of Allegiance until Flag Day, 1954. That represents an entirely different religious dispute.

[171] Minersville School Dist. v. Gobitis, 310 U.S. 586, 592 (1940).

The Court invoked its recently decided, and near contemporaneous, decision in *Cantwell* to state that "[T]he Constitution assures generous immunity to the individual from imposition of penalties for offending, in the course of his own religious activities, the religious views of others, be they a minority or those who are dominant in government."[172] And yet religious views may conflict with wider secular expectations, with that which is socially perceived as for the common good or, conversely, with that which may be seen as a common danger. The *Gobitis* Court sought to reconcile two competing rights without destroying either. Individuals are not typically relieved of the requirements of general laws when such laws are not aimed at the promotion or restriction of religious beliefs—religious *beliefs*, notably, rather than personal behavior that might express such beliefs.

The Court observed in *Gobitis* that, "In a number of situations, the exertion of political authority has been sustained, while basic considerations of religious freedom have been left inviolate," citing the *Reynolds v. U.S.* decision which found that a law prohibiting polygamy did not inappropriately infringe upon a Latter-day Saint's religious freedom regardless of the group's religious views on polygamy.[173] Given that religious freedom can only exist in an "orderly, tranquil, and free society," the government has the power to promulgate general laws to protect society from chaos and disorder that might threaten the wider freedoms of that society and its members. This power to police

---

[172] *Gobitis*, 593.

[173] *Gobitis*, 594–595.

an orderly society effectively trumps religious scruples incidentally affected by the government's actions or expectations.

How does the legal maxim in *Gobitis* about maintaining social order translate into the situation of two school children refusing to stand and say the Pledge of Allegiance? "A society which is dedicated to the preservation of these ultimate values of civilization [i.e., order and tranquility] may, in self-protection, utilize the educational process for inculcating these almost unconscious feelings which bind men together in a comprehending loyalty, whatever may be their lesser differences and difficulties."[174] In other words, the school can make the children stand and recite the pledge, under the threat of expulsion and the possible denial of the benefit of a public education.

The *Gobitis* decision was written by Justice Felix Frankfurter, a well-known defender of civil rights who was also a founder of the American Civil Liberties Union in 1920. And yet the *Gobitis* decision upheld the state's power to demand a physical act of allegiance arguably at odds with the religious sensibilities of Jehovah's Witnesses. Interestingly, Frankfurter offered a dissenting opinion when the Supreme Court overturned *Gobitis* a few years later, writing:

> Saluting the flag suppresses no belief, nor curbs it. Children and their parents may believe what they please, avow their belief and practice it. It is not even remotely suggested that the requirement for saluting the flag involves the slightest restriction against the fullest opportunity on the part both of the children

---

[174] *Gobitis*, 600.

and of their parents to disavow, as publicly as they choose to do so, the meaning that others attach to the gesture of salute.[175]

These *Cantwell* and *Gobitis* decisions were issued in 1940. During that same year, the armies of Nazi Germany had invaded and conquered France and the neutral countries of Norway, the Netherlands, Denmark, and Belgium. The first peacetime military draft would be instituted in the United States, a nation not at war quite yet, but probably not feeling entirely at peace. President Roosevelt became the first and only three-term president, a vote for stability perhaps. If one can psychoanalyze a country, the United States probably felt anxious, threatened on all sides by a world at war. The protests of Pennsylvania schoolchildren and the sensibilities of a minority religious group would not be readily accommodated when the order, tranquility, and freedom of the land were at risk.

In 1942, the U.S. Congress enshrined the Pledge of Allegiance into federal law, in Public Law 77-623, Section 7:

That the pledge of allegiance to the flag, "I pledge allegiance to the flag of the United States of America and to the Republic for which it stands, one Nation indivisible, with liberty and justice for all", be rendered by standing with the right hand over the heart; extending the right hand, palm upward, toward the flag at the words "to the flag" and holding this position until the end, when the hand drops to the side. However, civilians will always show full respect to the flag when the pledge is given by

---

[175] West Virginia State Bd. of Educ. v. Barnette, 319 U.S. 624, 664 (1943).

merely standing at attention, men removing the headdress. Persons in uniform shall render the military salute.[176]

The *Gobitis* decision inspired civic action in some local governments. For example, the West Virginia legislature passed a law requiring the recitation of the Pledge of Allegiance by teachers and students in all schools: *public, private, and parochial.*[177] In addition to requiring the pledge and saluting of the flag, the law required the teaching of history and civics "for the purpose of teaching, fostering, and perpetuating ideals, principles and the spirit of Americanism, and increasing the knowledge of the organization and machinery of government."

Education was inextricably linked to action. Refusal to salute the flag could be regarded as student insubordination, resulting in expulsion. While expelled, the child could be deemed unlawfully absent from compulsory education and therefore treated as a delinquent, potentially subject to incarceration in a reformatory for the criminally inclined. The child's parents or guardians could then be liable to prosecution. Conviction could result in fines of up to $50 and a jail term of up to thirty days. These events could happen and, indeed, did happen in West Virginia.[178]

Which may bring up a nagging question: what is the big deal? Just stand up and say the pledge. Why make a federal case out of something so seemingly minor? Roll with it. Now imagine saying

---

[176] This may seem similar to the salute used in Nazi Germany. It was. The form of salute for the Pledge of Allegiance was changed as a result.

[177] *Barnette*, 624, 626.

[178] *Barnette*, 629–630.

any one of these statements: It's a ham sandwich—eat it. What's the big deal? It's a few beers—drink them. What's the big deal? It's Sunday morning—just go to work. What's the big deal?

If you are a Jehovah's Witness and saluting the American flag reminds you of paying homage to a graven image, it might be a big deal. If you are Jewish or Muslim and the school lunch is filled with pork, it might be a big deal. If you are Baptist or Latter-day Saint and you are expected to drink alcohol at a work function, it might be a big deal. If you are Christian and your job requires you to labor on Sunday, it might be a big deal. From the outside looking in, requiring someone to do something that they find religiously unacceptable may not seem terribly consequential. But as a person of faith faced with the prospect of being compelled to do or to say something, it is a far greater concern.

This thought experiment is asking the dear reader to imagine requiring someone by force of law to act in accordance with the beliefs or expectations of someone else, the majority or those who happen to be in power. Conversely, the government may have clear and non-religious reasons for requiring people to act in certain ways, such as receiving compulsory vaccinations, refraining from taking hallucinogenic drugs, or limiting yourself to one spouse. With those reasons in mind, the Supreme Court in *Gobitis* declared that the government had the right to force children to say the Pledge of Allegiance.

In *West Virginia State Board of Education v. Barnette*, just three years later and with two new Supreme Court justices on the bench, the Court dramatically changed its mind. The Supreme Court reversed the *Gobitis* decision. It did so again to support the objectives of public education, but now with a different emphasis:

Free public education, if faithful to the ideal of secular instruction and political neutrality, will not be partisan or enemy of any class, creed, party, or faction. If it is to impose any ideological discipline, however, each party or denomination must seek to control, or, failing that, to weaken, the influence of the educational system. Observance of the limitations of the Constitution will not weaken government in the field appropriate for its exercise.[179]

Public schools could become battlegrounds for religious or political disputes, as seems to have been the conclusion about West Virginia's spree of civic-mindedness. The Bill of Rights was adopted to shield certain subjects from the "vicissitudes of political controversy." The Court also noted that Congress had made its flag observances like the Pledge voluntary and even took into consideration matters of religious conscience with respect to conscription during a time of war.[180] If Congress could make religious allowances in matters of national defense, "village tyrants" could and should make allowances in matters more trivial. The Court did not name names, but the West Virginia Board of Education was probably on the short list of tyrannical suspects. Furthermore, the Court may have been reacting to waves of violence against Jehovah's Witnesses around the United States: by one account, over 2,500 attacks were made against Jehovah's Witnesses between 1940 and 1945.[181]

---

[179] *Barnette*, 637.

[180] *Barnette*, 638.

[181] Zoe Knox, "Jehovah's Witnesses as Un-Americans? Scriptural Injunctions, Civil Liberties, and Patriotism," *Journal of American Studies* 47, no. 4 (2013), 1089.

The Court went on to say that the freedoms of speech, the press, assembly, and worship may not be infringed upon lightly. They may be restricted to prevent "grave and immediate danger to interests which the State may lawfully protect."[182] The American experiment with democracy was evolving from the time of the Bill of Rights being set down in the eighteenth century: "We must transplant these rights to a soil in which the *laissez-faire* concept or principle of noninterference [of that century] has withered, at least as to economic affairs, and social advancements are increasingly sought through closer integration of society through expanded and strengthened governmental controls." With such changes in the social environment, the reliability of past legal precedents must be reviewed and potentially reconsidered.

The *Barnette* Court seems to have reacted to the extent and severity of West Virginia's efforts. People were being put in jail because their children were not saying the Pledge of Allegiance. Students were being shipped off to reform schools. The "What's the big deal?" question can be answered in two ways: therefore just obey the rules or therefore the government should pick its battles. The Supreme Court chose the latter answer:

> [The ultimate] futility of such efforts to compel coherence [of belief] is the lesson of every such effort from the Roman drive to stamp out Christianity as a disturber of its pagan unity[;] the Inquisition, as a means to religious and dynastic unity, the Siberian exiles as a means to Russian unity, down to the fast failing

---

[182] *Barnette*, 639.

efforts of our present totalitarian enemies [the Axis Powers in World War II].[183]

The Court declared a "fixed star in our constitutional constellation," that no government official can decide what is orthodox in politics, religion, or other matters of opinion. And critically, they cannot force a citizen to confess faith in such orthodoxies by word or by action. *Barnette* stands for the proposition that no one can be forced to act or to speak in violation of their convictions. This is both in the context of freedom of speech, for which *Barnette* is generally remembered, and the free exercise of religion, for which the implications of *Barnette* are significant.

The prohibition against declaring a religious orthodoxy might more rightly fall under the column of antiestablishment, but the right of an individual to stay silent, or to remain seated, was firmly established by the Supreme Court in 1943. And the crystallization of that right in the evolving landscape of U.S. democracy was the result of the religious determination of the Jehovah's Witnesses in the face of widespread violence and social condemnation.

---

[183] *Barnette*, 641.

CHAPTER 12

The Sin in Sincerity

THE U.S. SUPREME COURT long held the view that the Bill of Rights did not apply to the states, there being no textual evidence to the contrary.[184] In the 1920s, however, the U.S. Supreme Court began the process of incorporating various pieces of the Bill of Rights so as to apply them against the states; the legal term "incorporating" is not always used in these decisions, but the judicial process has been dubbed so over time. This has been an iterative endeavor, with freedom of speech and freedom of the press leading the way.[185] This piecemeal approach has been in practice slow and selective, but remains legally dramatic—the Second Amendment would controversially be "incorporated" in 2010.[186]

---

[184] Barron v. Baltimore, 32 U.S. (7 Pet.) 243 (1833). ("These amendments contain no expression indicating an intention to apply them to the State governments.")

[185] Gitlow v. New York, 268 U.S. 652 (1925) (freedom of speech); Near v. Minnesota, 283 U.S. 697 (1931) (freedom of the press).

[186] McDonald v. Chicago, 561 U.S. 742 (2010).

The shift relies upon the Fourteenth Amendment and its broad language. The text was intended as a curative against racially motivated discrimination, though for that purpose the 1868 amendment sat mostly unused in the legal cupboard for a century. The Amendment requires that:

> No State shall make or enforce any law which shall abridge the privileges or immunities of citizens of the United States; nor shall any State deprive any person of life, liberty, or property, without due process of law; nor deny to any person within its jurisdiction the equal protection of the laws.

Prior to the Supreme Court's 1940 decision in *Cantwell v. Connecticut* and its 1947 decision in *Everson v. Board of Education*, the First Amendment's religion clauses did not control what the states could do on matters of religion.[187] A religion could be established, or otherwise supported, by the local government. Religious believers theoretically could be restrained from freely exercising their religious beliefs or convictions, assuming the state had no First Amendment-like protections in place. Many states had some semblance of religious freedom in their respective laws, but there were differences. Massachusetts notably maintained the last established church system. And Massachusetts has the similar distinction of hosting the last conviction for heresy in the United States.[188]

---

[187] Everson v. Board of Education, 330 U.S. 1 (1947).

[188] Charles Lee Smith, an atheist activist, was actually the last person convicted of heresy in the United States, but he never served time for that charge.

Abner Kneeland was born in Gardner, Massachusetts. His religious journey involved much wandering. He was a Baptist and then a leading Universalist clergyman, then a pantheist, then a freethinking utopian.[189] When and how these various "thens" overlap is for a Kneeland biography rather than the current brief treatment. Kneeland knew enough from his stint as a Universalist to develop varied opinions about their religious beliefs. He stated in one article that:

> 1. Universalists believe in a god which I do not; but believe that their god, with all his moral attributes (aside from nature itself,) is nothing more than a chimera of their own imagination. 2. Universalists believe in a god, which I do not; but believe that the whole story concerning him is as much a fable and a fiction, as that of the god Prometheus, the tragedy of whose death is said to have been acted on the stage in the theatre of Athens, five hundred years before the Christian era. 3. Universalists believe in miracles, which I do not; but believe that every pretension to them can either be accounted for on natural principles or else is to be attributed to mere trick and imposture. 4. Universalists believe in the resurrection of the dead, in immortality and eternal life, which I do not; but believe that all life is mortal, that death is an eternal extinction of life to the individual who possesses it, and that no individual life is, ever was, or ever will be eternal.[190]

---

[189] See Stephan Papa, *The Last Man Jailed for Blasphemy* (Franklin: Trillium Books, 1998).

[190] *Kneeland* case materials were reprinted in Peter Oxenbridge Thacher's *Reports of Criminal Cases*, 346–347 (1834).

The Sin in Sincerity

The primary point of divergence of Universalists from other Christians was and is the belief that God is by nature so fundamentally good that God therefore would not condemn to infinite punishment someone who committed finite sin. What that ultimately means in terms of heaven and hell, salvation and forgiveness, the nature of God and the meaning of scripture would be a good and lengthy intramural conversation among Universalists.

In his diatribe against Universalists, in whose clergy he had previously served, Kneeland criticized a portrayal of God that would be recognized and perhaps embraced by a large percentage of avowed Christians. His views seem focused on Universalism, but their brush strokes are wide enough to paint all of Christianity. He published those views in various newspapers to which he contributed or worked as an editor. And these publications got Kneeland into a spot of trouble. Kneeland was indicted for heresy and convicted, which conviction was upheld.[191]

The state law Kneeland broke was well established, though subject to a few major events in the intervening years. It was the 1782 Act Against Blasphemy, which provided:

> If any person shall wilfully blaspheme the holy name of God, by denying, cursing, or contumeliously reproaching God, his creation, government, or final judging of the world, or by cursing or reproaching Jesus Christ or the Holy Ghost, or by cursing or contumeliously reproaching the holy word of God, that is, the canonical scriptures as contained in the books of the Old and

---

[191] Commonwealth v. Kneeland, 37 Mass. 206 (1838).

New Testaments, or by exposing them or any part of them to contempt or ridicule, he shall be punished.

And it was hard to argue about Kneeland's contumeliousness, meaning his scorn for many key aspects of the Christian religion: God as a chimera, God as a fiction and fable, miracles as merely tricks and impostures, and eternal extinction rather than eternal life. Kneeland was nothing if not thoroughly scornful.

He had been a preacher, among many other jobs. His increasingly radical stances regarding religion made some of those stints in the pulpit shorter than they might otherwise have been. He eventually helped found the "First Society for Free Inquirers," a gathering of rational thinkers. Whether they could be called "atheists" may be hard to assess across the centuries. But Kneeland's publication was atheistic enough to be charged as heresy.

Massachusetts had disestablished its churches in 1833, the same year Kneeland's fateful article about the Universalists had been published in Boston. The controversies and contentions between Unitarians and Congregationalists were likely still fresh and raw. And Kneeland's words may have been heard as salt being applied liberally to an already aggravated wound.

It took a few tries, with four appeals in all, but eventually Abner Kneeland was convicted. The original trial judge had presented the case to the jury, but his comments suggest a foregone conclusion: "[T]he poor stand most in need of the consolations of religion, and the country has the deepest stake in their enjoying it, not only from the protection which it owes them, but because no man can be expected to be faithful to the authority of man, who revolts against the government of God."[192] The presiding Judge Thacher apparently was a deacon in the Brattle Street Church, by then a Unitarian congregation—an observation without any absolute consequence but, at the very least, one of context.[193]

Kneeland's counsel argued against conviction of several grounds. He mightily argued the grammatical contours of the article, a high-stakes diagramming of sentences if ever there was one. He also questioned the validity of the blasphemy statute in light of the religious protections afforded under the Massachusetts constitution, which had recently been amended in 1820. The Chief Judge of the Supreme Judicial Court, Lemuel Shaw, had been involved with those amendments, however, and had no concerns about the ongoing efficacy of the blasphemy statute. Shaw ruled that blasphemy was "speaking evil of the Deity with an impious purpose to derogate from the divine majesty, and to alienate the minds of others from the love and reverence of God."[194] Legalities aside, this was seemingly Kneeland's intent.

Consistent with this definition, and allowing for the conclusion on the statute's constitutionality, Kneeland was convicted of blasphemy. He was imprisoned for sixty days. Leading liberal lights of Boston, such as William Ellery Channing, Ralph Waldo Emerson, and Theodore Parker (all Unitarians), wrote on his behalf seeking his release, but to no avail.

---

[192] Leonard W. Levy, "Satan's Last Apostle in Massachusetts," *American Quarterly* 5, no. 1 (Spring 1953), 35 (quoting Judge Thacher's charge to the jury).

[193] Levy, 34.

[194] Levy, 38.

Justice Morton questioned the result against Mr. Kneeland and the prospect of the state prosecuting blasphemy:

> To allow and encourage discourses and arguments in proof of the existence of the Deity and in support of the Christian religion, and to prohibit arguments on the other side, would appear to imply a want of confidence in the truth, power, and efficacy of these great doctrines which . . . would lead to scepticism and infidelity. These essential and all-important truths are too deeply rooted, and have too strong a foundation, to need or admit of the dangerous aid of human legislation.

How can the government legislate truth with regard to the nature of God? Massachusetts had been founded as a colony on religious grounds and as a state it had maintained an established church. But to send a man to prison for his expressed beliefs by assessing them against a common frame of reference, one adopted by the government, stands squarely opposed to the notions of freedom of religion, freedom of speech, and freedom of the press (Kneeland was the editor of the blasphemous newspaper in question).

And all that would change. Over a century later, the Supreme Court held in *Cantwell* that the Free Exercise Clause affects the states. In *Cantwell*, Jehovah's Witnesses had been convicted of a breach of the peace by extolling their views to the detriment of the sensibilities of a neighborhood of Catholics, but the Supreme Court reversed those criminal convictions as being fundamentally at odds with the requirements of the First Amendment.

How far does this freedom go? To what degree will, or must, society defer to the beliefs of those in the minority? If the government cannot legislate religious truth, as in the case of blasphemy, how can a court determine the truth, sincerity, or centrality of those beliefs in cases in which those questions might be relevant?

When I was graduating from seminary, I was nervous about the prospect of finding gainful employ as ordained clergy—a momentary lack of faith, perhaps. I must confess that I would occasionally joke to my classmates that if this whole mainline ministry thing did not work out, I could always make big money by starting a cult.

There is, of course, nothing funny about being controlled by or taken advantage of by anyone, let alone a cult. Further, there is nothing humorous about religious leaders who use their positions of trust and authority to take advantage of others in financial, physical, or emotional ways. And yet the balancing of religious freedom against the right not to be defrauded becomes complicated. Because even if a religious belief may seem absurd, if it is nonetheless earnestly held, how can acting upon it be declared a fraud?

Which leads us to the strange case of *U.S. v. Ballard*.[195]

Guy Ballard was a mining engineer, perhaps a metaphoric occupation for what he would become religiously. He was a student of the occult and theosophy. Theosophy is a school of religious thinking that holds that there are divine "Masters" who possess great spiritual powers and who have existed across human history, often enduring through multiple reincarnated lives. This is similar to the Buddhist notion of bodhisattva, a

---

[195] 322 U.S. 78 (1944).

being that compassionately refrains from entering nirvana in order to save others.

Ballard claimed to have had an encounter with such a personage on the slopes of Mount Shasta in California. It was Saint Germain, an allegedly divine entity and one of the so-called Ascended Masters, who would become a cornerstone of Ballard's religious movement. Ballard was deemed an Accredited Messenger of St. Germain, as was his wife Edna Ballard and their son, Edona Eros "Donald" Ballard. Edna was also well read in matters theosophical.[196]

They formed the "I AM" movement, which by the movement's own claims swelled to over a million members worldwide. The Ballards's efforts were based in the Chicago area and began with lectures, at times called "I AM Activity." The name "I AM" is attributed to the encounter between God and Moses in the Book of Exodus, in which God's name is "I am who I am." The movement is syncretic, blending theosophy, Buddhism, and Christian texts, ideas, and imagery. One can become free by embracing the Violet Consuming Flame, or God's Flame of Divine Love. Bright light and colors play a role in the movement, with the Ballards often dressed entirely in white tuxedoes and evening gowns while holding forth before crowds of believers.

The Ballards also claimed storied pedigrees, if only perhaps of the metaphysical variety. The court in *U.S. v. Ballard* declares Guy Ballard's aliases as including "Saint Germaine, Jesus, George Washington, Godfre Ray King." (The encounter on Mount Shasta

---

[196] See Marie Failinger, "United States v. Ballard: Government Prohibited from Declaring Religious Truth," in *Law and Religion: Cases in Context*, ed. Leslie C. Griffin (New York: Aspen Publishers, 2010).

was perhaps greatly simplified by Ballard's communing with himself.) Later followers and adherents to the Ascended Masters have suggested that Edna Ballard was previously Joan of Arc, Elizabeth I of England, and Benjamin Franklin. It is predictable that such recitations of past lives never include being a bus driver from Queens or a giraffe.

The Ballards, as Accredited Messengers of the Ascended Masters, are said to have possessed spiritual abilities, notably the power to heal. As the Court set forth a relevant portion of the Ballards' criminal indictment:

> that Guy W. Ballard, during his lifetime, and Edna W. Ballard and Donald Ballard had, by reason of supernatural attainments, the power to heal persons of ailments and diseases and to make well persons afflicted with any diseases, injuries, or ailments, and did falsely represent to persons intended to be defrauded that the three designated persons had the ability and power to cure persons of those diseases. . . .[197]

The Ballards had offered to heal people in exchange for money or other property. Those healings apparently did not always work out. The I AM Movement also advocated an austere lifestyle, advising adherents to refrain from smoking and drinking, or having sex for anything other than procreative reasons even between married couples. Higher-level followers were to forgo meat, garlic, playing cards, narcotics, and insurance. Why insurance? Perhaps it shows a lack of faith, but also because death was merely

---

[197] U.S. v. Ballard, 322 U.S. 78, 80 (1944).

the next step toward one's own Ascended Mastery.[198] And yet that life of austere living did not seem to be embodied in the Accredited Messengers's day-to-day. For example, Guy Ballard died in 1939, a death surprising both because of his seeming divine status and avowed healing abilities and because it was attributed to heart disease and cirrhosis of the liver, pathological indicia of less-than-abstemious tendencies.

The Ballards were prosecuted on federal charges of mail fraud. Over the span of proceedings, there were dismissed charges and mistrials, but finally convictions. One witness, Margaret Schall, the wife of U.S. Senator Thomas Schall of Minnesota, testified that the Ballards failed to heal her husband's blindness and that she had failed "to experience the 'sparkles' she was told she would experience if she followed the Ballards's instructions, despite the expenditure of significant funds for the sect."[199] Edna was fined $8,000 and was given a one-year suspended sentence while Donald was fined $400 and given a thirty-day suspended sentence. Once again, someone was not feeling the sparkles, so the Ballards appealed.

The primary basis for appeal had to do with the Ballards's beliefs and how those factored into allegations of fraud. The trial judge had been in a difficult situation, trying to avoid the trial becoming a referendum on religious beliefs, akin to a heresy trial, rather than an assessment of whether the defendants' behavior rose to the level of fraud. The court directed the members of the jury to focus their attention on the question of the Ballards's good faith:

---

[198] Failinger, *Law and Religion*, 38.

[199] Failinger, 39.

The Sin in Sincerity

Now, gentlemen, here is the issue in this case: First, the defendants in this case made certain representations of belief in a divinity and in a supernatural power. Some of the teachings of the defendants, representations, might seem extremely improbable to a great many people. For instance, the appearance of Jesus to dictate some of the works that we have had introduced in evidence, as testified to here at the opening transcription, or shaking hands with Jesus, to some people that might seem highly improbable. . . . Whether that is true or not is not the concern of this Court and is not the concern of the jury. . . . As far as this Court sees the issue, it is immaterial what these defendants preached or wrote or taught in their classes. They are not going to be permitted to speculate on the actuality of the happening of those incidents. . . . Therefore, the religious beliefs of these defendants cannot be an issue in this court."

The issue is: did these defendants honestly and in good faith believe those things? If they did, they should be acquitted. I cannot make it any clearer than that. If these defendants did not believe those things, they did not believe that Jesus came down and dictated, or that Saint Germain came down and dictated, did not believe the things that they wrote, the things that they preached, but used the mail for the purpose of getting money, the jury should find them guilty. Therefore, gentlemen, religion cannot come into this case.

Religion cannot come into the case, which is daunting in a case about alleged fraudulent conduct perpetrated under the guise of religion. Interestingly, it was the Ballards who had sought to bring considerations of the truth of their religious beliefs into the court proceedings. Whether this was an act of faith or a legal strategy to multiply the appealable issues is unclear. The Court focused attention on their good faith, their sincerity.

The Supreme Court agreed with the trial judge's approach. Under the *Barnette* decision involving the Jehovah's Witnesses, Americans are free to believe in what others might consider heretical. "Heresy trials are foreign to the Constitution. Men may believe what they cannot prove. They may not be put to the proof of their religious doctrines or beliefs. Religious experiences which are as real as life to some may be incomprehensible to others."[200] The Court noted that it would seem an equally high hurdle for someone to defend a belief set out in the New Testament, whether it be miracles, the divinity of Jesus, or the power of prayer.

This is noteworthy for several reasons. First, it would have been a complete vindication for poor old Abner Kneeland a century before. Second, it forbids the courts from trying to assess such religious questions. And third, the First Amendment prohibits selecting one religious group or one type of religion for preferential treatment.[201]

After being sent back to the lower appeals court for further review, the Ballards's underlying indictment was later thrown out by the Supreme Court, after a second appeal. The fly in the ointment was alluded to in the jury charge when the judge had addressed the panel: "Now gentlemen..." Women had been systematically excluded from both the grand and petit juries

---

[200] *Ballard*, 86.

[201] *Ballard*, 87.

that had returned the Ballards's indictment and convictions,[202] which was in violation of the jury-selection scheme set forth by Congress.[203] After the indictment was deemed invalid after a second appeal to the Supreme Court, the government did not seek to prosecute the Ballards further, though they were prohibited by the U.S. Postal Service from using the U.S. mails until the 1950s.[204]

Why is any of this of enduring interest? Religious belief has in one sense been declared a black box, mysterious in content and sealed away from consideration. But didn't the Supreme Court declare that one may inquire into the sincerity of one's beliefs, if not their content or consistency? True in theory, but how might that work in practice? "Mr. Ballard, do you honestly believe that you are the reincarnation of Jesus Christ and George Washington?" Effectively, the dissent by Justice Jackson describes the trajectory post-*Ballard*. For prosecutions of religious fraud and religious speech, there is a narrow stretch of territory in which the government might take action—proving that the accused doesn't *really* believe that.

The specifics of the religious belief system are not to be disputed, only whether this person sincerely holds them to be true. Again, in theory, that legal approach is possible after *Ballard* but practically speaking, the *Jackson* dissent's "hands off" approach is more likely. In light of that tighter scope, the prosecution effectively must prove material misrepresentations, such as whether

---

[202] *Ballard*, 187, 189–190.

[203] *Ballard*, 193.

[204] Failinger, *Law and Religion*, 43.

the money sought was diverted to illicit use.[205] Short of that, they might need a recording of an accused saying, "Watch me milk these chumps out of their money—who could believe such nonsense?" It is said that confession is good for the soul, but recording devices are not always handy.

The shadow of the *Ballard* decision will stretch across the coming decades as the courts become frequently embroiled in cases involving religious freedoms. And as that line of cases coalesces around greater protection for religious minorities, it will also bedevil the ability of federal, state, and local governments to implement seeming neutral programs and policies that adversely affect, or particularly advantage, certain religious groups. The courts cannot easily assess religious beliefs on account of *Ballard*, but that will not stop the steady flow of religious cases onto court dockets.

---

[205] Failinger, 44.

CHAPTER 13

Lemony Thicket: Modern Rules About Establishment

RELIGIOUS STRUGGLES OVER supporting private versus public schools did not end in the nineteenth century. However, they were further complicated in 1947 with the Supreme Court's decision in *Everson v. Superintendent of Schools.*[206] A state program in New Jersey allowed parents to be compensated for the costs of transportation for their children to travel to and from private schools. The state expenditure was challenged to the extent it allowed reimbursement for transportation to sectarian schools. In its examination of this program, the *Everson* Court spelled out the parameters of the Establishment Clause:

---

[206] 330 U.S. 1 (1947).

The "establishment of religion" clause of the First Amendment means at least this: neither a state nor the Federal Government can set up a church. Neither can pass laws which aid one religion, aid all religions, or prefer one religion over another. Neither can force nor influence a person to go to or to remain away from church against his will or force him to profess a belief or disbelief in any religion. No person can be punished for entertaining or professing religious beliefs or disbeliefs, for church attendance or non-attendance. No tax in any amount, large or small, can be levied to support any religious activities or institutions, whatever they may be called, or whatever form they may adopt to teach or practice religion. Neither a state nor the Federal Government can, openly or secretly, participate in the affairs of any religious organizations or groups, and vice versa. In the words of Jefferson, the clause against establishment of religion by law was intended to erect "a wall of separation between church and State."[207]

The New Jersey program was found to be free of such problems, and therefore it did not violate the Establishment Clause of the First Amendment. The program was specifically about transportation; there was no effort to hinder or help the schools' efforts to teach children about religion or to foster religious activities (though one could quibble that getting children to the schools helped achieve that end). It was a policy devoid of subject matter, its aim merely to assist children getting to school and back home safely. And, as a legal legacy, the *Everson* decision served to

---

[207] *Everson*, 15–16, citing in part *Reynolds v. United States,* 98 U. S. 164.

incorporate the Establishment Clause so as to affect state governments. The states were now fully subject to both the Establishment Clause and, as previously seen in *Cantwell v. Connecticut*, the Free Exercise Clause.

The attempt to help schools needed to be handled in a neutral fashion. The list of potential problems spelled out in *Everson* could well have easily been by triggered by a less well-crafted effort toward aiding private schools. That was to be the result 24 years later in the landmark case of *Lemon v. Kurtzman*.[208] Two school programs were examined, one in Pennsylvania and the other in Rhode Island. Both were found to violate the Establishment Clause.

The Superintendent of Public Schools was authorized in Pennsylvania to allocate state funds for textbooks, educational materials, and teacher salaries in private schools. Teacher salaries could be supplemented, provided certain criteria were met: the teachers had to be teaching the same courses as taught in public school, using the same materials, and *not* teaching religion courses. While written generically, the program effectively only benefited Catholic schools, which at the time represented 95 percent of Pennsylvania's private schools and 25 percent of its total schools. A similar program in Rhode Island would provide up to 15 percent salary supplements for private school teachers, again primarily helping teachers in Catholic schools.

The *Lemon* court found these school aid programs to be far more problematic than the *Everson* case. And, in a moment of judicial humility, the Supreme Court mused that it was a difficult

---

[208] 403 U.S. 602 (1971).

area of the law to discern: "Candor compels acknowledgement . . . that we can only dimly perceive the lines of demarcation in this extraordinarily sensitive area of constitutional law."[209] Through a glass darkly, as it were.

The Establishment Clause is broadly worded, and perhaps intended, but the Court teased out three main "evils" to be protected against: the sponsorship, financial support, and active involvement of the "sovereign" (i.e, the government) in religious activity. And so the Court created what became known as the pun-inspiring *Lemon* test for assessing such situations:

> First the statute must have a clear secular legislative purpose; second, its principal or primary effect must be one that neither advances nor inhibits religion . . . [and] finally, the statute must not foster "an excessive government entanglement with religion."[210]

Three factors were compiled for a court's examination of the permissibility of a governmental statutory effort: (1) have a secular purpose, (2) neither advance nor hinder religion, and (3) not foster excessive entanglement.[211] The *Lemon* Court found that the two programs ran afoul of these criteria. It acknowledged that while some relationship is inevitable between government

---

[209] *Lemon,* 612.

[210] *Lemon,* citing *Walz v. Tax Commission,* 397 U.S. 664 et seq.

[211] By some accounts, the second and third parts have been contracted into one, as helping or hindering seem to be at the root of any entanglement and not every entanglement is potentially problematic. See, e.g., *Agostini v. Felton,* 521 U.S. 203, 233 (1997).

and religion, the object of the Establishment Clause is to prevent the intrusion of one into the precincts of the other.

How about a not immediately relevant legal tangent for illustration purposes? There is a concept in the law called equity, or equitable relief. Equity is a mechanism for addressing unfairness in a situation, a thumb placed knowingly on the scale of justice to make the result come out "right," whatever that means. Equity historically had been a magic power of the Chancellor of England, who also historically had been a member of the clergy.

In a sense, equity was a form of mercy, the "conscience of the King," to be applied in situations where the result under the law was considered unfair or excessively punitive. That power eventually devolved to the courts and equitable relief is one form of potential judicial intervention, like a preliminary injunction against a public nuisance or to stop some pending action. The concept of equity can be unpredictable, however, often changing from judge to judge. For that reason, equity in the form of the King's conscience was criticized for being more akin to the length of the Chancellor's foot—meaning, it offers an arbitrary and selective remedy.

The *Lemon* test is a bit like equity: often hard to anticipate and even harder to implement. The *Lemon* test could be described as a religious gut check, a feeling of religious unease a judge has about a statute or program. The metrics of the test are not particularly helpful.

Requiring a law to have a secular purpose seems sensible. But generic language used in a statute may not openly manifest the underlying reasons for passing the law. There is a "nudge, nudge, wink, wink"[212] process of legislation, after which the product is cleaned up for public consumption and the possibility of judicial review. The two *Lemon* programs did not need to say in the text of the law "and we really want to help the Catholic schools" because the effect of the law could have been predicted. The states must have examined who would benefit, how much the programs would cost, and whether the programs would reach their targeted population. Whether the intended effect is the *stated* effect can be as much a detective story as it is a courtroom drama.

Similarly, determining whether a statute or program advances or hinders religion is a judgment call, one about resulting effects as much as planned consequences. Is the statute acceptable under the Establishment Clause if those effects were not intended? Or if they could not have been anticipated? If one were to assume an underlying goal of helping or hindering religion, does that make it convenient for the legislature or a municipality not to look too deeply into the details of a program? "Okay, everyone just act naturally and maybe the court won't notice what we were really trying to do." A cynical view, perhaps.

The question of entanglement is particularly complicated. The more that the program sought to police that there was no entanglement with religion, the more it looked like the program was entangling itself with religion. The salary supplements in

---

[212] It may seem unorthodox to cite a phrase from a Monty Python sketch as a means for describing the intricacies of the legislative process. I also once cited in a court argument an episode of the "Seinfeld" television show, describing the allegedly fraudulent activity of the opposing side in a case as akin to the efforts of George Costanza to earn commissions by selling computers to himself. The comparison was apt, and the judge laughed, but my client still lost. Such is life.

Pennsylvania and Rhode Island could arguably be considered to be helping religious schools. But the oversight imposed on the funding intruded upon how the supported teachers did their jobs: what they taught, the books used, etc. In order to assure that you are not helping the schools, you succeed in showing that you are hindering them.

The changing roster of the U.S. Supreme Court, however, has made *Lemon* vulnerable to being overruled. That lineup now includes a majority of members who are identified as Roman Catholic: J. Samuel Alito, J. Amy Coney Barrett, J. Brett Kavanaugh, C.J. John Roberts, J. Sonya Sotomayor, and J. Clarence Thomas. Justice Neil Gorsuch was raised Catholic, though seems currently to identify as Episcopalian. This observation is more than a passing point of trivia. One of the recurring objections about *Lemon* is an underlying sense of anti-Catholicism, a general concern that has endured since the nineteenth century through the Blaine Amendments added to state constitutions.

The modern political litmus test for the Supreme Court has tacitly been where a judicial nominee stands on the 1973 *Roe v. Wade* decision, the landmark case legalizing abortion in the United States. For example, the 2016 National Republican Party platform not so tacitly stated:

Only such appointments will enable courts to begin to reverse the long line of activist decisions—including *Roe [abortion]*, *Obergefell [same sex marriage]*, and the Obamacare cases—that have usurped Congress's and states' lawmaking authority, undermined constitutional protections, expanded the power of the judiciary at the expense of the people and their elected representatives, and stripped the people of their power to govern themselves. [213]

As a long-standing matter of church doctrine, Roman Catholics are taught that abortion is an unacceptable practice, without exception, at any stage of a pregnancy and is an automatic basis for excommunication.[214] The outsized weight given this social issue has, arguably, given outsized prominence to Catholic jurists among political and religious conservatives.[215]

How could the pitfalls spelled out in *Everson*, such as taxpayer funding for religious purposes or government oversight of religious activities, be avoided if not through the *Lemon* test? Given the Court's changing makeup, this is not merely a thought exercise. There are several Supreme Court cases since the time of *Lemon* signaling a shift toward a theory of *neutrality*.

What would that look like? For example, school vouchers are one recent means for creating an appearance of legal neutrality while also allowing financial support to sectarian schools. The trick is to avoid having the government make the choice about where the funds are going. Instead, parents are given a voucher,

---

[213] Bracketed text not in original. "2016 Republican Party Platform," The American Presidency Project, presidency.ucsb.edu/documents/2016-republican -party-platform.

[214] "A person who procures a completed abortion incurs a latae sententiae excommunication." Canon 1398 of 1983 Code of Canon Law. Restrictions on abortion are long-standing. See, e.g., Papal bull *Apostolicae Sedis,*1869.

[215] The test is not merely for the courts or for Republicans. Lisa Lerer, "Abortion Is New Litmus Test for Democratic Attorneys General Group," *New York Times,* November 18, 2019, nytimes.com/2019/11/18/us/politics/democratic -attorneys-general-abortion.html.

a portable form of funding, to be presented to a school to pay for or to supplement the cost of their child's education.

In the 2002 case of *Zelman v. Simmons-Harris*, the Supreme Court upheld a program of vouchers established for the struggling school system of Cleveland, Ohio.[216] Families would be awarded vouchers based upon need and then through a lottery. Those vouchers could be used at any schools that joined the voucher program. Notably, over 80 percent of those participants were religious schools. The amount of aid linked to the voucher varied depending on several factors. Public schools from surrounding suburbs could receive the full amount of per-pupil state funding plus a $2,250 tuition grant. And yet no such schools chose to join the program. Private schools, including religious ones, would only receive the $2,250 tuition grant and the parents would then be required to pay any additional costs.[217]

The Supreme Court found, 5–4, that the Cleveland program did not violate the Establishment Clause.[218] The government was not directing the aid to religious schools; it was the parents who made the choice. The program was not limited to religious schools and yet the majority of schools participating were religiously based. The wider community of public schools from the surrounding suburbs chose not to join up—whatever concern or bias steered any of those schools away from accepting Cleveland schoolchildren is for some other book to analyze.

---

[216] 536 U.S. 639 (2002).

[217] *Zelman*, 645.

[218] For those keeping score at home: Rehnquist, O'Connor, Scalia, Kennedy, and Thomas in the majority versus Stevens, Souter, Ginsberg, and Breyer in a pair of dissents.

The Court distinguished between the government aiding schools directly, as in *Lemon*, from "true private choice," as seen in *Zelman*.[219] The Court had allowed in cases prior to *Zelman:* (1) tax deductions for school expenses (including private tuition), (2) vocational scholarships that permitted someone to study to become a pastor, and (3) the federal funding of sign language interpreters to assist children enrolled at religious schools.[220] In each case, the financial benefit to the schools flowed in accordance with the choices of someone other than the government. The programs were neutral in language, though that openness in turn served to allow their utilization by parents and students for religious schools.

This form of "neutrality" and "free choice" was worrisome to some members of the Supreme Court. Justice David Souter in his *Zelman* dissent suggests that *Zelman* serves effectively to overrule the Establishment Clause framework set down in *Everson*.[221] Again, this is a difference between the neutrally ascribed intent of a statute versus its less-than-neutral effects. A voucher system could be established with the stated goal of free choice and the trappings of neutrality but be implemented in a real-world situation in which there are literally no alternatives between the existing public schools and the nearby religious schools. Is that free choice at play in a program's application or a religious bias baked into the design?

---

[219] *Zelman*, 649.

[220] *Zelman*, 649–651, respectively discussing *Mueller v. Allen*, 463 U.S. 388 (1983); *Witters v. Washington Dept. of Servs. for Blind*, 474 U.S. 481 (1986); and *Zobrest v. Catalina Foothills School Dist.*, 509 U.S. 1 (1993).

[221] *Zelman*, 686.

This is not an outlandish concern. According to data from a U.S. Department of Education survey from 2013–2014, Catholic schools account for nearly 20 percent of all private schools and 41 percent of total private school students.[222] Other religious schools make up over 48 percent of the remaining schools and an additional 37 percent of the student population. Conversely, less than a third of such private schools are nonsectarian in nature and only about one fifth of the private student population attend such schools.

Assuming no massive shift in these numbers over time or by geographic area, a government-funded school voucher program will disproportionately support religious schools. The one note-worthy change from the nineteenth century is that there are many more religious schools that do not happen to be associated with the Roman Catholic church. Recall that the chief divide between public and parochial schools had been the perception of an undercurrent of Protestantism flowing through the curriculum of the public schools. Protestants supported the schools as "neutral" while Catholics objected to their partisan religious nature.

In 1962, however, the generic Protestant content of school curricula began to change. In *Engel v. Vitale*, the Supreme Court decided that it was inappropriate for the New York State school system to require the recitation of a prayer.[223] The committee-drafted prayer was: "Almighty God, we acknowledge our dependence upon Thee, and we beg Thy blessings upon us, our parents,

---

[222] Office of Non-Public Education (ONPE), "Statistics About Nonpublic Education in the United States, 2013–2014," U.S. Department of Education, ed.gov/about/offices/list/oii/nonpublic/statistics.html.

[223] 370 U.S. 421 (1962).

our teachers and our country. Amen." Though simple, and a mite bland as even public prayers go, the Regents' Prayer was found to be objectionable.

New York argued in support of their policy, claiming that students were not asked to observe any specific religion, that the heritage of the nation was religious, and that the prayer was voluntary. The Court held, conversely, that prayer is an inherently religious activity, one the governments of this nation should avoid: "It is neither sacrilegious nor anti-religious to say that each separate government in this country should stay out of the business of writing or sanctioning official prayers and leave that purely religious function to the people themselves and to those the people choose to look to for religious guidance."[224]

The Court alluded in its arguments to American colonists fleeing from the state-run Church of England and its imposition of certain prayers and other requirements in the official Book of Common Prayer. And yet the meaning of history and the relative importance of traditions is a subjective process, even when used by judges to anchor their legal opinions. The Puritans did leave England to follow their religious sensibilities. But it would be difficult to argue that the expression of those sensibilities was to encourage freedom of religious conscience in the Massachusetts Bay Colony. Look to the examples of Mary Dyer, hanged as a Quaker heretic, or Roger Williams, expelled from Massachusetts for his radical ideas about religion.

Supporters of religious freedom turn to history to convey a sense of religious openness among the early European colo-

---

[224] *Engel*, 435 (1962).

nists that may never have existed, or was limited to discrete geographic areas, for example, Rhode Island. And advocates for religious traditionalism declare the United States' ironclad Christian origins but leave quietly aside the similar historic traditions of those in charge being white, rich, and male—though, sadly, some don't even leave those aside. The Bill of Rights was in many ways an effort to keep the federal government's nose out of the business of the states, but that foundational barrier against federal involvement came into question after ratification of the Fourteenth Amendment.

The next school shoe to drop was in 1963. In the case of *Abington v. Schempp*, the Supreme Court struck down school-sponsored Bible readings.[225] The practice in the Abington schools was to have readings from the Bible and recitation of the Lord's Prayer. The Schempps objected to these requirements as Unitarian Universalists[226] who did not consider either the Bible or the Lord's Prayer as anchors of their personal religious beliefs.[227]

Unlike the nineteenth-century state court cases which supported the reading of the Bible, the U.S. Supreme Court found that the recitation of Bible verses, even without any commentary, was problematic. The Court remarked:

---

[225] School Dist. of Abington Township v. Schempp, 374 U.S. 203 (1963).

[226] The Unitarian Universalist Association was formed through the merger of the American Unitarian Association and the Universalist Church of America in 1961.

[227] Some Unitarian Universalists do consider the Bible and the Lord's Prayer to be anchors of their religious beliefs. It's complicated. But in general, Unitarian Universalists ardently believe in the personal freedom to make those choices without the impositions of governments or anyone else.

The wholesome "neutrality" of which this Court's cases speak thus stems from a recognition of the teachings of history that powerful sects or groups might bring about a fusion of governmental and religious functions or a concert or dependency of one upon the other to the end that official support of the State or Federal Government would be placed behind the tenets of one or of all orthodoxies. This the Establishment Clause prohibits. And a further reason for neutrality is found in the Free Exercise Clause, which recognizes the value of religious training, teaching and observance and, more particularly, the right of every person to freely choose his own course with reference thereto, free of any compulsion from the state. This the Free Exercise Clause guarantees.[228]

The reading of Bible passages and in-school prayer are inconsistent with these versions of government neutrality: freedom *from* governmental religious overtures under the Establishment Clause and freedom to follow a *chosen* religious path without government intrusion under the Free Exercise Clause.

The *Schempp* Court directly addressed and rejected the idea that the end result of this change would be a "religion of secularism" and expressly stated that the Bible could be studied for its literary and historic qualities as part of a secular program of education.[229] The Court also disregarded the argument that the implications of *Schempp* led to a denial of religious freedom to the majority, those who might effectively control the schools

---

[228] *Schempp,* 222.

[229] *Schempp,* 225.

by dint of political numbers and votes. This is the minority veto of the Bible alluded to by nineteenth century state courts. As set forth in Schempp, deference to a religious majority was never the intended result of the First Amendment: "While the Free Exercise Clause clearly prohibits the use of state action to deny the rights of free exercise to *anyone*, it has never meant that a majority could use the machinery of the State to practice its beliefs."[230]

And yet, over time, the Supreme Court has drifted from its 1963 sentiments. The move toward "neutrality" as an overarching concept marked the beginning of a reconfiguration of the Court's position on the Establishment Clause, shifting into a more *laissez-faire* approach. That same desire to foster neutrality, and to remain neutral with regard to government regulations affecting religion, also transformed the Court's views on the Free Exercise Clause. And so we move from *Lemon* to *Sherbert*.[231]

---

[230] *Schempp*, 226 (emphasis in the original).

[231] I.e., *Sherbert v. Verner*, 374 U.S. 398 (1963). It has been said that puns are the lowest form of humor. Having worked my way through law school as a bouncer in a comedy club, I can assure the gentle reader that there are much lower forms. Case in point: ventriloquism.

CHAPTER 14

Sherbert and Yoder: Religious Freedom and the Limits of the Law

ADELL SHERBERT WORKED in a textile factory in South Carolina. Two years prior to the events in question, she had become a Seventh-day Adventist, a Christian tradition arising from the Millerite "Great Disappointment" of the 1840s along with the Jehovah's Witnesses. For present purposes, the group's sabbath practices are the most relevant: Seventh-day Adventists observe Saturday as their day of rest and worship. During the term of her employ in 1959, the factory expanded its work schedule from five to six days, including Saturdays. It had previously been an optional day for work, but no longer. Sherbert refused to work on Saturdays, explaining it violated her religious beliefs. She was fired.

Sherbert tried to find another job, but her Saturday restriction made this difficult. She then applied for unemployment benefits. One obligation imposed upon those receiving benefits was to show efforts toward finding gainful employment. Consistent with her original job loss and prior to applying, Sherbert had turned down positions that would have required her to work on Saturdays. She was therefore denied unemployment benefits because she would not accept available work. Sherbert sued the state and prevailed.

The following statute was applicable in South Carolina during the pendency of the *Sherbert* case:

> No tradesman, artificer, laborer or other person whatsoever, shall do or exercise any worldly labor, business, or work of his ordinary calling upon Sunday or any part thereof, work of necessity or charity only excepted, and any person of the age of fifteen years or upwards offending in the premises shall, for every such offense, forfeit the sum of one dollar.[232]

The Supreme Court in *Sherbert* invoked its 1940 decision of *Cantwell v. Connecticut* to reset the bar for government regulation affecting religion. The Court considered whether the state's denial of benefits imposed a restriction on Sherbert's free exercise of her religion. The Court concluded that the state's unemployment policy regarding Saturday work infringed upon her religious rights. The effect of the implicit requirement to take Saturday work was to force a choice between receiving benefits and maintaining her religious observations. Whether unemployment benefits are considered a legal right or a privilege, the

---

[232] Code of Laws of South Carolina, §64-2 (1952 Code).

denial of benefits was impermissible as it "produced a result which the State could not command directly,"[233] meaning the state could not act to hinder the religious rights of those who take their sabbath on Saturday.

The government could nonetheless apply such a law, or follow such a policy, if it serves or supports a compelling state interest and thereby can survive such strict scrutiny. What is "strict scrutiny"? A heightened level of review by a court when constitutional rights are involved: "There may be narrower scope for operation of the presumption of constitutionality when legislation appears on its face to be within a specific prohibition of the Constitution, such as those of the first ten amendments, which are deemed equally specific when held to be embraced within the Fourteenth."[234] Only a compelling state interest might warrant an infringement of a constitutional right, a threshold not reached in the *Sherbert* case. Even with such a compelling state interest at issue, the infringement must be narrowly tailored to achieve that purpose through the least restrictive means.

Triggering a constitutional right, as with the First Amendment, forces the government to have a high measure of justification for its law or policy, permissible only for the "gravest of abuses, endangering paramount interests."[235] In defense of the policy, South Carolina in *Sherbert* offered concerns about false claimants, those seeking benefits while feigning to be followers

---

[233] Sherbert v. Verner, 374 U.S. 398, 405 (1963), citing *Speiser v. Randall*, 357 U.S. 513, 526 (1958).

[234] United States v. Carolene Products Co., 304 U.S. 144 (1938), n. 4.

[235] *Sherbert*, 406, citing *Thomas v. Collins*, 323 U.S. 516 (1945).

of a Saturday sabbath. The Court found this to be an insufficient basis for the work requirement.

The building blocks of a new sense of religious freedom have been slowly gathered over the years since *Reynolds v. U.S.*, which elevated the interests of the government over the individual's free exercise of religion (i.e., there is no religious exemption to bigamy laws). In *Cantwell v. Connecticut*, the Court for the first time applied the Free Exercise Clause of the First Amendment against the states, allowing Jehovah's Witnesses the right to proselytize without permits. In *Everson v. Superintendent of Schools*, the Court cautioned state governments against financially supporting religious schools in violation of the Establishment Clause, also now affecting the states. The right to believe had frequently been distinguished from the right to act, but the long-term implication of the *Sherbert* decision is that government restrictions on the right to act on one's religious beliefs require a heightened level of justification.

The *Sherbert* Court opined that it was underscoring the government's obligation to remain neutral with regard to religion. Unemployment recipients who kept a Sunday sabbath were unhindered by the work requirement while Saturday Sabbath-takers were burdened. The provision of exceptions would become a theme in religious freedom cases: allowing an exception for one group opens a policy up to questions about why other groups should not be afforded similar exceptions. The exceptions might arise because of long-standing traditions, such as for Christians who follow a Sunday sabbath. They might also represent enduring preferences for certain well-known or culturally familiar religious groups, like the historically advantageous place maintained for Protestant-preferred Bible translations over Catholic translations in the public schools.

And such traditions and history were a-changing. The 1960s and 1970s represent a time of societal introspection and outright social upheaval in the United States. It was a time of political dualism, though who stood on each side is dependent on one's perspective. Mutually opposed left- and right-wing cultures clashed across the country and around the world. It was in the midst of the Cold War, with the capitalist lands of the United States and Western Europe in a tense standoff with the communist nations of the Soviet Union, China, and the Warsaw Pact. The Vietnam War was a proxy battle in a global conflict, which polarized American society into supporting and opposing camps.

Religion was felt to be of paramount importance in that wider struggle, a core societal difference lifted up by American politicians and pundits against "godless Communism." For example, the Pledge of Allegiance had been amended in 1954 to insert "under God" for this reason. Objecting to such acts of personal patriotism was criminally punishable before the 1943 *Barnette* decision. Reservations against the Pledge remained culturally suspect, if not legally sanctionable, in the subsequent decades, and a religious line was drawn connecting love of country with love of deity.

As telegraphed by *Cantwell* and *Everson*, two seminal religious freedom cases of the 1940s, religious believers would find the Supreme Court in the 1960s and 1970s more amenable to protecting their rights. Even as the civil rights of other groups had earlier been bolstered under cases like *Brown v. Board of Education* (desegregation), *Loving v. Virginia* (interracial marriage), and *Griswold v. Connecticut* (contraception), religious minorities would turn to the Supreme Court to ensure their religious autonomy. Interestingly, the broadening of religious rights would find an unlikely champion, one not known for speaking out, making demands, or driving cars: the Amish.

The Protestant Reformation has several branches, the better known following the lineage of Martin Luther and John Calvin, respectively, the Lutherans and the various Reformed traditions. Another group are called Anabaptists, a term which arose as a criticism of the group, as many enduring religious names do. Anabaptist refers to those "who baptize again," which references the practice of baptizing adults only rather than infants.[236] Converts would be baptized in this manner, regardless of a previous baptism, a break from an ancient and widely followed tradition that all Christian baptisms are equally valid.[237] Amish traditions arose from Swiss German Anabaptists.

The Amish are particularly well known for eschewing technology and living simply without items like automobiles, tractors, telephones, and even zippers. Clothing and furnishings are

---

[236] *The Oxford Dictionary of the Christian Church (3 rev. ed)* (Oxford: Oxford University, 2005), 55.

[237] How did this tradition arise? Christians in the fourth century trying to avoid Roman persecution might renounce their faith under duress, only to seek return to the fold at a later (and safer) time. Some religious authorities suggested that these folks required rebaptism, while others suggested that baptism was an indelible event. The latter group won that argument, which is known as the Donatist controversy. See *Oxford Dictionary of the Christian Church,* 503. Rebaptism is routinely practiced by Anabaptists, like the Amish and Mennonites, as well as Latter-day Saints, Seventh-day Adventists, and Jehovah's Witnesses. The reasons for this difference are either because of a requirement of "believer's baptism," meaning for adults, or, more pointedly, the inefficacy of baptism outside of a specific religious group.

modest, and work is tied closely to the land, whether farming, raising livestock, or creating household items. It is a community apart, often an enclave-like collection of households working together without major contact with or involvement from the wider society. This desire to be a people independent of worldly influences is where our legal story begins.

Like many states, Wisconsin has mandatory requirements for children to attend schools up to a certain age. This requirement ran afoul of Amish beliefs, which focus educational efforts on practical occupational and domestic matters. There were also direct cultural conflicts—for example, schools requiring girls to wear immodest athletic clothing to take physical education classes. Amish parents established their own schools, but these were in various cases deemed insufficient by state authorities. Some families resisted, particularly declining to send children to school after eighth grade or the age of fourteen. Some Amish families were convicted of violating the state's compulsory school-attendance laws, which convictions were overturned by the U.S. Supreme Court in *Wisconsin v. Yoder*. The Amish won the day.

The *Yoder* case involved the concerted use of anthropological testimony about the Amish to familiarize the court with the practices of the Amish religion and the traditions of the Amish community. One might, and I will, call the Court's description an Amish "lovefest" in which the hardworking and sensible Amish toil idyllically in their fields, an inspiring vista being examined amidst the relative seeming chaos of the United States in 1972. Cue an unpopular war, a controversial president, and a kaleidoscopic culture: the Amish stand in stark and likeable counterpoint.

The U.S. Supreme Court sided with the Amish families, over-ruling the legislature's purview and notably substituting the Court's preference for one religious group's practices. The Amish are therefore not required to comply with compulsory education laws for their children beyond the age of fourteen, a timeline determined by the Amish and adopted by the Court. The logic of that limit arises from the Amish considering high school lessons to be particularly inconsistent with their core values. The *Yoder* Court noted:

> The high school tends to emphasize intellectual and scientific accomplishments, self-distinction, competitiveness, worldly suc-cess, and social life with other students. Amish society empha-sizes informal "learning through doing;" a life of "goodness," rather than a life of intellect; wisdom, rather than technical knowledge; community welfare, rather than competition; and separation from, rather than integration with, contemporary worldly society.[238]

Again, the Court is straying well into the realm of the legis-lature. The government could, and did, reach a different educa-tional conclusion. Sending these Amish children to high school comes at the formative time of adolescence, when they are on the one hand expected by their religious community to be learn-ing Amish attitudes of self-reliance and hard work while on the other hand the State of Wisconsin is advancing competing val-ues of social integration and cooperation learned explicitly or

---

[238] Wisconsin v. Yoder, 406 U.S. 205, 211 (1972).

implicitly in the halls of the local high school. During this critical period of development, the Court adopted the argued position of the families that Amish youth must acquire the skills and mental discipline "to perform the adult role of an Amish farmer or housewife."[239] The legislature advanced its policies toward a different set of societal goals—does the Court have the authority to reject these conclusions in favor of the religious choices of the group?

In 1940, the Supreme Court previously upheld a different vision of government's role in education. In the *Gobitis* decision, Jehovah's Witness children were compelled to say the Pledge of Allegiance. Society had a role in instilling certain common values: "A society which is dedicated to the preservation of these ultimate values of civilization [i.e., order and tranquility] may, in self-protection, utilize the educational process for inculcating these almost unconscious feelings which bind men together in a comprehending loyalty, whatever may be their lesser differences and difficulties."[240] *Gobitis* would be overturned by *Barnette* a few years later, avoiding the rather draconian prospect of sending children to reform schools for delinquency for failing to say the Pledge of Allegiance. But what of the underlying notion that government has a role in instilling certain civic values, ones necessary to encourage social cohesion? Public schools were considered a vehicle for social cohesion in the nineteenth century, a point of fierce contention between Protestants and Catholics.

---

[239] *Yoder,* 205, 211.

[240] *Gobitis,* 600.

With the *Yoder* decision, religious groups could now object to the values being taught in public schools. The move toward greater reliance upon sectarian schools, and paying for them with school vouchers, is one response to that concern. Homeschooling is another. Even if a state requires children and young adults to take comprehensive tests to meet required proficiencies in academic subjects, there seem to be legal limits being placed on any goal of ensuring social integration into the wider society.

The Amish are unusual in that they fundamentally do not wish to integrate, a self-segregated and exclusionary group that does not wish to join society or to ask much of it. The Supreme Court found Amish values and self-sufficiency to be commendable traits. And the rights of parents to direct the religious upbringing and education of their children is afforded a "high place in our society."[241] The Court in *Yoder* fundamentally shifts the emphasis, however, moving the locus of control away from the needs of the government and society at large toward the preferences of the parents as to the education needs and social integration of children. The Amish way of life is integral to their religious values, but are there any societal values that are being lost or social needs shortchanged?

The State of Wisconsin sought to justify its requirement that children attend school until the age of sixteen. First, echoing Thomas Jefferson, the state had a right to ensure that citizens are able to participate effectively and intelligently in the political system if as a nation we are to preserve freedom and independence. Second, education prepares an individual to be self-reliant

---

[241] *Yoder*, 214–215.

and self-sufficient *within* society. The Court accepted those premises, but then substituted its judgement for those of the State of Wisconsin: "an additional one or two years of formal high school for Amish children in place of their long-established program of informal vocational education would do little to serve those interests."[242]

Wisconsin further argued that it was trying to protect school children from languishing in ignorance, to ensure that they would be able to function within the state in the event that they ever left the Amish community. The Court discounted this concern, declaring that the "Amish community has been a highly successful social unit within our society," both productive and law-abiding and that Amish children would still possess readily marketable skills to function in modern society should the need arise.[243] This was again a dramatic displacement of legislative authority.

The uniquely appealing nature of the Amish may have opened the door for further, and less appealing, objections to government policies. The Court had previously declared that parents are not required to send their children to public schools[244] and by further extension in *Yoder* they are not necessarily subject to either the values the public schools might teach or the length in years of those lessons. Furthermore, the states do not have the right to "standardize" children, whether through public schools or, arguably, public values.

---

[242] *Yoder*, 221–222.

[243] *Yoder*, 223, 225.

[244] Pierce v. Society of Sisters, 268 U.S. 510 (1925).

In a dissent, Justice Douglas questioned the result in *Yoder* because it did not take into account the *children's* underlying right to an education. The religious rights of the parents, and their possible conviction, understandably give the parents standing to object to Wisconsin's system of public education. But the religious rights of the children were also invoked. Those rights stand silent while the rights of the parents are affirmed. An Amish child could object in theory and seek a public school education, but how would society ever discover such an objection within a separatist religious community? Perhaps it is beyond the desirable reach of the government to inquire too deeply, but it is worth a moment of pause to consider a child who wishes to choose differently from within a subculture that offers little to no instruction about those choices, rumspringa notwithstanding.

Subsequent to the *Ballard* decision, it is arguable, the Supreme Court stepped away from delving into inner religious justifications. Your dear author is under no such compunctions. Parents can make indelible decisions within their children's lives, religiously and otherwise. They are charged with the care of children and are offered much deference in their decision-making. But those decisions are not absolute. For example, in the case of *Prince v. Massachusetts*, a Jehovah's Witness parent was found to have violated labor laws by sending out a child to sell religious literature.[245] The *Prince* court broadly stated, "Parents may be free to become martyrs themselves. But it does not follow they are free, in identical circumstances, to make martyrs of their

---

[245] Prince v. Massachusetts, 321 U.S. 158 (1944).

children before they have reached the age of full and legal discretion when they can make that choice for themselves."[246]

Should children be subject to potential risk arising from their parents' religious decision-making on their behalf? Another older decision, *Jacobson v. Massachusetts*, allowed a state government to compel an adult to receive a vaccination.[247] That same case suggested that even the religious rights of an individual would be subject to the needs of the government to address the health and safety of the public. This reflects the so-called "police power" inherent to any government which can in theory override even religious convictions.[248] The *Jacobson* case, however, predates many landmark decisions about the growing judicial deference to individual religious liberties as in *Barnette*, *Sherbert*, and *Yoder*. And even the *Prince* holding regarding child labor laws and the limits on religious exemption seems in tension with *Yoder*. One might even wonder about whether religious objections to vaccinations for schoolchildren would be upheld or set aside by a federal court.[249]

Does society have the right to impose restrictions on religious freedom when the consequences of religious behavior might

---

[246] *Prince*, 170. For example, Jehovah's Witness evangelizing by adults had led to neighborhood conflict in the *Cantwell* case.

[247] Jacobson v. Massachusetts, 197 U.S. 11 (1905)

[248] *Jacobson*, 25, 29.

[249] The U.S. Supreme Court refused to review a decision of the Second Circuit Court of Appeals regarding mandatory vaccinations for school children. See *Phillips v. City of New York*, 775 F.3d 538, 542-44 (2d Cir.), cert. denied, 136 S. Ct. 104 (2015). Whether that compulsory policy would withstand legal challenge for a *religious* objection is an open question, particularly under new religious rights legislation, such as the federal Religious Freedom Restoration Act, which will be discussed in a subsequent chapter.

adversely affect others? Would the same be true for actions that run afoul of general public safety laws that are ostensibly neutral regarding such religious sensibilities? The implication of the *Sherbert* and *Yoder* decisions perhaps leaves lingering question marks. The Supreme Court did try to simplify matters, however, and attempted to shift the legal balance back to the government and away from individual religious freedom. That effort arose from a case about a cactus—a very special cactus.

CHAPTER 15

The *Smith* Case: The Peyote Road and the First Amendment

LONG BEFORE THE U.S. CONSTITUTION, long before the Pilgrims set foot in the Massachusetts Bay Colony, the continent that was to become known as North America was a busy place. For thousands of years, Indigenous peoples lived in various styles of communities, some close to the land and others in settings as dense and urban as any in Europe. It was a complex landscape, filled with different cultures and different religions. There was nothing "new" about the New World.

Unfolding in the shadow of the many sectarian fights detailed prior, the religious struggle of Indigenous peoples is often an afterthought. North and south, Protestant and Catholic, colonists were accompanied by Christian missionaries, the former seeking to claim the land and the latter striving to claim the souls of

Indigenous people. No library full of books could contain all those tragic stories of loss or convey the depth of what was lost. So, we will make do in the immediate chapter with one fairly recent story that found its way into the highest court of a conquered land.

In 1919, Alfred Leo Smith was born on a Klamath Indian reservation in Oregon, near the Cascade Mountains.[250] Smith had a difficult life, one of poverty, without a father or access to his culture. Like many children on reservations, he was pressed into assimilation programs. In his case, Smith was placed into Catholic schools, where neither the Klamath language was spoken nor Klamath culture learned. Smith rebelled in his schools and in his life, beginning to abuse alcohol in his teenage years.

Drafted into the military in 1941, his substance-abuse issues did not change. He was dishonorably discharged and sent to prison. In the 1950s, he entered Alcoholics Anonymous and, eventually, stopped drinking and became a drug-and-alcohol-abuse counselor. Smith also sought to reconnect with his lost tribal background and to integrate such cultural content into his treatment efforts. He took part in Indigenous rituals and ceremonies. And he became involved with the Native American Church, which religious road would unexpectedly lead him to the Supreme Court.

The Native American Church (the NAC) is an intertribal faith tradition, dating from the late nineteenth century but

---

[250] Biographical materials were drawn from Carolyn N. Long, "Employment Division, Department of Human Resources of Oregon v. Smith: The Battle for Religious Freedom," in *Law & Religion: Cases in Context* (New York: Aspen Publishing, 2010), 107.

incorporating aspects of religious traditions long pre-dating American colonialism. It is a syncretic tradition, a blending of Indigenous peoples' and Christian religions. It has also been described as "Peyotism" or the "peyote way," as one of its signature rituals involves the use of peyote, a cactus indigenous to Mexico and the American Southwest which has psychedelic properties. Peyote usage was originally linked to Indigenous tribes from those geographic areas but has spread in large part because of the expansion of the NAC.[251]

Smith was working as a counselor at a drug rehabilitation facility in Oregon and faced a quandary. There was a workplace policy against taking controlled substances, which in Oregon included peyote. But as a follower of the NAC, Smith felt obligated to partake in this central ritual of his faith. And so he did and he was fired. He then sought to obtain unemployment benefits from the State of Oregon. His application was denied because he was discharged for engaging in illegal activity. Smith sued and he lost, a surprising result given past case law such as the *Sherbert* decision.

Smith's situation seemed nearly identical to that of Adell Sherbert in South Carolina, who was denied unemployment benefits because of her religious observances, which were in turn restored because of her right to the free exercise of her religion. Two people were following their religious beliefs. Two people were denied unemployment benefits for having done so. One

---

[251] For an account of the Half-Moon tradition within the Native American Church, see, Vincent Catches, "The Native American Church: The Half-Moon Way," *Wicazo Sa Review* 7, no. 1 (Spring 1991), 17–24. The article is also contemporaneous with the *Smith* decision.

was a white woman who was a member of the Seventh-day Adventist denomination. The other was an Indigenous man who was a member of the Native American Church. One was fired because she wanted to go to church on Saturdays. The other because he was engaged in the ancient tradition of taking peyote. One received those benefits after a trip up to the Supreme Court; the other did not. What were the differences?

The State of Oregon, for its part, focused on the illegality of peyote use. Because peyote was a controlled substance, Smith did not have a right to use it regardless of his religious sensibilities. In this sense, Smith's situation was distinguishable from the *Sherbert* case. The courts of Oregon, however, sided with Smith and not surprisingly focused on his religious rights under the First Amendment. Oregon appealed to the Supreme Court, seeing the underlying decision on Smith's behalf as a potential law-enforcement nightmare of religious exemptions cropping up for all manner of otherwise illegal activities. And the Supreme Court sided with Oregon.

Although the *Sherbert* case from 1963 might have suggested a different result, the trajectory of the Supreme Court's First Amendment jurisprudence had begun to shift in the 1980s. With the advent of the Rehnquist Court and, in particular, the appointment of conservative Justice Antonin Scalia, the Supreme Court gradually curtailed religious exceptions to otherwise neutral-seeming laws and regulations. For example, the Court upheld a military policy that religious head coverings were not permitted indoors for general military personnel, including a yarmulke by an Orthodox rabbi.[252] It further refused to set aside a New Jersey

---

[252] Goldman v. Weinberger, 475 U.S. 503 (1986).

prison policy that effectively forced Muslim inmates with jobs outside the facility to miss Friday services.[253] In these cases, specialized circumstances had led to deferential treatment of government policies in strictly controlled environments. With the *Smith* decision, the Supreme Court threw out the baby with the bathwater, and tossed in the tub for good measure.

As in these other cases, the strict scrutiny standard applied in *Sherbert* was set aside for a far lower standard, one of general reasonableness. The *Smith* decision does not apply strict scrutiny to the religious use of peyote, instead focusing on the state's interest in reducing drug use under a statute of general applicability that relies upon language that is neutral on its face. The burden of making the argument has shifted. Instead of the government having to meet a high hurdle of justifying and tightly tailoring its law or policy, the aggrieved believers in *Smith* needed to demonstrate that the law somehow excessively undermined their free exercise of religion or was otherwise not neutral.

After a few procedural twists and turns, the Supreme Court issued its final *Smith* decision, upending the twentieth-century decisions of *Sherbert* and *Yoder*, by reembracing the belief/behavior distinction established in the nineteenth-century *Reynolds* decision.[254] Justice Scalia wrote the *Smith* decision. He declared that the Court's decisions had never shielded a religious objection from the effects of an otherwise neutral law: "We have never held that an individual's religious beliefs excuse him from compliance with an otherwise valid law prohibiting conduct that

---

[253] O'Lone v. Estate of Shabazz, 482 U.S. 342 (1987).

[254] Employment Div. v. Smith, 494 U.S. 872 (1990).

the State is free to regulate. On the contrary, the record of more than a century of our free exercise jurisprudence contradicts that proposition."[255]

Justice Scalia cited back to the *Reynolds* case, which clearly stood for this proposition. Then however he relied upon the *Gobitis* decision which had effectively forced Jehovah's Witness schoolchildren to say the Pledge of Allegiance: "Conscientious scruples have not, in the course of the long struggle for religious toleration, relieved the individual from obedience to a general law not aimed at the promotion or restriction of religious beliefs."[256] An aptly salient quote for the point being made, notwithstanding that the policy from *Gobitis* was overturned three years later by the Supreme Court in its landmark *Barnette* case.

Justice Scalia distinguishes cases like *Barnette* as hybrid cases, coupled with concerns about free speech, and *Sherbert* as dealing solely with unemployment compensation, unsullied by the threat of peyote use and its portending cactus madness. *Yoder* narrowly involved the rights of parents to direct the education of their children, a right of arguably high importance which however, unlike religious freedom, is not mentioned in the United States Constitution.

By changing the level of judicial inquiry in Free Exercise cases, the *Smith* decision flipped the analysis. Under strict scrutiny, such as used when laws have a negative racial impact, the burden is on the government. The *Smith* Court instead declares, "We have never held that an individual's religious beliefs excuse

---

[255] *Smith,* 878–879.

[256] *Smith,* 879 (citing *Gobitis,* 594–595).

him from compliance with an otherwise valid law prohibiting conduct that the State is free to regulate."[257] The religious person or group must argue that the statute or subject matter was in some manner invalid or that the statute as adopted was intended to be religiously neutral. This is not a question of unintended, collateral effects but whether the law was passed because of, or against, this religious use. After the *Smith* decision, the effects of a neutral seeming law or government policy of general applicability upon a religious community would no longer be subject to strict scrutiny.

And this line of thinking came from the Justices of the United States Supreme Court, not from the State of Oregon. The state had not briefed the case to reach this result, meaning submitted arguments to the court along these lines. While the state obviously wanted to prevent religious exemptions for drug use, it had never been its intention to overturn decades of First Amendment jurisprudence. The Attorney General of Oregon at that time, David Frohnmayer, was surprised by the result, claiming that he "had no clue that the Court would reconsider free exercise doctrine."[258] If one were looking around for an example of the dreaded term "judicial activism," one need look no further than the *Smith* case, which seems to have served the purposes of one faction of the Supreme Court far more than it addressed the concerns of the parties to the case.

Why this change? Compare the result in *Smith* and its undermining of *Sherbert* and *Yoder* with another decision, the decid-

---

[257] *Smith*, 878–879.

[258] Long, *Law & Religion*, 121.

edly pro-school voucher case *Zelman* and the slow but steady decline of the antiestablishment protections offered under the *Lemon* test. Under *Smith*, the ability of religious folks to object to the effects of laws and government programs has been reduced, weakening rights under the Free Exercise Clause. Conversely, under cases like *Zelman* and others, the power of the government to support religious activity, such as in religious schools, has been increased, diminishing protections under the Establishment Clause.

Arguably, the net effect of these two lines of judicial activity is to give the government power. Power to support preferred religious activities. And power to protect its promulgations and prerogatives against religious objections from less-preferred religious groups. It could be characterized as a clandestine form of creeping establishment, duly sanctioned and perhaps initiated by the Supreme Court.

For example, the Supreme Court has in recent decades produced a "tradition" line of cases, relying upon long-standing practices of reciting prayers and erecting religious symbols to justify continuation of those practices or the use of those symbols. In *Town of Greece v. Galloway*, the Supreme Court held in 2014 that a town council meeting could begin with a prayer.[259] That practice had been established in 1999 but invoked a longer standing practice in the New York state legislature. The clergy delivering the prayers served the local community and, significantly, were all Christian. This may seem an ecumenical result, and it is literally so. But the objective of reinforcing broad Christian themes

---

[259] Town of Greece v. Galloway, 572 U.S. 565 (2014).

on the governmental landscape is another facet of religious establishment, even in this homogenized form.

The rationale in *Town of Greece*, and in earlier cases, relies in part upon the historical fact that Congress had passed the First Amendment while also retaining the services of chaplains who offered prayers to the assembly. This singular example does not limit the effect of the exception to chaplain-like matters. Instead, it bolsters a developing line of jurisprudence in *Town of Greece* and elsewhere that the Establishment Clause must be interpreted "by reference to historical practices and understandings." The courts may then look at the traditions surrounding the current or proposed practice and see how they might line up with past practice. Tradition becomes a shiny new yardstick for Establishment inquiry. Whether that yardstick applies to non-traditional religious groups, or recent religious arrivals, is an open question.

This trend toward tradition creates problems of judicial consistency across historical events. There could not have been First Amendment objections to these practices or symbols in the states before the Fourteenth Amendment was ratified in 1868. And there was no immediate effect of that change, not until long afterwards when the Supreme Court began to expand the scope of religious freedom directly to the states. State traditions of the eighteenth and nineteenth centuries developed prior to the incorporation of the Free Exercise Clause and the Establishment Clause in the 1940s. These traditions were not being permitted across the Union *in spite* of the First Amendment, making their ongoing nature somehow logically valid. They had been legally permissible before the First Amendment kicked into effect against the states, making their ongoing presence legally questionable.

The difficulty is even greater for the use of symbols. In 1918, the American Legion, a veterans' organization, erected a memorial to those who died during the First World War. The 32-foot-high memorial took the form of a "Latin cross" constructed of white stone and visually echoing the rows of white crosses used to mark the graves of fallen soldiers in Europe. The monument was built and maintained by the American Legion and it was placed on public land. An objection to the cross was made in 2012 by the American Humanist Association. The Supreme Court sided with the American Legion in a complicated patchwork of a decision, which wide-ranging constellation of opinions and concurrences has become par for the judicial course.

Justice Alito wrote the primary opinion of the Court, at one point waxing poetic about Flanders field and mining the symbolic history of crosses in general—even judges get bored.[260] He also begins tolling the bell for the Court's *Lemon* test, which has been ignored or trimmed over the years. He seems to be seeking to replace *Lemon's* three-part test with the *American Legion's* four-step vivisection of past precedents, instead adopting traditions and historical continuity as touchstones for decision-making.

First, he offers that monuments like the American Legion cross were erected many years before and therefore ascertaining the original purposes for the project might be difficult or impossible. Second, over time, the original purposes associated with a monument may change, expanding over time, like monuments that depict the Ten Commandments serving as reminders of

---

[260] See *American Legion v. American Humanist Association*, 588 U.S. ___; 139 S. Ct. 2067 (2019), supreme.justia.com/cases/federal/us/588/17-1717.

great lawgivers—such a memorial to Moses is not coincidentally painted above the Supreme Court justices' heads in their courtroom. The understanding of those religious ideas might have been transformed in some civically minded manner and could be maintained for their historically significant content.

Third, even as the purposes change, so might the message of the monument, like the religious name of a municipality that was religious originally, like Providence, Rhode Island, or Corpus Christi, Texas. Those overtly religious names may now appear religiously neutral. Over time, "religiously expressive monuments, symbols, and practices can become embedded features of a community's landscape and identity." And fourth, when over time the symbol's meaning within a community has changed, the actual removal might appear not to be religiously neutral. To take down the cross, to paint over the Supreme Court's depiction of Moses, would be perceived as a critique of that religion or of religions generally.

All of which goes to show, it pays to be early to the party. If you want to avoid the rules, break them as soon as possible and with any luck, no one will object and you get to declare it a tradition. Unless, of course, you happen to be Indigenous. . . .

The logic of the *American Legion* case is an effort of jurisprudential retrojection: impose a desirable framework on the past to bootstrap the conditions of the present. Use the trappings of tradition and history to make acceptable what should no longer be permitted because it has been around since 1776 or so. By this logic, Sunday as the traditional day of rest is now a civic reality rather than a religious preference. Compare that with the *O'Lone* decision in which a prisoner's Friday observances as a Muslim would not be accommodated. Even the *Sherbert* decision, now narrowed down to a case about unemployment, might no longer be a sturdy bulwark for those who observe a Saturday sabbath.

There were quite a few turns in the road before we get to that present worry, however, so back to *Smith*. How would the Supreme Court interpret a Free Exercise case in light of its return to the good old days of *Reynolds*?

The case of *Church of the Lukumi Babalu Aye, Inc. v. Hialeah* was the first examination of the Free Exercise clause post-*Smith*.[261] It offers an important insight into the Court's developing thought processes. The Church of Lukumi Babalu Aye is a Santeria church. Santeria is a religion originating in the Caribbean, a synthesis of the Yoruba belief system from Africa and Roman Catholic traditions. What Santeria is and is not is an energetic topic for cultural and academic discussion, though a bit out in the weeds for present purposes.[262] For us, dear reader, the salient issue is that Santeria is a religious tradition that prescribes the sacrifice of animals as a part of its worship practices.

The Supreme Court in *Lukumi* offered the following characterization:

This case involves practices of the Santeria religion, which originated in the 19th century. When hundreds of thousands of members of the Yoruba people were brought as slaves from western Africa to Cuba, their traditional African religion absorbed

---

[261] 508 U.S. 520 (1993).

[262] See, e.g., John P. Bartkowski, "Claims-Making and Typifications of Voodoo as a Deviant Religion: Hex, Lies, and Videotape," *Journal for the Scientific Study of Religion* 37, no. 4 (December 1998), 559–579.

significant elements of Roman Catholicism. The resulting syncretion, or fusion, is Santeria, "the way of the saints." The Cuban Yoruba express their devotion to spirits, called *orishas*, through the iconography of Catholic saints, Catholic symbols are often present at Santeria rites, and Santeria devotees attend the Catholic sacraments.[263]

One key element of Santeria is to nurture relationships with the *oris ha*, or orishas, powerful spirits. These relationships are in part cultivated through the offering of animal sacrifices. The Supreme Court also noted that such sacrifices were historically part of the Jewish tradition prior to the destruction of the Second Temple, and of the Islamic tradition as a commemoration of Ibrahim, or Abraham, offering to sacrifice his son Ishaq, or Isaac, to God.[264]

Followers of Santeria were persecuted in Cuba, leading to their practicing their religion in secret. And then some Santeria adherents arrived in Hialeah, Florida, where they sought to practice openly. They applied to obtain customary permits and utilities for their congregation. Some members of the public were less than enthused about this prospect, however, and the city council of Hialeah gathered in an emergency session to address the proposal.

The Council leaped into action against this new unknown. It made a resolution acknowledging the neighbors' concerns and declaring its commitment to a prohibition against any and all

---

[263] Church of the Lukumi Babalu Aye, Inc. v. Hialeah, 508 U.S. 520, 524 (1993).
[264] *Lukumi,* 524–525.

acts of any and all religious groups which were "inconsistent with public morals, peace or safety." They then incorporated Florida's animal cruelty law into their ordinances, seeking clarification from the state as to whether that law would prohibit the sacrifice of animals. The state attorney general's office opined that the unnecessary killing of an animal would be prohibited and further suggested that killing an animal not for consumption was unnecessary. The religious killing of animals was against state law, as this line of thinking suggested, and therefore Hialeah could seek to ban the practice.

The Council passed three ordinances against animal sacrifice. Sacrifice was defined as "to unnecessarily kill, torment, torture, or mutilate an animal in a public or private ritual or ceremony not for the primary purpose of food consumption," and prohibited owning or possessing an animal "intending to use such animal for food purposes." The ordinance was limited in scope to the killing, slaughtering, or sacrificing of "animals for any type of ritual, regardless of whether or not the flesh or blood of the animal is to be consumed." The sacrifice of animals in the city limits of Hialeah was declared by the municipality to be a safety concern. Exceptions were made for exemptions provided by state law. Violations were punishable by jail terms of up to 60 days and fines of up to $500.

The Lukumi congregation filed suit for a violation of their religious rights and the Supreme Court found in its favor. The decision is a remarkable jigsaw of opinions, with justices supporting some colleagues but not others, concurring in part and diverging on others. But once the scorecards were tabulated, the congregation won.

Animal sacrifice cannot be deemed "bizarre or incredible," presumably because of its long-standing history and its associations with Jewish and Islamic practice.[265] However, a similar argument could easily have been made in the case of Latter-day Saint polygamy in *Reynolds v. U.S.* The *Lukumi* case involved a direct ban of a religious practice, with ordinances specifically targeting the use of animals in rituals. The ordinances were therefore not neutral laws of general applicability as required under *Smith*. There was also an exception carved out for kosher butchers—one might argue whether one is ritual slaughter or sacrifice versus the other, but the exception underscores that the Santeria congregation was being singled out.[266]

Comments by public officials made it clear that the congregation was a less than desirable presence in Hialeah. The most energetic seem to have come from the chaplain of the Hialeah Police Department. He opined to the city council that "Santeria was a 'sin,' 'foolishness,' 'an abomination to the Lord,' and the worship of 'demons.'" He advised that "We need to be helping people and sharing with them the truth that is found in Jesus Christ." He offered a telling assessment: "I would exhort you . . . not to permit this Church to exist."

One might conclude from *Lukumi* that, "See, the system is not broken." Or one might surmise that it took flagrant and hyperbolic abuse of municipal power, singling out one house of worship to prevent it from coming into existence, to invoke the meager protections of the Free Exercise clause left after *Smith*.

---

[265] *Lukumi*, 531.

[266] *Lukumi*, 536.

To trigger scrutiny, the law in question would need to be lacking in neutrality or general applicability, bear a high expectation of proof for the aggrieved party, and be easy to meet by all but the most injudicious or inflammatory of government bodies.

An enduring perception of government is that it is secretly out to get us, plotting against the citizenry—the entrenched "Deep State," as it were. This observation makes the assumption that state, local, or federal governments care enough to plot and further assumes that elected officials are at any time competent enough to do so. In my personal experience, such efforts are typically more like the City of Hialeah, not well thought out or particularly well executed. Conversely, a capable group of well-educated and patient lawyers, with decades of experience in the law and lifetime appointments to wear velvety robes, might just be able to impress its will onto the landscape of U.S. constitutional law. One's political perspective might determine onto which decades of the Supreme Court that jaundiced eye might be cast. But something is clearly afoot.

Smith was an unexpected turn in First Amendment law, and for some it was an unwelcome change. Obviously, members of the Native American Church like Mr. Smith would be displeased. Anyone with a situation below the foaming-at-the-mouth legislation of the *Lukumi* case might have cause for alarm. But one group took particular notice of the *Smith* decision and had the power to address it: the United States Congress.

CHAPTER 16

The Religious Freedom Restoration Act

IT IS THE 1990S. There is upheaval in the Persian Gulf and Iraq. An impeachment trial looms. A new wave of feminism is cresting in response to allegations of sexual harassment against powerful men. And a conservative Supreme Court has made dramatic changes to First Amendment law. *Smith* reduced judicial discretion to offer relief from legislation or government policies of general applicability that are neutral in language (if not effect).[267] While the case is silent on the question of specific exemptions, the implicit effect of the decision is to remove the courts from the position of crafting exemptions as in *Sherbert* and *Yoder.*

---

[267] Michael W. McConnell et al., *Religion and the Constitution* (New York: Wolters Kluwer, 2016), 146.

The Religious Freedom Restoration Act

In 1990, the Supreme Court effectively gutted the holdings of *Sherbert* and *Yoder*, greatly reducing the protections available for religious groups in matters of Free Exercise. The United States Congress did not agree with that result and promulgated a new law to revive those old cases: the Religious Freedom Restoration Act of 1993 (RFRA). Passage was unanimous in the House of Representatives and all but three members of the Senate voted in favor.[268] *Smith* had been condemned by a wide range of groups across the religious and political spectrums, including the American Civil Liberties Union, the Christian Legal Society, and the American Jewish Congress.[269]

The express purpose of the law was to restore the legal standards from *Sherbert* and *Yoder*. It provides:

> Government shall not substantially burden a person's exercise of religion even if the burden results from a rule of general applicability, except . . . [g]overnment may substantially burden a person's exercise of religion only if it demonstrates that application of the burden to the person (1) is in furtherance of a compelling governmental interest; and (2) is the least restrictive means of furthering that compelling governmental interest.[270]

This statute is unusual. It seeks to manifest through legislation the court-crafted test set out in *Sherbert* and echoed in *Yoder*. It is written so as to encompass all state and federal law,

---

[268] H.R.1308—Religious Freedom Restoration Act of 1993, congress.gov/bill/103rd-congress/house-bill/1308.

[269] McConnell at 146–147.

[270] 42 U.S. Code § 2000bb-1.

statutory or regulatory. It places a significant policy burden on government legislators and regulators and requires compliance notwithstanding anything short of an express opt-out by Congress. As enacted, it originally covered every state or any subdivision thereof. RFRA was an attempt to turn back the clock to the religious freedom "salad days" before *Smith*. And, arguably, the law was designed to convey Congressional displeasure with the Supreme Court.

Given the often-long process of federal appeals, the Supreme Court may not respond to such legislative matters for years, waiting silently for a relevant legal case to wend its way through the court system. Eventually, one such case did emerge, three years later. The City of Boerne, Texas, denied a building permit for the remodeling of a Catholic church for failure to comply with applicable historic preservation restrictions. The Archbishop of San Antonio sued, relying upon RFRA as one defense against the denial. The Supreme Court found on behalf of the city. It also pointedly struck down RFRA to the extent it sought to dictate the actions of state governments. RFRA remains applicable as a bar against the *federal* government, but for the states the holding of *Smith* still applies.

The *Boerne* decision is complicated, and not unanimous, but the justices seem to agree on one thing: Congress, you are not our boss. "Our national experience teaches that the Constitution is preserved best when each part of the Government respects both the Constitution and the proper actions and determinations of the other branches." [271] Even as the justices disagree over

---

[271] City of Boerne v. Flores, 521 U.S. 507, 535 (1997).

the *Smith* decision, the interpretation of the U.S. Constitution is the sole province of the Supreme Court. The *Boerne* Court concluded that Congress has remedial power to protect constitutional rights under the Fourteenth Amendment, but it does not have the power to *define* the extent of those rights. Such remediation must be congruent with and proportional to the injury suffered while substantive legislation might define, interpret, or even create the underlying matter.[272]

The purpose of RFRA is described in its text as restoring the pre-*Smith* mode of thinking, but that was not the complete picture. Rather than simply recreating a standard of strict scrutiny, RFRA imposed a "least restrictive means" requirement. Strict scrutiny is a high hurdle for the government to meet, as the name suggests. But the term "least restrictive" narrows the options of government down even further, arguably removing the government's discretion to weigh and to choose among available legislative possibilities.[273] This again suggests that Congress is not acting remedially but trying to redraw the boundaries of religious rights.

The *Boerne* decision limits the reach of RFRA as per the states, though the statute remains a restriction on the federal government. RFRA becomes a Congressionally imposed "one hand tied behind the back" approach to legislation and executive action. Assuming Congress or a federal agency does not pursue the least restrictive option, so as not to infringe upon religious freedom, RFRA offers an open and potentially blanket exception to those laws for religious individuals and groups.

---

[272] *Boerne,* 519–520.

[273] *Boerne,* 535.

How might this be applied?

In the Amazon rainforest, there is a religious sect that relies upon a special tea as a part of its communion services; this may sound vaguely familiar.[274] Unlike the peyote users of the Native American Church who lost out in *Smith*, Christian Spiritists of Brazil use hoasca (pronounced "wass-ca"), a blend of plants that notably contain the compound dimethyltryptamine (DMT), which is a controlled substance. An American branch of O Centro Espírita Beneficente União do Vegetal (UDV), one such Spiritist community, shipped drums of hoasca to the U.S. They were discovered by U.S. customs officials. UDV was threatened with prosecution for violation of the Controlled Substance Act, and UDV in turn sued the federal government under RFRA. UDV succeeded.

The federal government invoked the controlled nature of hoasca as a compelling state interest, and the law enforcement implications thereof. But the requirements of RFRA mandate that the government impose the least restrictive means in any instance when the exercise of religious rights might be affected. And when Congress sought to protect religious rights, and specifically those of the Native American Church, they had not put all of their legislative eggs in one statutory basket. They exempted the religious use of peyote under an amendment to the American Indian Religious Freedom Act. But why exempt one such drug and not others?

---

[274] Gonzales v. O Centro Espírita Beneficente União do Vegetal, 546 U.S. 418 (2006).

Having carved out an exemption for one religious group, and one hallucinogenic substance, the least restrictive option available to the government was to apply a similar exemption to UDV and hoasca. Moreover, RFRA was created in response to *Smith* and its implication for peyote use. *Smith* was not a criminal case, but RFRA was not restricted in its scope or its implications and was effectively premised on an exemption for the use of a controlled substance. It would be difficult for the federal government to argue that RFRA therefore did not anticipate courts carving out exceptions even to criminal statutes such as the Controlled Substance Act—tuck that notion away for later musing.

The effects of RFRA, even if limited to the federal government, are significant: whenever a religious right is implicated or a religious practice affected, by design or by chance, the federal government must offer its compelling interest and take the least restrictive pathway to achieve that interest. Moreover, many states created their own versions of RFRA, patterned after the statute but not always entirely identical to it. This creates a potentially bewildering puzzle of considerations when dealing with a law that affects the free exercise of religion somewhere in the United States.

Let us turn back the clock to 1975 and reconsider the Tennessee snake handlers who were forced to stop their religious practices. Tennessee has worded its 2010 version of RFRA differently, but in pertinent part it provides:

> No government entity shall substantially burden a person's free exercise of religion unless it demonstrates that application of the burden to the person is: (1) Essential to further a compelling

governmental interest; and (2) The least restrictive means of furthering that compelling governmental interest.[275]

Recall that members of the Holiness Church handled poisonous snakes and drank poisonous substances pursuant to their interpretation of the concluding verses of the Gospel of Mark. The State of Tennessee moved to block these practices due to their inherent dangers. How might that police power protection effort fare under this new statutory framework? Keeping members of the public safe and secure from death or injury likely remains a cornerstone aspect of the project that is government. However, is a ban against those dangerous religious practices the *least* restrictive means for meeting those objectives? The lower Tennessee courts had tried to craft restrictions short of an outright ban. For example, could they allow the handling of snakes, but require that children and unsuspecting members of the public not be present? Could there be an area closed off from the larger congregation, a "steel cage" match of sorts with direct participants and snakes inside but not others?

Drinking poison seems harder to be less restrictive about, though there is an unmentioned matter of religious faith that might bolster the argument: the right to die. If I have the legal right to die voluntarily according to my religious wishes, how is it any different to have the right to test my faith at the risk of my life? It is a personal act and choice, one that the person in question does not believe will result in death but which they are willing to chance as a religious undertaking (no pun

---

[275] Tennessee Code 4-1-407(c).

intended). The right to die is not allowed in most states, or under federal law, but RFRA is a broad exception to practically every aspect of federal law and could have a similar effect in states with local RFRA laws like Tennessee. In any case, it is likely that revisiting the facts surrounding *Swann v. Pack*[276] would result in greater freedom for members of the Holiness Church to follow the traditions of their faith, including the handling of snakes. And, it is worth pointing out, there are still groups of polygamous Latter-day Saints.

Depending on your perspective, this trend is scoring one for the little guy, striking a blow for religious freedom at the margins of society. But RFRA does not exist in a vacuum, legally or politically. Separation of church and state implies there are two worlds to keep separate. The Establishment Clause protects against government sponsored or supported religion. The Free Exercise Clause guards against government interference with religion. Two sides of a coin, two strands of the law.

But what if these begin to overlap? RFRA allows a religious group to express its grievances against a law or policy, including if it is denied access to funds or consideration for government programs. A law intended to protect rights under the Free Exercise Clause can be used in ways that tread closely upon the concerns of the Establishment Clause. If the government can sidestep establishment questions with maneuvers like school vouchers, if prayers at public meetings can be sanctioned under the auspices of "tradition," and if religious symbols can be maintained or even

---

[276] 527 S.W.2d 99.

used afresh because of their being embedded in history, how is the government barred from effectively establishing religious preferences in its budgets, programs, or messaging?

Even seemingly neutral laws and programs can be nudged in favor of certain religious groups by positively disposed lawmakers. School vouchers help religious groups that have already organized schools, giving groups like the Catholic Church and Evangelical Protestants an advantage in accessing the funds. Public prayers will tend to be given by existing religious groups in communities. Traditional religious symbols, like white crosses as memorials, will be accepted as historically familiar. The programs and policies are neutral on their face but geared toward these familiar groups. On balance, that could lead in time to desired support finding its way to preferred religious groups. When does that rise to the level of Establishment?

Similarly, RFRA is not merely in place as a last resort for the plucky Jehovah's Witnesses or the admirable Amish. It is a wide-open exception available to majority and minority religions alike. It has been used by corporations, some quite large, to deny healthcare benefits to their employees. By the way, how does a corporation have the right, or even the ability, to have a religion? Gather round to hear the tale.

Once upon a time, there was a law entitled the Affordable Care Act. It was a comprehensive plan for ensuring Americans had greater access to healthcare in every state. For some this was a happy ending in itself, while for others it was the Big Bad Wolf swaddled in grandma's legislative pajamas. One particular objection to the ACA was that it required employers who provided health insurance to include contraceptive coverage.

The Religious Freedom Restoration Act

One aggrieved company in particular was the Hobby Lobby Stores, Inc. Hobby Lobby is a chain of arts and crafts stores with thousands of employees. It was founded by David Green and owned and operated by his family, who are Evangelical Christians of a conservative stripe. They objected to the requirement of providing forms of birth control which they consider abortifacients, meaning drugs that by the Greens' definition result in an abortion or similar result after a human egg has been fertilized. Failing to provide such coverage under the ACA could result in the imposition of multi-million-dollar fines. Hobby Lobby sued and won.[277]

The obvious question again is how can a commercial for-profit corporation possess a religion? These corporations were "closely held," which is a legal term for a corporation owned and operated by a small group of shareholders who are often family members. The ACA and its regulations provided similar exemptions for offering contraceptives to nonprofit corporations, such as religious institutions or charities. The local Catholic diocese need not offer birth control and is likely an incorporated entity. Once again, exceptions to the rule made for one religious group can be the basis for exceptions to the rule for any religious group or religious person.

The plaintiffs in *Hobby Lobby* are for-profit companies, but that was deemed an insufficient distinction to obviate the requirements of RFRA. They are closely held corporations and therefore are tightly enmeshed with the persons who own and run them. A large, publicly traded corporation would be an unlikely candidate

---

[277] Burwell v. Hobby Lobby Stores, Inc., 573 U.S. 682 (2014). This case also included a related Green family company and a Mennonite furniture company.

for RFRA status, but not so for the local bakery company seeking to avoid baking a cake for a same-sex wedding couple.

This is also a factor to bear in mind if the result of *Hobby Lobby* and its kin seem like too little separation of church and state. If a corporation can have a religion because it is so closely identified with its owners, are those owners so fundamentally entwined with the corporation that the figurative veil between them must fall away and leave them as legally identical? This may seem an esoteric observation. But as will be discussed, that result would be less of a fairy tale and more of a horror story for your friendly neighborhood corporate lawyer. Because under such a scenario, the plaintiff Big Bad Wolf has access to defendant grandma's personal bank account.

CHAPTER 17

RLUIPA and the Case of *Jehovah v. Clarke*

THERE ARE DAYS when it may seem like the whole world is against you. Now, imagine opening your mail and discovering that you are being sued by God.

Harold Clarke, Director of the Virginia Department of Corrections (the VDOC), was named as a defendant in a lawsuit brought by Jesus Emmanuel Jehovah.[278] The latter individual is a prisoner in the Virginia corrections system, also known as Robbert Gabriel Love and Gabriel Alexander Antonio.[279] He is referred to by the defendants as "Jehovah" throughout the case

---

[278] See, e.g., *Jehovah v. Clarke*, 798 F.3d 169 (4th Cir. 2015).

[279] The spelling of "Robbert" is an allusion to the prisoner's contention that he is the Messiah, having been found between two robbers. This may be a literary allusion to the Passion story of Jesus and the two crucified thieves (see Matthew 26:39), or it may have been the literal event resulting in Jehovah's incarceration.

materials and I will maintain that designation, otherwise reserving judgment as to its accuracy or propriety. Jehovah seems to have written his own "Bible" and reports to be the Messiah. He follows a specific—one might say idiosyncratic—set of beliefs and practices. In all likelihood, he is a religion of one.

Jehovah filed a series of complaints with the VDOC as to the conditions of his incarceration. These related to the withholding of certain medical treatments, restricting his religious freedom in various ways, and imposing inappropriate roommates upon him in violation of his religious sensibilities. Focusing on the religious claims, Jehovah is particularly concerned about maintaining his version of the Sabbath, taking his style of communion, and determining the moral fitness of his cellmates.

Jehovah was assigned a prison job cleaning, which required work seven days per week. Jehovah's sabbatarian practices, however, dictate that he observe the "'Old Jewish Sabbath' (Friday sundown to Saturday sundown) and the 'New Christic Sabbath' (Sunday at sunset to Monday at sunrise)."[280] He lost his cleaning job, and there are few jobs that would allow for this nearly full weekend of Sabbath-taking at the prison. With this restriction in place, prison officials have not assigned him any new jobs, ironically giving Jehovah seven days to rest.

Jehovah also seeks accommodation of his personal form of communion. Communion is the practice of taking bread and wine in commemoration of the last supper Jesus of Nazareth spent with his disciples. This is a common ritual across Christian denominations, but the introduction of wine into a prison

---

[280] *Jehovah*, 174.

setting is a concern for officials. Moreover, Jehovah's specific requirements add to the logistical issues: "Jehovah's religion mandates that he take communion by drinking red wine and consuming bread dipped in honey, olive oil, sugar, cinnamon, and water."[281] Palatability aside, the prison was unwilling to supply wine.

Finally, Jehovah was concerned about the moral and theological suitability of his cellmates, an understandable concern in a maximum-security prison. He was by his account housed with anti-Christians and unbelievers, including "an atheist, an agnostic, a worldly Muslim, a false/non-practicing insincere Christian, a racist black anti-Christian atheist, a self-proclaimed 'Hell's Angel' biker, and a black anti-Christian from an anti-white gang."[282] Prior Virginia prisons had been able to accommodate these roommate requests, but the officials at the Sussex I Prison apparently were not so inclined.

Jehovah filed a series of grievances about these matters. Neither the prison grievance process nor the courts yielded much success. A federal judge did further examine the complaint about denial of access to communion wine, meaning it was not dismissed outright. But the case was allowed to proceed to summary judgment, when the court held that the prison officials had articulated sufficient reasons to restrict access to communion wine.

There are at least three possible motivations behind Jesus Emmanuel Jehovah's series of religious grievances. One, that he

---

[281] *Jehovah*, 173.

[282] *Jehovah*, 174.

is suffering from some form of mental illness, operating under the delusion that he is the Second Coming of Jesus. Two, that he is attempting to tweak prison officials using the grievance system and to gain whatever benefits he can as a result. Or three, that these are sincerely held religious beliefs, ones that have been self-generated from a broad understanding of Christian sources.

As to the first point, prison officials state that Jehovah had refused to meet with mental-health providers in the belief that such examinations would be used to diagnose him as being mentally ill, a diagnosis he denies.[283] As to the second, it would not be surprising to find someone in long-term incarceration exercising what little power he has at his disposal to access desirable objects or privileges. The VDOC briefs suggest that the officials consider Jehovah either mentally ill or an annoyance (or both). The third possibility, that these are sincerely held beliefs, is not actively disputed by the VDOC, perhaps owing either to an internal conclusion that Jehovah is more unbalanced than calculating or their desire to dispose of the matter well short of a trial in which the sincerity of those beliefs would be examined.

It is conceivable that Jehovah's complaints are a complex expression of all three possibilities. And, to be honest, that would be this author's conclusion. If that is the case, the concerns of Mr. Jehovah would indeed require careful examination. Why? Because sincerely held beliefs, regardless of these collateral matters, regardless of his mental state or strategic objectives, are to be given a high level of discretion and deference under federal law and procedure. There are several factors involved.

---

[283] Brief of Appellees at note 2.

RLUIPA and the Case of *Jehovah v. Clarke*

This case is a *pro se* complaint of civil-rights violations. *Pro se* is a legal term which means "for oneself." A non-lawyer is seeking to resolve a matter in the courts, and judges are generally required to construe *pro se* pleadings liberally. It can be a procedural headache for judges and opponents alike. This is also a case of religious rights, potentially subject to state and federal constitutional protections. Add to the mix the even more stringent protections contained within the Religious Land Use and Institutionalized Persons Act (RLUIPA)[284] and the claims of Mr. Jehovah become far more difficult to brush aside.

RLUIPA was passed in response to the Supreme Court's refusal to apply the RFRA statute to state governments in the *Boerne* case. Rather than a blanket restriction on all government infringement on religious rights, as arguably attempted with RFRA, RLUIPA focuses on certain places and people. If a municipality were to try through local zoning to prevent religious uses from being set up in certain areas, RLUIPA could be invoked to protect the religious use. Why might a municipality do this? Houses of worship are often tax exempt and would be less desirable in prime commercial locations. If a local government sought to exclude uses that are important to certain religious groups, but not clearly provided for under a narrow definition of religious use, RLUIPA could be used to expand the permitted uses. For example, food pantries, daycares, homeless shelters, or so-called "sanctuary" locations might be blocked because of zoning, health regulations, or the like—RLUIPA could be used to override the restrictions. Some religious organizations have even used

---

[284] 42 U.S.C. § 2000cc.

RLUIPA to overcome limitations on the inclusion of solar panels on historic buildings.[285]

RLUIPA avoids the problems of RFRA by a narrower focus linked to federal areas of concern such as interstate commerce and the provision of federal funds. States, universities, municipalities, and of course prisons accepting federal funds would be subject to this law as "governments." Conversely, the federal law's intervention into local land use and zoning is a broad invocation of ill-defined (or nonexistent) federal power. As such, certain aspects of RLUIPA could be subject to a challenge of the federal government's overreach, as in RFRA, but such a challenge has not been successful to date.

The *Jehovah* appeal was halted at one point because a relevant and subsequently controlling case was being heard before the U.S. Supreme Court in *Holt v. Hobbs*.[286] Another prisoner had brought a claim under RLUIPA, this time because prison officials had refused to allow a Muslim prisoner to grow and to maintain a half-inch long beard. The prison officials in *Holt* were concerned that contraband could be hidden in beards and only permitted an exception for one-quarter-inch beards for inmates with specific medical conditions. Factually, neither the *Holt* federal magistrate nor the U.S. Supreme Court found it likely that a prisoner could hide contraband in such a beard and, further, the prison did not require haircuts of similar short length rendering the restriction nearly pointless.[287]

---

[285] Heather Beasley Doyle, "On Religious Grounds," *UU World*, August 19, 2019, uuworld.org/articles/religious-grounds.

[286] Holt v. Hobbs, 574 U.S. ___, 135 S.Ct. 853 (2015).

[287] *Holt*, 10 (slip opinion).

While the *Holt* magistrate ultimately deferred to the prison officials' arguments, the Supreme Court refused to do so under the exacting requirements of RLUIPA. Under RLUIPA, the petitioner, in this case a prisoner, must meet the initial hurdle of showing a substantial burden on religious exercise. Then the government, in this case a prison, must establish that the complained-of policy is the least restrictive way to meet or to further a compelling governmental interest. As the Supreme Court held in *Holt*, "The least-restrictive-means standard [of RLUIPA] is exceptionally demanding, and it requires the government to show that it lacks other means of achieving its desired goal without imposing a substantial burden on the exercise of religion by the objecting party."[288]

The prison officials in *Holt* suggested that this one burden on beards was small in context when the inmate was otherwise permitted other religious accommodations, such as access to a prayer rug, being able to maintain religious fasts, etc. But "substantial burden" focuses on the specific practice: the "inquiry asks whether the government has substantially burdened religious exercise (here, the growing of a ½-inch beard), not whether the RLUIPA claimant is able to engage in other forms of religious exercise."[289] This "half a loaf is better than none" balancing test would otherwise be a consideration for any prison governance, except as overridden by RLUIPA in which each metaphorical slice of bread matters.

---

[288] *Holt*, 10–11.

[289] *Holt*, 7–8.

In the *Jehovah* case, Jesus Emmanuel Jehovah sets out a list of beliefs and a series of practices at odds with the vast majority of Christians. And yet the prison officials did not challenge the sincerity of his beliefs, perhaps because it would have been too prolonged and chaotic a process to argue with a plaintiff who wrote his own religion. The prison was likely relying upon its working practice of broad discretion with regards to prison discipline. As described in the 1987 case *Turner v. Safley*, "when a prison regulation impinges on inmates' constitutional rights, the regulation is valid if it is reasonably related to legitimate penological interests."[290] And then came RLUIPA in 2000.

RLUIPA is by definition not geared toward the efficiency of government practice. It is not limited to beliefs shared by all the members of a religious sect, such as "Christianity" on the whole, as if one could readily generalize from Protestant to Catholic, Evangelical to Episcopalian. It is not the role of the courts to question the centrality of particular beliefs and practices, or even the validity of the interpretations of those beliefs and practices made by the complaining party. The courts are not equipped to draw such religious lines, which is perhaps one reason why the Supreme Court sought to remove itself from such matters through the *Smith* case, thereby spawning RFRA and RLUIPA. And so, the religious beliefs and practices need not be broadly held, centrally important, or even "correctly" interpreted by whatever standard.[291] Once the court determines that a belief or practice is sincerely held, it is the government's turn to begin explaining its position.

---

[290] 482 U.S. 78, 89 (1987).

[291] Hernandez v. Comm'r of Internal Revenue, 490 U.S. 680, 699 (1989).

RLUIPA and the Case of *Jehovah v. Clarke*

What does this mean for Mr. Jehovah? After *Holt*, the Fourth Circuit remanded, or returned, all of the religious claims of Jehovah to the district judge. The issues about his expansive Sabbath and cellmate concerns had been dismissed, a ruling that essentially states that even if everything you say is assumed to be true, there is no law to support your desired outcome. Jehovah had no constitutional right to a prison job or the selection of his cellmates. However, he had articulated an argument that the prison was operating out of a spirit of animus, meaning they were punishing him in some manner for being a nuisance. That was enough to get back into court.

The communion question had made it to a further level of review, summary judgment. There needs to be a genuine issue of material fact to warrant going on to trial. The assumptions about facts at these early stages avoids the detailed fact-finding process of a trial and focuses instead on the judge-specific task of interpreting the law. The *Jehovah* lower court found that the prison officials had articulated a legitimate legal basis for their decision to keep communion wine out of the prison, which was the pre-RLUIPA standard. However, the rights of a prisoner under RLUIPA require an even more exacting analysis than applied by the lower court. The prisoner had, for example, offered several examples for how wine could be used in this setting under close control and by doing so at least alleged a less restrictive way of handling his religious requests. The prisoner had made his case, at least to a point, and the lower court would have to continue examining what to do about Jehovah.

RLUIPA is an effort to balance the power of government against the religious rights of people and organizations. Along with RFRA, it provides a useful tool for religious folks to respond to government laws, regulations, and policies that burden the exercise of religious briefs and practices. As the *Holt* decision suggests, it requires a high standard of review and, if properly invoked, a high hurdle for the government to clear, particularly when other exceptions to the rules are already allowed.

CHAPTER 18

If You Can't Beat Them, Join Them

HARKENING BACK to the opening pages of this project, in recent decades liberal and progressive religious folks have more often than conservatives sought to delineate a clear wall of separation between church and state. Whatever the reasons for that sensibility, cultural or religious, that wall is not what it used to be. Realistically, it was a hastily erected structure, with the recognizable legal foundations loosely laid in the 1940s and cases about religious rights fashioned like bricks to be stacked up in the 1960s and 1970s. Those dissimilar legal pronouncements were mortared together with a broad goal of tolerance for religious minorities and resistance to government-supported religion. That has changed.

The Free Exercise Clause was powerfully defended in cases like *Sherbert* and *Yoder*. There was a setback in the *Smith* case, one seemingly "fixed" by the Religious Freedom Restoration Act and its state progeny. And yet the emphasis has changed. The Free Exercise Clause used to be the refuge of minority religions beset by majority sensibilities: different sabbath days, different holy books in schools, different cultural virtues. But now, calls for religious liberty have been transformed into the desire to broaden the presence of religion generally against the perceived secularization of society. As in the *Hobby Lobby* case, the religious beliefs of a corporation can now be protected, inflicting the net effects of those personal beliefs onto the employees of a for-profit corporation—no birth control for you because we bosses object.

In 2019, the Attorney General of the United States, William Barr, warned a group at Notre Dame University about the problem of secularism.[292] He argued that:

> Catholicism and other mainstream religions were the target of 'organized destruction' by 'secularists and their allies among progressives who have marshalled all the force of mass communications, popular culture, the entertainment industry and academia . . . the traditional Judeo-Christian moral system' of the United States was under siege by 'modern secularists' who were responsible for every sort of 'social pathology,' including drug abuse, rising suicide rates and illegitimacy.

Furthermore, Barr obliquely attacks progressive support for social change, particularly regarding LGBTQ folks: "Militant secularists today do not have a live-and-let-live spirit—they are not

---

[292] See, e.g., Philip Shenon, "'A threat to democracy': William Barr's speech alarms liberal Catholics," *The Guardian*, October 20, 2019, theguardian.com/us-news/2019/oct/19/william-barr-attorney-general-catholic-conservative-speech.

content to leave religious people alone to practice their faith. Instead, they seem to take a delight in compelling people to violate their conscience."[293]

To leave religious people alone: how might this form of religious freedom take shape? By shopkeepers being allowed to turn away gay customers and medical providers being permitted to forgo providing treatment for transgender patients? By municipal buildings and public schools being authorized to declare which bathrooms can be used by which persons? By protecting religious groups from the possibility of seeing same-sex marriages performed and same-sex couples living freely on their own in society? Leaving someone alone is not the same as requiring someone else to hide. The traditional "Judeo-Christian" moral system touted by Barr can in practice be as much an Establishment Clause concern as the Standing Order of the Massachusetts Bay Colony.

Furthermore, he makes the assumption that within the broad confines of Judaism and Christianity those same moral questions would be answered in the same way. This is a false presumption of unanimity by Attorney General Barr for his intended audience of religious conservatives. This is not a fight between secularists on the one side and the religious on the other, or at least it should not be. Religious liberals and progressives have an obligation to engage these arguments and to end the effective

---

[293] For a less than subtle critique of the speech, see, e.g., Jeffrey Toobin, "William Barr's Wild Misreading of the First Amendment," *The New Yorker*, October 17, 2019, newyorker.com/news/daily-comment/william-barrs-wild-misreading-of -the-first-amendment.

retreat into silence while relaxing behind an ineffective wall of spotty separation.

It is as much a violation of the conscience of religious liberals and progressives to abandon the fight for racial and gender inequality or to forsake the welcome that has been offered to LGBTQ folks as it would be to require the Catholic Church to offer contraceptive health coverage to its employees or force a Seventh-day Adventist to work on a Saturday. Conservatives have never been the sole source of moral guidance for American society. And recent political trends suggest that many religious conservatives have traded away that long-standing appeal to religiously anchored morals in exchange for immediate access to the halls of power.

And it is worth pointing out the absurdity of attempting to leave every social problem at the feet of "secularists." Sexual abuse by clergy ran rampant in the bastions of rectitude petitioned by Barr. Opioid addiction arose more from corporate greed, lax regulations, and worsening social struggles than giving people a choice of bathrooms or the right to love in peace. Sadly, however, these equally lofty religious ramparts have not always been carefully guarded by liberals and progressives. It is not a betrayal of social ideas to convey them into a religious context. It is rather a way of articulating one's core ideals and values for a large percentage of society.

Why does it have to be set down in religious language rather than in terms of social theory or philosophical perspectives? Because religion is safeguarded under the United States Constitution while social theories and personal philosophies are not—the right to believe and the right to speak plus the *right to act*.

Religious liberals and progressives have access to an often-untapped ability to champion these ideals and values, and to act in keeping with them, in a way that is legally protected. Religious freedom is a cherished right and it belongs as much to those on the Left as to those on the Right. It has not been as frequently articulated as such, or embraced in practice.

Mainline religious groups did not always seem to require protection. And progressive religious groups did not always seek to work within the system. And yet, even if the masters' tools will never dismantle the masters' houses, these tools may at least temporarily allow one to beat them at their own game (apologies to Audre Lorde). The luxury of being left alone is no longer an option, and every tool in the box will be needed if liberals and progressives are to be true to the goals they would pursue and the morals and values they would see lived out in American society.

Similarly, the Establishment Clause had been vigorously used to strike down government financial support to religious groups and sectarian schools. The *Lemon* test stood for decades as a clumsy barrier against such interference. But the game has changed. Instead of direct support to a school as in *Lemon*, state and federal programs have been made nominally neutral, without reference to or direct language regarding religion. Funds are generically available, but lo and behold, they somehow mostly end up in the hands of religious schools as in *Zelman*. The effects of these programs can be anticipated—that is how budgeting works—and therefore they can be tacitly calculated to support religious objectives while masked behind straight-faced neutrality. Again, it is time for liberals and progressives to enter the religious debate and to press for the same supports being offered to other religious groups. That may be a challenge for those who have made principled decisions to the contrary. Religious groups have always been faced with social challenges that require triaging their efforts and reimagining their mission to the wider world. The funding is open to all, allowing all religious groups to lay claims.

Consider the decision of *Trinity Lutheran*.[294] It is a banal little case about fixing a church playground that somehow found its way up to the Supreme Court. It also became the engine of judicial destruction for a century-old thorn in the side of those who sought to provide greater support for religious organizations and schools: the Blaine Amendments. The original purpose of these amendments to state constitutions was to prevent religious schools from receiving state funds to support their efforts. The amendments were initially anti-Catholic in their focus, though support for them may have been drawn from secular-minded supporters of the public schools. But neither perspective, anti-Catholic or pro-secular, is currently in favor in the evolving jurisprudence of the Supreme Court.

The Trinity Lutheran Church of Columbia, Missouri, wanted to fix their playground. There was an on-site preschool and daycare center at the church, one of the ongoing ministries of that institution. The organization applied for a state program that would reimburse groups that replaced their playground surfaces with those made from recycled tires, the desired state goal being to reduce the impact on landfills. The church's application was

---

[294] Trinity Lutheran Church of Columbia, Inc. v. Comer, 582 U.S. ___ ; 137 S. Ct. 2012 (2017), supreme.justia.com/cases/federal/us/582/15-577/.

one of the top candidates for the program, but it was disqualified under Missouri's strict policy against supporting religious organizations set out under the Blaine Amendment to its state constitution.

The *Trinity Lutheran* case lies at the crossroads of the shifting jurisprudence under both the Free Exercise Clause and the Establishment Clause. Under Free Exercise, religious parties are protected from unequal treatment. "[D]enying a generally available benefit solely on account of religious identity imposes a penalty on the free exercise of religion that can be justified only by a state interest 'of the highest order.' "[295] In the *Everson* case, a general state program supporting the transportation of children to schools, public or private, was permissible. Now under *Trinity Lutheran*, the denial of support for religious schools would be *impermissible*.

Under *Smith*, religious believers were not permitted special dispensation under general laws. But the Court conversely did not permit special disabilities against religious believers. Denying Trinity Lutheran access to the state program would be such a disability. Like a school voucher available to any student, generic support from the state to a group or program is not invalid because it happens to flow to a religious organization. Or, at least, it is not so now.

The *Sherbert* case resulted in a Seventh-day Adventist receiving unemployment benefits even though she would not work on Saturdays, violating an implicit requirement of the state program

---

[295] *Trinity,* Section II. The court relies obliquely on the *Yoder* case, notwithstanding the effects of *Smith*.

to take on an available job. In other words, there can be no exclusion from a public benefit that revolves around religious identity. The playground program is a public benefit and therefore it cannot be conditioned on being a non-religious applicant. In this way, the Free Exercise Clause has been used to invalidate the long-standing protections of Missouri, and other states, against violating the Establishment Clause. Blaine Amendments are at best now legally questionable and at worst effectively overruled across the country. Best or worst depends on one's perspective.

Justice Sotomayor thought *Trinity Lutheran* was overall in the "worst" category. In her dissent, she reviewed the history of disestablishment in the United States and found that the states had developed across history a tradition of avoiding financial support for ministers and houses of worship. Preventing the use of funds for these religious purposes was a long-standing goal of state governments, a tradition the *Trinity Lutheran* Court has placed firmly aside.

Now what? The Supreme Court has made it difficult, if not impossible, for state governments to restrict the use of taxpayers' funds from supporting religious purposes. If a program is of generally applicability, like a school voucher or a college scholarship, it cannot be conditioned on secular use. Could the same challenge be made for a school building fund made available to public schools versus private ones? Could the financial support given to public charter schools under various programs be redirected to private schools? Legal creativity knows no bounds.

The public schools are once again a "playground" for these fundamental constitutional arguments. Sectarian schools were traditionally Catholic schools with a few others of limited number. Coincidentally, the overhaul of First Amendment cases on the Supreme Court level in the 1980s and 1990s overlaps with an increase in Conservative Christian migration to private academies.[296] Evangelical Christian academies have increased the religious diversity of such schools, though arguably not broadened the "left-right" spectrum terribly much.[297]

Catholics moved away from the public schools because there was a sense that those schools offered a broadly Protestant education. When prayers and Bible readings were eventually pulled from the schools, the migration of other conservative-leaning religious groups followed. Liberal and progressive religious groups were less inclined to do so because the separation of church and state within the school curriculum was not as much a point of concern, though that is speaking in broad generalities and assumptions. Homeschoolers tend to be more conservative, though that does not mean that all homeschoolers are conservative.

This is not intended as a generalized lament over the changing shape of the public schools. The growing availability of state funding and support for religious schools and other institutions requires a rethinking of how liberal and progressive religious groups engage with municipal, state, and federal programs,

---

[296] "You can't have a Bible in the public schools. If you are a teacher, you can't talk to people about your faith and you can't pray in school," quoting Ed Gamble, the executive director of the Southern Baptist Association. Mary Ann Zehr, "Evangelical Christian Schools See Growth," *EducationWeek*, December 7, 2004, edweek.org/ew/articles/2004/12/08/15private.h24.html.

[297] Per government statistics, in 2013–2014, there were over 4,200 Conservative Christian schools in the U.S. compared with 6,700 Catholic schools. Office of Non-Public Education (ONPE), "Statistics About Nonpublic Education in the United States, U.S. Department of Education, aboed.gov/about/offices/list/oii/nonpublic/statistics.html.

including the public schools. There should be a lower threshold for seeking financial support from the government, and it is obviously not unheard of for religious groups to develop private schools that support their values. The perennial worry, of course, would be that the government would impose restrictions on the use of the funds or would intrude upon the nature and scope of the work being performed. That has been and remains a worry, but it is also an opportunity. If public funds are available generally, under *Trinity Lutheran* they are available implicitly for religious organizations.

And yet the government still faces Establishment Clause issues if it seeks to intrude upon the inner workings of an organization like a church, synagogue, or mosque. To give a common New England example, a historic preservation grant might require approval of any changes to a congregational building. Those directives risk shaping how a house of worship operates. A similar restriction dictating whether banners or messages may be affixed to the exterior of the building run the same establishment gauntlet. State RFRA laws and the federal Religious Land Use and Institutionalized Person Act might limit whether or how far a state or local authority may delve into the life of a religious community.

I offer these and other observations with a heavy dose of caution—recall the early lesson that the answer to every legal question is "It depends." That remains the case here. If such a situation presents itself in the life of a congregation, I strongly advise seeking legal counsel from someone who specializes in this area of the law. Retaining your well-intended lawyer or sibling-in-law who usually performs house closings to spearhead your First

Amendment case has some built-in pitfalls. And presenting this book to the court as the basis of your case would be momentarily amusing for the judge and court officers, but not overly effective. So, lawyer up.

But with those cautions in place, it is equally important to consider the implications of these changes to the case law surrounding the First Amendment. In the next few chapters, I will dig into special situations about the literal use of houses of worship to reflect religious values, the allowance of religious displays in public places, and the ability of people of faith to challenge laws and regulations that fall short of the religious values of their traditions. The hope is to offer a few different frameworks for organizing liberal and progressive religious responses to moral questions facing our communities and our nation.

CHAPTER 19

Going to and Fro: Religion on Display

YEARS AGO, while I was in college, I played rugby. Having played football in high school, I decided to give up on all that protective equipment and come by my concussions honestly. Actually, it was a wonderful time and a wonderful group, plus the injuries are fewer once you realize the only thing standing between you and a head injury is your haircut.

Twice yearly, the rugby club would travel to the woods for a party: the roast. We would buy a lamb or a pig (or both), build a fire, imbibe with abandon, and commune with nature while the meat cooked. My senior year, I was busy with academics and a serious girlfriend, so I decided to skip the festivities. I missed an exciting time.

Some non-rugby civilians were passing by, unaware of the gathering, and they noted the ash-covered men, the fire, and the preponderance of animal carcasses in a clearing. They called the police, as one might. The party ground to a halt, or so I gathered once I read the campus newspaper, which read something along the lines of "Rugby Team Mistaken for Devil Worshippers." The president of our club was quoted in the paper, saying that, "This could not have come at a worse time." And this observation got me thinking—when *would* it have been a good time to have been mistaken for a devil worshipper? Many years later, I have finally come across a situation when that was the desired result.

The Satanic Temple is an American religious organization that is notable in many ways, including a lack of belief in either Satan or anything terribly supernatural. Frankly, they are decidedly atheistic, strongly humanist, and more than occasionally funny in their message. Why then use the name "Satanic Temple" when that name does not fit the underlying views? To be "mistaken" for devil worshippers. To capitalize on the moral panic that the name "Satan" stirs. It is like calling yourself the "Puppy Kicking Society" or the "Charles Manson Glee Club." Someone is bound to take notice and take offense, and therefore mission accomplished.

The Satanic Temple is an advocacy group that supports various causes, particularly religious freedom inclusive of freedom *from* religion. They are satirical, humorous, and occasionally litigious. In Oklahoma, a monument to the Ten Commandments was installed on the grounds of the state house in 2012. Three years later, the Oklahoma Supreme Court tersely declared that the monument had to come down as it was obviously religious in nature and therefore its presence violated the Oklahoma Constitution.[298]

---

[298] Prescott v. Oklahoma Capitol Preservation Comm., 2015 OK 54, Case Number: 113332 (2015), law.justia.com/cases/oklahoma/supreme-court/2015/113332.html.

During the statue's short time on public land, the Satanic Temple had filed a petition to add its own monument to the state house grounds: an enthroned statue of Satan, with ram's horns and angel wings, backed by a pentagram and flanked by children.[299] The logic for the request was that the erection of the Ten Commandments monument opened the door for other religious groups to seek placement of their various symbols in public spaces. The Satanic Temple has shopped the statue around to other states in response to similar monumental disputes.

The Oklahoma Supreme Court's reliance upon the state constitution seems to have been an implicit effort to avoid the issues in *Van Orden v. Perry*, a Supreme Court case in which a similar monument in Texas was found not to trammel upon the Establishment Clause.[300] One might guess that the judges were trying to avoid a prolonged battle all the way up to the Supreme Court, a sensible decision if not one overtly made. Nevertheless, that trip to Washington might have been complicated, even if it avoided letting the issue out of Oklahoma's direct control.

The *Van Orden* case does not necessarily make it easy for religious monuments or similar displays to go up. The Texas State Capitol grounds are well appointed with numerous monuments and historical markers. The Ten Commandments monument is placed within that busy context, and its embedded symbols are varied:

---

[299] Abby Ohlheiser, "The Satanic Temple's giant statue of a goat-headed god is looking for a home," *The Washington Post*, July 1, 2015, washingtonpost.com/news/acts-of-faith/wp/2015/07/01/the-satanic-temples-giant-statue-of-a-goat-headed-god-is-looking-for-a-home/.

[300] Van Orden v. Perry, 545 U.S. 677 (2005).

The monolith challenged here stands 6-feet high and 3-feet wide. It is located to the north of the Capitol building, between the Capitol and the Supreme Court building. Its primary content is the text of the Ten Commandments. An eagle grasping the American flag, an eye inside of a pyramid, and two small tablets with what appears to be an ancient script are carved above the text of the Ten Commandments. Below the text are two Stars of David and the superimposed Greek letters Chi and Rho, which represent Christ. The bottom of the monument bears the inscription "PRESENTED TO THE PEOPLE AND YOUTH OF TEXAS BY THE FRATERNAL ORDER OF EAGLES OF TEXAS 1961."[301]

The Supreme Court suggested that the Texas monument was more passive than other cases in which a display was struck down, such as cases when the Commandments were ordered to be displayed in every public school classroom. *Van Orden* was a patchwork of concurring opinions, which effectively places greatest weight on that of Justice Breyer, the fifth vote for the result of the decision if not the entirety of the logic of that lead opinion. Breyer noted from the *Schempp* decision that under the Establishment Clause, the government may not engage in or compel religious practices, show favoritism among religions, or seek to deter religious belief. The Texas monument in its context provides both a religious and a secular message, yet when divorced from that context, it would be singularly religious. The monument represents one ideal among many scattered

---

[301] Ibid.

about the grounds. Such a religious monument can therefore be secularized.

It can also be placed in a context of diversity. Imagine the Oklahoma monument had stayed in place. Next to it would potentially have been a statue of Satan surrounded by frolicking children, a result that would have no doubt inspired a range of responses. Another group, this one of Hindus, had also sought to have a display.[302] *Van Orden* is one of the "tradition" cases that arguably relies upon aspects of U.S. history to privilege certain religious messages over others, such as the memorial cross monument in *American Legion* or opening prayers at government meetings as in the *Town of Greece.*

The Satanic Temple has decidedly not been a fixture of U.S. history. And yet the opening of the public square to religious symbols and messages under the auspices of history also opens that same door to the possibilities of diversity. That is the core message of the Satanic Temple as they shop their statue around the country looking for a home, but in reality using it as a bludgeon to keep public spaces free from such religious appropriation. They have similarly challenged the practice of allowing religious materials to be passed out at public schools, including the distribution of Bibles in the Orange County, Florida, area. Rather than seeking to deny the practice, the Satanic Temple threatened to embrace it with their own Satanic religious materials and even coloring books, such as the "Satanic Children's

---

[302] Abby Phillip, "Oklahoma's Ten Commandments statue must be removed, state Supreme Court says," *The Washington Post,* June 30, 2015, washingtonpost .com/news/acts-of-faith/wp/2015/06/30/oklahomas-ten-commandments -statue-must-be-removed-state-supreme-court-says/.

BIG BOOK of Activities." Again, this is more about tweaking those susceptible to such worries than indoctrinating the masses.

A founder of the Satanic Temple described the situation as follows:

> We would never seek to establish a precedent of disseminating our religious materials in public schools because we believe our constitutional values are better served by respecting a strong separation of Church and State. However, if a public school board is going to allow religious pamphlets and full Bibles to be distributed to students—as is the case in Orange County, Florida—we think the responsible thing to do is to ensure that these students are given access to a variety of differing religious opinions, as opposed to standing idly by while one religious voice dominates the discourse and delivers propaganda to youth.[303]

If one religious voice or organization is allowed to dominate the public square or to distribute its message in the public schools, the response can be two-fold: seek removal or seek inclusion. Perhaps, as with the Satanic Temple, it is best to try both paths at once.

These monument examples are indicative of the issue, but they may seem few in number and rather distant from local concerns,

---

[303] Valerie Strauss, "Satanic Temple challenges policy allowing religious materials to be distributed at public schools," *The Washington Post,* washingtonpost .com/news/answer-sheet/wp/2014/11/17/satanic-temple-challenges-policy -allowing-religious-materials-to-be-distributed-at-public-schools/.

depending on where one is a local. Another far more common example of this conflict is the annual holiday season. Religious displays of nativity scenes are common around Christmas time. Where they are located can trigger these same legal questions about exclusion or inclusion in public spaces.

A few years ago, I was a decision-maker in such a case. A local synagogue had requested the right to place a menorah on the common of my New England town—a "common" is usually a big green lawn with picturesque buildings and churches all around. It is often also a public space for municipal events or displays. The rabbi was seeking permission to put up the menorah for one night. Never willing to leave well enough alone, I shared my recollection that Hanukkah lasted for eight nights and opined that the board would have no issue with the display being there for that time period. Everyone agreed.

The next year, I was not on the board, having left the halls of local government to take on my life in ministry. The synagogue returned to request permission to place the menorah on the common for eight nights. However, in the intervening year, a new policy had gone into place, limiting any such displays to one night. This policy seemed limiting and might have been construed as a reaction to the prior year's display and its religious sponsors. A "guerilla" nativity scene had also one year appeared on the common without discussion or permission. In response to the denial of the eight-day display, many of the other houses of worship in town banded together to each request permission to display a menorah on the town common for one night, filling in the remaining seven days. A holiday miracle of a different sort—the town allowed the menorah.

The moral of that story? People of faith are often people of good faith. The prospect of a local synagogue being denied the right to display a menorah seemed inconsistent with the values of that small suburban community. Being selective about who can offer such displays is an inherently corrosive decision that will inspire thoughts of resentment. The Catholics of the nineteenth century were not wrong to feel excluded from the decision-making about what could be taught in the United States' public schools. The non-Christians of the twentieth century were not wrong to feel preached at through the use of Bible readings and recitations of the Lord's Prayer in the public schools. Eventually, those tensions were removed from the schools, but were re-centered in public conversations about the perceived decline of society's sense of morality. And yet the monuments cases provide a similar logic for approaching these questions: exclusion or inclusion.

Legal decisions about holiday displays turn on strange and interesting factors. If a nativity scene is displayed by itself on public lands, or through public sponsorship, it will likely be found to violate the Establishment Clause. A similar nativity scene within a diverse display, such as one with a menorah and other holiday items, has been upheld.[304] This has been archly referred to as the "Three Plastic Animals" rule, though Frosty the Snowman has served in a pinch. There is a concern that this policy leads to a "profanation" of religious symbols, as suggested by Justice Alito

---

[304] Compare *County of Allegheny v. ACLU*, 492 U.S. 573 (1989) (nativity scene alone not allowed) with *Lynch v. Donnelly*, 465 U.S. 668 (1984) (nativity scene in holiday display allowed).

in a dissent from before he rose to the Supreme Court.[305] The Establishment Clause does not require that the sacred be made profane. Conversely, having the government elevate one representation of the sacred over others is *expressly* not permitted.

The *Van Orden* case relies upon the same process, the sacredness of a symbol or display being lost in translation, such as in the many monuments and markers surrounding the Texas State House. The *American Legion* case regarding a memorial cross monument to veterans similarly utilized arguments regarding historic secularism and faded religious sentiment to allow the monument to remain. Under these various lines of cases, the religious meaning of the symbol must either be lost or diffused in context to such an extent that the primary meaning cannot be perceived as religious and therefore as establishing a religious preference.

Allowing religious symbols in a public setting requires a loss of the symbol's overt religiousness. Profanation is not the goal, but it is the result. That consequence may be upsetting to those who cherish that symbol, that language, or that message. Similarly, placing symbols next to each other in a display of diversity can seem jarring for those who have made distinct religious choices in their lives. That is the point: having a cross in a public square, having the Ten Commandments on the courthouse steps, can give an impression of political support for one religious tradition or family of traditions. If you want one, the other may follow, so prepare to be jarred.

The alternatives are exclusion or inclusion. Either do not have the government allow those symbols within public spaces or

---

[305] ACLU ex rel. *Lander v. Schundler*, 168 F.3d 92, 98 (3rd Cir. 1999).

expect that other symbols may be placed adjacent to them. Do not have the government begin its meetings with public prayers or expect that other voices might be permitted to offer those prayers. The discomfort one might undergo seeing an unfamiliar symbol or hearing an unfamiliar prayer is a familiar feeling for those who do not ascribe to a majority form of religion, such as American Protestantism. The First Amendment protects religious freedom and freedom of speech. It does not guarantee access to public spaces to affix advertisements for those religious beliefs or opinions.

The image of a statue of Satan on the courthouse lawn may fill someone with dread, which is the initial goal. The ultimate goal is to have no such symbols in the shared places of a democracy that has since its inception sought to avoid government entanglement with religion. The Satanic Temple does not worship Satan, by their own account, but they do value religious freedom: the freedom to act according to their beliefs and freedom from the imposition of the beliefs of others. Such freedom is always in flux, and it needs to be monitored and protected by conscientious folks willing to let their voices be heard and, on occasion, willing to commission unusual sculptures to make a point.

CHAPTER 20

The New Sanctuary Movement

The towns that you give to the Levites shall
include the six cities of refuge, where you
shall permit a slayer to flee. . . .

NUMBERS 35:6

THE IDEA OF SANCTUARY is ancient. In the Book of Numbers, the Levite cities of refuge were set up to create places to which a "slayer" might flee. These were indeed killers, though it is unclear whether they were murderers, to highlight the distinction between bringing about someone's death and being legally responsible for doing so. Israelite justice was often outsourced to the families of victims, meaning the only justice available was through blood feud. The cities of refuge were protected places, controlled by the Levite priestly class, where those responsible for the death of another might find peace from the mob. This did not necessarily prevent finding the accused responsible for a crime, but it did offer time to examine events. Sanctuary in this ancient sense did not absolve one of anything, but it potentially provided a pause in a cycle of violence.

Centuries later, the concept of sanctuary changed in medieval Europe. Rather than whole cities of refuge, many Catholic churches became designated places for retreat. In an example of the deeply rooted nature of the practice, after William the Conqueror took over Saxon England, there was concern that the Normans might eliminate this key principle of law. The people had little to worry about; William did nothing of the sort, for sanctuary was also an ancient right in Normandy.

Some contemporary charters for English churches nonetheless contain express grants of the right to offer sanctuary, some actually fraudulent, forged to increase the stature of the church. This form of religious sanctuary was often more fundamental than that offered by the Israelites. It was not a pause but a *pardon*—those making it into the church would be absolved of the crime. As in Ancient Israel, the practice of sanctuary was a response to weak or nonexistent systems of justice. At the time, a "trial" could be a familiar weighing of evidence, but it could also be a trial by fire, meaning only an innocent would remain unburned by flames, or trial by combat, meaning God would not let the guilty prevail in mortal combat. The escape valve of offering religious sanctuary provided an element of mercy within a harsh and arbitrary system.

Over time, however, Europeans grew less fond of the practice. The offering of sanctuary was seen as allowing enterprising criminals to break the law with impunity, at times mere steps away from a church. As law and order became more regulated, though often no less harsh, support waned for the idea of sanctuary as outright forgiveness of a crime and disappeared almost entirely by the time of the Protestant Reformation in the 1500s.

In the 1980s in the United States, a sanctuary movement began in response to the wars in Central America, conflicts alternately sponsored and opposed by the U.S. government. Refugees from the conflict sought asylum in the U.S., but not with equal success. As often a silent partisan in these wars, the United States government did not necessarily recognize that there was anything from which to flee in certain countries.

The risk of returning home to war-torn countries was so great that religious communities sought ways of helping refugees. And thus the Sanctuary Movement was born. Church buildings were opened to asylum seekers, who lived for varying periods in seclusion. Immigration officials, then called the Immigration and Naturalization Service, had to contend with a growing movement of churches and synagogues across the political spectrum opening their doors to migrants fleeing violence in El Salvador and Guatemala (Nicaraguans and Cubans fleeing leftist regimes were more acceptable to the Reagan Administration).

The federal government did not simply let this movement unfold, as evidenced by the case of *U.S. v. Aguilar.*[306] A network of U.S. Americans developed a system for finding and sheltering Central American refugees, in association with churches in the U.S. Southwest. Rev. John Fife of Southside Presbyterian Church in Tucson, Arizona, was a leader of the movement which was in many ways patterned after the Underground Railroad movement

---

[306] 883 F.2d 662 (1989).

of the nineteenth century, whose mission was to liberate enslaved people to Northern states. Fife would later say in response to more recent struggles over immigration to the U.S.:

> In the 1980s, people were fleeing death squads and massacres in Guatemala and El Salvador, and our government was refusing to acknowledge them as refugees and deporting them back to those same death squads—because those countries were allies of the U.S. Now the government is threatening human rights and family integrity, and parents are the disappeared from the workplace. U.S. policy is to use death in the desert as a deterrent to coming here, and that is a violation of international law and human rights. Churches ought to stand up for the right of people to work and feed their families.[307]

In the 1980s, Fife and others were prosecuted and convicted of violating U.S. immigration laws. These crimes took the form of shielding migrants from detection within the U.S. and assisting their passage through Mexico to the relative safe harbors of the sanctuary community. This was not merely an effort to house asylum seekers in religious buildings but also to organize a complex international system for finding, moving, and supporting these immigrants. As Fife suggests in his remarks, there is more to sanctuary than a building.

Notably, Fife's organization was infiltrated by federal law enforcement, leading to his prosecution. The defense's efforts to

---

[307] "No More Deaths: An Interview with John Fife," *Reflections* 95, no. 2 (Fall 2008): 48, reflections.yale.edu/article/who-my-neighbor-facing-immigration/no-more-deaths-interview-john-fife.

explain the moral and theological bases for the sanctuary movement were suppressed during the court proceedings as irrele-
vant to the primary question of whether the accused intentionally
violated federal law, a governmental legal tactic that may face
stiffer response under subsequent federal laws like RFRA. The
Aguilar defendants were convicted and placed on probation.
In 1986, the Reagan Administration declared a general amnesty
for many undocumented migrants, relieving much of the immigration tensions. This did not however eliminate the convictions,
confirmed on appeal in 1989, though no time was served.

Tensions over immigration have returned. They have been
fostered by post-9/11 terrorism concerns as discussed by Rev.
Fife in his remarks from 2008. More recently, a highly visible
nationalist surge in U.S. politics culminated in the election of
President Donald Trump, a vocal opponent of immigration and
asylum-seekers. One rallying cry of the Trump campaign had
been a call to build a wall across the U.S. border with Mexico.
Practicalities and economics aside, the morality of cutting off the
flow of people seeking to come to the United States is Biblically
questionable for those who attend to such questions. During the
1980s, a wide range of denominations rallied to the sanctuary
movement, across the liberal and conservative spectrum. And
now, the calls for sanctuary have resumed.

The Church of the Covenant in Centerville ("Covenant") is a
pseudonymous case study of a Midwestern congregation from
the 1980s.[308] Bear in mind that some of the activities of being or

---

[308] Nelle Slater, ed., *Tensions Between Citizenship and Discipleship: A Case
Study* (Cleveland: Pilgrim Press, 1989).

supporting a sanctuary location potentially violate federal immigration law, as seen in the case of Rev. Fife, so anonymity prevents those interviewed from being seen as confessing to federal crimes. Again, this has become more complicated as federal and some state laws protecting religious liberty like RFRA have come into existence after *Aguilar.*

Covenant was a Reformed church, one on the traditional and conservative end of the religious spectrum. Faced with the humanitarian plight of Central American refugees, Covenant began an internal process to consider becoming a sanctuary location. There were struggles. One key issue was whether the proposed program would be intended as an effort to help others or as a political statement. People left the church over the initial conversation, let alone the program. As one of the supporters of the sanctuary effort described it: "I think we were taking a hard look at what the idea of social justice meant and also a hard look at whether we want to take a risk or not. Was this issue worth taking a risk for or not? And how do we really sort through the ideas of gospel versus law?"[309]

Gospel versus law: the context for this decision was the overall framework of Christian and Jewish practices and moral expectations. The ancient reference in the Book of Numbers is an interesting artifact in that discussion, a source of ancient law and a foundational statement. But the ongoing tradition of sanctuary is an effort both to recall traditions and to instill ongoing practices in keeping with Biblical outlooks.

---

[309] Slater, 6.

Concerns about the expectations of faith seemed to be front and center for the Covenant congregation. They wrestled with how to live out their faith within their religious community and the larger society. The scholar and theologian Walter Brueggemann provided his own analysis of the Covenant case study, noting this religious tension in his observations.[310] Brueggemann focused in particular on the Biblical supports offered within Covenant's process of becoming a sanctuary congregation. He categorized these supporting texts, distinguishing the wide "neighborliness" of the Beatitudes from the greater, more direct action called for in the parable of the Good Samaritan. It is one thing to love thy neighbor from afar; it is quite another to carry him to safety and to tend to his wounds.

Brueggemann also highlighted the more subtle influence of "rendering unto Caesar," a sense of needing to divorce the obligations of a citizen from those of a congregant. Neighborliness in this context becomes a pleasant and socially acceptable form of compassion bounded by a system of social expectations. This compassionate neighbor falls short of the more radical messages in the Bible, those that counsel for upheaval within any social systems that fall short of God's law.

The compassionate citizen in this manner can thrive within a traditional religious setting and a traditional cultural landscape. But this bounded form of compassion makes for a "shy disciple," a term of Brueggemann's, someone reluctant to stray from the well-beaten path of religious and cultural expectations. No money-changing tables overturned in the Temple, no challeng-

---

[310] Slater, 48.

ing Pharaoh to let the people go. This is not a religious or spiritual impulse, but a dampening of such urges to action to remain in line with social expectations and worldly legal concerns.

Paul the Apostle himself wrote of obedience to authority: "Let every person be subject to the governing authorities; for there is no authority except from God, and those authorities that exist have been instituted by God. Therefore whoever resists authority resists what God has appointed, and those who resist will incur judgement."[311] Which leads to an impasse. If the citizen is prevented from being a disciple, if the culture and social structure circumscribe any urgency of action, compassion for others becomes constrained, tailored to fit into a familiar role. In the Church of the Covenant example, the congregation struggled with how to reconcile a political message born out in the offer of sanctuary with their adherence to civic religion, to a devoted "Americanism" that counseled loyalty to country and obedience to its legal workings.

In Covenant, conversely, the leadership of the church seemed to be operating out in front, beyond where the people might be comfortable, emulating the radical call of Moses against Pharaoh, and Jesus with the moneychangers, more so than the conservative efforts of David and Solomon building up a kingdom. The Covenant congregation settled into this program through an acceptance of the compassionate work of the sanctuary movement while maintaining a distant (or oblivious) attitude toward the political implications of that work. Interestingly, the senior minister of Covenant was *not* an advocate for the

---

[311] Romans 13:1–2.

effort, effectively placing the Covenant pulpit in a neutral position relative to the discussion. Brueggemann noted this as a lost opportunity to embrace the deeper message of the Gospels—though Brueggemann did not stand to get arrested.

Covenant carefully drafted its policies and resolutions. It defined "sanctuary" as "spiritual, emotional, legal, and educational assistance, and financial support for provisions of housing, furnishings, food and clothing."[312] Covenant was providing a range of services to those in need, not always or primarily a place of refuge. It also sought links among other congregations, seeking support and shared resources for the sanctuary effort. The congregation would host a family, or a group of no more than three people. The election to become a sanctuary congregation would be communicated to the community and directly to the federal government. The decision was to be described as an open act of Christian concern in response to the plight of the refugees and the perceived injustice of the INS policies, but not as an overt stand against U.S. policies.

That was the 1980s. Currently, there are ongoing conversations about a New Sanctuary Movement, responding to the recent immigration surge along the Mexican border prompted by unstable Central American governments and, arguably, the effects of climate change on subsistence farming. There are any number of ways of approaching that unfolding conversation, but many of them would be little more than an internet search in print. Instead, I would like to present a sketch of the legal framework for offering sanctuary to immigrants.

---

[312] Slater, *Tensions Between Citizenship and Discipleship*, 12–13.

The New Sanctuary Movement

Please, please do not think of this as legal advice, meaning advice to be followed without retaining the services of competent legal advisors. As previously mentioned, there is only one answer to every legal question: *it depends*. It depends on what state you live in, the layout of a building to be used, the content of the programs, the legal status of the entities or individuals involved, what the judge had for breakfast, etc. There is a lot to be considered, as seen in the thorough process undertaken by places like Covenant.

I offer this conversation as a "heads up" because the call to resist is often attractive because it is transgressive. Being arrested at a demonstration sometimes becomes a point of pride rather than serving as a constructive step toward achieving a goal. Sometimes it will be better and more effective to be boring. In any event, it is worth knowing what can be done within the bounds of the law.

There are many political and philosophical reasons for protecting those seeking shelter and a new life in the U.S. I do not mean to ignore those or to diminish their importance. But I will focus on the religious reasons for doing so. I select these reasons over others for the very technical purpose central to this work: to use existing federal law protecting religious freedom to formulate legal protections for those churches, synagogues, and other houses of worship that seek to create sanctuaries for undocumented immigrants in the United States.

Much of the sanctuary movement, and the larger movement for resistance against new and not so new authoritarian tendencies in the U.S., is couched in terms of defiance of systematic oppression. Those oppressive tendencies are said to be "baked in" or enshrined in the laws, policies, and practices of the federal government and law enforcement. I do not mean to disagree with or to embrace that perspective, but to offer another avenue for religious individuals and organizations using existing federal law.

As described across the prior chapters, the evolution of First Amendment law has played out and changed across two centuries. Regardless of one's feelings about these changes, how might these efforts to protect religious liberty be used to support a New Sanctuary Movement? The notion of sanctuary is ancient, enshrined in the text of the Bible and the history of European Christianity. There is little legal mileage needed to show the vintage of these articles of faith, let alone the centrality of them to a religious group's practices.

INS is now referred to as the U.S. Immigration and Customs Enforcement, or ICE. ICE currently has a policy regarding the entry into "sensitive locations." These locations include schools, hospitals, churches, synagogues, and mosques.[313] The locations are highlighted as places in which ICE activities are curtailed. Enforcement actions are not to occur at or to be focused on these sites. Please note this is a policy statement from 2011 during the Obama Administration, not a regulation or a statute. More recent ICE raids have pressed near to, if not yet into, sensitive locations.[314] Past policies might be discarded and even the old policy allowed for exceptions for matters of national interest,

---

[313] John Morton to Field Office Directors, memorandum, "Enforcement Actions at or Focused on Sensitive Locations," October 24, 2011, U.S. Immigrations and Customs Enforcement, ice.gov/doclib/ero-outreach/pdf/10029.2 -policy.pdf.

[314] To my knowledge, that is.

terrorism, etc. U.S. immigration policies have become pointedly more aggressive. There are no guaranties that ICE will stand quietly outside the sanctuary doors, but there are arguments to be made that when it comes to a church, synagogue, mosque, or other house of worship, ICE should not be allowed to enter.

Consider the context of sanctuary. A congregation invites a person into a facility, an undocumented immigrant there seeking asylum. The federal government through its agency, ICE, is charged with enforcing immigration laws that would ostensibly require the detention of the person being hosted. What now?

The federal government has broadly limited itself under RFRA: "Government shall not substantially burden a person's exercise of religion *even if* the burden results from a rule of general applicability."[315] In this scenario, the congregation and its members are exercising religious rights. The offer of sanctuary itself is a religious act. The government would counter, however, that it is exercising its police powers in a manner unrelated to and neutral as regarding the religious rights of the church—the immigrant seeking sanctuary is not exercising religious rights.

The right being violated, however, is not only the right to house an immigrant *per se*, but the right not to have someone enter into one's house of worship without permission. That right seems to be in keeping with ICE's own policy regarding sensitive locations—there needs to be a good reason for going into these sites requiring a particular analysis of the circumstances, timing, and location of the planned enforcement action. For this reason, it is *critical* that an offer of sanctuary be made within a church,

---

[315] Emphasis added.

synagogue, mosque or other house of worship. Not the parson-age, not a congregant's house, not even a *rented* location used by a congregation. A house is not a sensitive location in this sense. A rented space could be entered under the authority of a land-lord or another tenant. The hope would be to offer the toughest choice, the highest hurdle.

Without question, these arguments are "maybes" rather than certainties. There is no reason necessarily to believe that ICE will honor its prior policy or pause to comply with the pastor at the door declaring "None shall pass!" In the criminal case of *U.S. v. Aguilar*, the organizers went far beyond housing asylum seekers, travelling to Mexico to assist them in their efforts to get to the U.S. This was a full-blown conspiracy to circumvent U.S. immi-gration controls, and it was found to be such. Notably, however, these convictions in 1989 predate the passage of RFRA in 1993, so who knows what the impact might be on a current effort to offer sanctuary. That being said, it would be legally wise not to replicate *Aguilar.*

There are many reasons to offer sanctuary to those in need. Two stand out in particular in this consideration of the legalities of such a program: *support* and *time*. Sanctuary needs to be far more than a place to sleep. It requires a range of supports, spiri-tual and financial, and a careful organization of resources often in conjunction with other religious organizations and people. Sanctuary also offers the precious commodity of time—time to seek asylum and time to prepare for the range of possible out-comes. A family can be separated unannounced, leaving children alone and spouses or partners grieving. Sanctuary in the 1980s was about slowing things down long enough to rally the support necessary to help someone fight to remain in the U.S. These were often refugees, rather than the long-term residents currently at risk for summary deportation. Their circumstances may differ, but the need for time remains. Time to consult with legal counsel, time to file the right paperwork, time to assure care for family members and particularly children. Unlike medieval Europe, there will be no amnesty waiting behind the stout doors of a church. In the modern United States, sanctuary is at best an effort to embarrass law enforcement enough to slow down the speedy wheels of deportation.

ICE might not hesitate to arrest a sanctuary seeker or to arrest those who sought to shield that person in alleged violation of federal immigration law. One person was charged with littering in a wildlife refuge, that is, leaving jugs of water in desert areas for migrants, and an appeals court struck down the conviction, holding that leaving water for others to use did not amount to littering.[316] Other volunteers have been charged with various felonies, such as Dr. Scott Warren of the "No More Deaths" organization, a Unitarian Universalist ministry affiliated with the Tucson, Arizona, congregation. Warren's first case ended in a mistrial but he was found *not* guilty of any felony on retrial in November 2019 (he was found guilty of the misdemeanor of operating a motor vehicle in a wildlife refuge).[317] Warren stated that he was acting out of empathy, motivated by his religious beliefs. He had originally been charged with conspiracy to violate

---

[316] U.S. v. Millis, 621 F.3d 914 (9th Cir. 2010).

[317] Jasmine Aguilera, "Humanitarian Scott Warren Found Not Guilty After Retrial for Helping Migrants at Mexican Border," *Time*, November 20, 2019, time .com/5732485/scott-warren-trial-not-guilty.

U.S. immigration laws, much like in *Aguilar*, and harboring someone in the country illegally so as to "shield" them from law enforcement.[318]

As in the Covenant case study, and without judging the complexities of the No More Deaths situation, the public nature of a sanctuary declaration and support for a sanctuary seeker is vitally important. Hiding someone from ICE is a crime, regardless of one's religious inclinations. Breaking the law to meet a moral obligation is a religious choice, but it is notably a choice that may result in worldly consequences. RFRA might serve as a defense. *Might.*

A legal argument is much like an arrow—you could get lucky and hit with one well-placed shot. More likely, you will need many arrows, many efforts, many people toiling along multiple fronts. And yet the sanctuary movement is a fundamentally religious argument, one familiar to American religious groups across the spectrums of tradition and politics. Breaking down the doors of a church to arrest a frightened soul hiding inside would be an open and obvious act of violence perpetrated against a house of worship, violence that may nonetheless be legally sanctioned, violence that is not unheard of in the darker corners of modern history. There may be few points of agreement on the United States political landscape. But that scene of a shattered doorway into a house of worship might well be one that even the most ardent supporter of immigration restrictions might hesitate to see.

---

[318] Miriam Jordan, "An Arizona Teacher Helped Migrants. Jurors Couldn't Decide if It Was a Crime," *New York Times,* June 11, 2019, nytimes.com/2019/06/11/us/scott-warren-arizona-deaths.html.

CHAPTER 21

Separation of Church and Politics

DR. REV. EDWARD EVERETT HALE, a Unitarian minister, was a chaplain to the U.S. Senate in the early twentieth century. He was once supposedly asked: "Do you pray for the senators, Dr. Hale?" He is said to have responded, "No, I look at the senators and I pray for the country."

In some congregations, a recurring prayer may be said during services for political leaders. One version used in a Massachusetts church I serve asks God "to behold and bless thy servants, the President of the United States, the Governor of this Commonwealth, and all others in authority . . . that they may always incline to thy will and walk in thy ways."[319]

The request is manifold. Watch these leaders. Nudge them along. Move them onto the righteous path. Or, perhaps, it could

---

[319] A little Elizabethan English to start off the week.

be understood as look out for them, protect them, and help them stay the course. The direction sought depends upon one's opinion of the leaders and their conduct. Which leads to a related question: is this sort of prayer *political*?

One occasional churchly complaint is indeed "That is too political." The subject in question might change, but the objection remains—things are straying too far into the realm of politics. Of course, that concern depends upon the definition of what is political. There is the technical definition that the government might use for determining whether a group has strayed too far into restricted matters (Spoiler: this is effectively a very narrow area of concern for most religious organizations). And then there is the unease within a religious group about whether a topic is too political within that community (Spoiler: this chapter will not help make any of those conversations more comfortable, but no one is likely going to jail). These are not the same questions, but they may become entwined when comments and objections begin to emerge about some new topic or initiative.

A minister might preach on a wide range of political-seeming subjects: abortion, capital punishment, immigration, or "demon rum." For example, Rev. John Pierpont was forced to resign from his Boston church when his advocacy for the temperance movement stood at odds with congregants who made their living in the liquor trade and stored rum in the church's basement.[320] Similarly, U.S. President Taft, after his term in office, helped orchestrate the ouster of his home church's minister, Rev. Alson

---

[320] Mark W. Harris, *The Historical Dictionary of Unitarian Universalism* (Lanham: Rowman & Littlefield, 2018), 428.

Robinson, a pacifist who failed to support the nation's efforts during World War I.[321] Politics do not sit easily in the pulpit. And if they do, the minister may not sit there for very long.

There are federal rules about religious groups intervening into political subjects, whether elections or legislation. These rules are not terribly clear, nor enormously helpful, for the conscientious planner. From a legal perspective, there are things that cannot be done, which is different than claiming they *should* not be done. But then again, there are things that can be done, which does not suggest that they should *ever* be done.

Let us consider how one gets onto the Internal Revenue Services' naughty list. In 1934, the U.S. tax code was amended to limit the ability of tax-exempt organizations, including church and religious organizations, from engaging in "propaganda" or other lobbying activities seeking to "influence legislation."[322] Might one religious group decry leafletting by another and declare it to be "propaganda"? Possibly, but this statute was only directed at efforts to influence legislation, not to evangelize the public for members.

This restriction was amended in 1954 by the so-called Johnson Amendment to also preclude any involvement at all in partisan political activity or campaigning for or against particular candidates for office. This is a far clearer restriction. If you say in the congregational newsletter "Vote for Truman" or "Don't Vote for Dewey" it is a violation of the law. If you post a sign at the church door that says, "Federalists Only" or "Whigs Need Not

---

[321] Harris, 536.

[322] See Revenue Act of 1934, § 101(6), Pub. L. No. 73-216 (1934).

Apply," there could well be an issue. If someone gets up during a service and tells a long story about their recent political activities, well, that is likely not a problem for the organization, but it may be really awkward.

The current restriction defines the nature of entities that may maintain tax-exempt status. In defining the permissible scope of activities for these entities, these two restrictions against "propaganda" and against partisan political activity are spelled out, albeit awkwardly: "no substantial part of the activities of which [entity] is carrying on propaganda, or otherwise attempting, to influence legislation . . . and which does not participate in, or intervene in (including the publishing or distributing of statements), any political campaign on behalf of (or in opposition to) any candidate for public office."[323] There is an option under a later section for an entity to elect to engage in a greater amount of lobbying or legislative activity (as distinct from endorsing or opposing candidates for office), but "churches" are not permitted to do so.[324] And in case you were wondering, the terms "no substantial part" and "greater amount" are not well defined in print or in practice.

The term "church" is specifically used.[325] Defining what a "church" is or is not under the U.S. Code would swamp this chapter beyond any utility.[326] But to be clear, or as potentially clear

---

[323] 26 U.S.C. §501(c)(3).

[324] 26 U.S.C. §501(h).

[325] 15 U.S.C. §501(h)(5)(B).

[326] For entry into that weedy corner of the legal briar patch, see, e.g., Charles M. Whelan, "'Church' in the Internal Revenue Code: The Definitional Problems," 45 *Fordham Law Review* 885 (1977).

amidst all this statutory imprecision, if your religious home defines as a "society" or a "congregation" or a "mugwump," please do not assume you are free from such political scrutiny in the eyes of the government.

Again, the scope of these restrictions is poorly defined. For example, an Episcopal church was investigated by the IRS during the second Bush Administration for an anti-war sermon given in 2004 before the presidential election.[327] The sermon was built around a fictitious debate among President George W. Bush, Candidate John Kerry, and Jesus. The investigation was closed without any penalty to the church, but it had been initiated because of what was described as an "implicit" intervention in the 2004 election. Does this mean one should never use the name of a candidate in a sermon? That is unclear. The mere existence of a closed IRS investigation offers no helpful guidance as to what the IRS might actually conclude in a different context or, more importantly, what a court might decide when presented with the competing interests of this statute and the protections of religion and speech afforded under the First Amendment and federal laws like RFRA.

Notice the statute's similarly murky limit on legislative activity. It does not require zero "propaganda" but no propaganda amounting to a "substantial part" of the entity's "activities." Some legislative activity is permitted. How much? Less than "substantial."

---

[327] See, e.g., "Los Angeles: Pasadena parish receives vindication from IRS," December 10, 2007, the Archives of the Episcopal Church, episcopalarchives.org/cgi-bin/ENS/ENSpress_release.pl?pr_number=121007-07; Ina Jaffe, "IRS Clears California Church, But Dispute Isn't Over," *NPR*, September 26, 2007, npr.org/templates/story/story.php?storyId=14715290.

Is that helpful? Not really. Some sources place that number at five percent of an organization's annual budget.[328]

The Internal Revenue Service has provided explanatory materials which are not entirely explanatory. It even tries to be definitive by offering a variety of "what if" scenarios.[329] It offers a number of publications that seem to gesture vaguely in the general direction of compliance but which are really no better than the underlying terms "substantial" or "propaganda." Legislative activities are distinguished from partisan political activities, the former being restricted by a vaguely worded amount while the latter are totally prohibited. If a religious organization would like to declare a preferred candidate for office, or a less preferred candidate, that seems to violate the statute. A member of the clergy can individually state a political preference for a particular candidate but may not do so in an official or organizational capacity. Not from the pulpit, not in the newsletter, not on the website. You're on your own, pastor.

What about "church" members? Is the president of the church board or one of the formal Elders speaking in their official role? Probably a problem. What about someone holding forth at coffee hour? Much less so unless they are setting up a table with campaign literature. Is it someone chiming in during a service, such as in the announcements, about the campaign they are

---

[328] "The Real Rules: Congregations and the IRS Guidelines on Advocacy, Lobbying, and Elections," Unitarian Universalist Association, updated October 2016, uua.org/sites/live-new.uua.org/files/the_real_rules_2016.pdf. This is a general and user-friendly guide for religious organizations.

[329] See, e.g., Rev. Rul. 2007-41, 2007-25 I.R.B. (June 18, 2007); *Tax Guide for Churches and Religious Organizations*, IRS Publication 1828 (Rev. 8-2015).

working with this election season? Forget the legalities for a moment—it is annoying, distracting, and liturgically suspect.

Many religious organizations, including churches, engage in legislative activities. Prison reform, marriage equality, immigration, the "right to die," abortion, birth control, universal healthcare: various social movements have religious and moral dimensions. And there are other aspects of the First Amendment, beyond the Free Exercise and Establishment Clauses, that underscore the importance of supporting or opposing such movements, including freedom of speech, freedom of the press, the right of assembly, and the right to petition the government. A statute that limits the ability of one group to pursue such rights brings into question the fairness, not to mention the constitutionality, of the law.

Conversely, no one is *prohibiting* speaking or assembling or petitioning. The consequence for violating the 501(c)(3) requirements is not a muzzle or a jail sentence, but the loss of tax-exempt status. The church or other organization would have to pay taxes on contributions made. Tax exemptions for religious organizations or purposes are long-standing in the United States but they are not universally loved or supported. For example, the Freedom from Religion Foundation sought to overturn a federal law that allowed "ministers of the gospel" to receive a tax exemption for housing allowances. A Wisconsin federal judge struck down the exemption, only to be reversed by the Seventh Circuit Court of Appeals.[330]

The loss of tax-exempt status would be an unwelcome event in the life of a religious organization, but does it amount to a

---

[330] See *Gaylor v. Mnuchin* 919 F.3d 420 (7th Cir., March 15, 2019).

violation of its rights? The loss of the deductibility of those dona-
tions by the donors might be equally unwelcome. But this brings
up the atypical tax treatment enjoyed by religious organizations.
If other taxpayers are required to pay, why not religious organizations? Charitable organizations, like churches, are also exempt
from paying taxes on contributions, so the point of comparison
is more aptly made between churches and similar nonprofits.
And yet, churches are nonetheless singled out for different, less
favorable treatment in some cases. For example, unlike some
other types of nonprofits, only churches are disqualified from
electing to make greater expenditures toward lobbying efforts
under Section 501(h).

The Supreme Court has upheld lobbying restrictions on tax-
exempt organizations.[331] The tax exemption is supporting charitable work being performed and is in that sense a government
subsidy of the work. The government has chosen not to subsidize
lobbying activity, which the Court concluded is not an infringement of the First Amendment right of free speech. And yet some
organizations, such as veterans' groups, are not subject to this
lobbying restriction.[332] The *Regan* Court in 1983 did not see this
restriction, or the exemption for veterans' groups, as a flaw in the
regulatory system.

That decision was made prior to the Religious Freedom Restoration Act, under which the federal government restricted its
own power as to legislative effects upon religious individuals

---

[331] Regan v. Taxation With Representation of Washington, 461 U.S. 540 (1983).

[332] "Qualifying veterans' organizations are permitted to lobby as much as they
want in furtherance of their exempt purposes." *Regan*, 461 U.S. at 546 & n.8 (citing
26 USC §§170(c)(3) & 501(c)(19)).

or organizations. Allowing one group an exemption from a law while denying a similar accommodation to religious individuals or organizations has been a basis for overturning such limitations, as when kosher butchers were exempted from restrictions placed on the ritual killing of animals by Santeria practitioners in *Lukumi*.[333] Additionally, the specific restriction placed on "churches" electing to make greater expenditures under Section 501(h) is more pointedly disparate in its treatment of one class of religious organizations. While there are never guaranties in a courtroom, the lobbying restrictions on "churches" and other religious organizations may be suspect under RFRA and these evolving standards (but see below).

On May 4, 2017, the Trump Administration issued an executive order "promoting free speech and religious liberty." In particular, the President ordered that, "All executive departments and agencies shall, to the greatest extent practicable and to the extent permitted by law, respect and protect the freedom of persons and organizations to engage in religious and political speech. . . ." The executive order may not have the efficacy intended by the administration, or survive the Biden Administration's review, but it brings up an interesting conundrum.

Under the U.S. Code, the IRS may not perform an investigation of a church—a "church tax" inquiry—unless "an appropriate high-level Treasury official reasonably believes (on the basis of facts and circumstances recorded in writing) that the church—(A) may not be exempt, by reason of its status as a church . . . or (B) may be carrying on an unrelated trade or business . . . or

---

[333] Church of the Lukumi Babalu Aye, Inc. v. Hialeah, 508 U.S. 520, 524 (1993).

otherwise engaged in activities subject to taxation under this title."[334] Could the Trump Administration have withdrawn the executive discretion of Treasury officials to act in this regard, substituting its own direct determinations? Stranger things have happened and this Congressional effort to tinker with the statute to insulate churches may bolster the effect of the executive order to shield them almost completely.

Does that mean one can lobby without limit? All it would take is a few years, a squadron of lawyers, and a large pile of money to fund the effort to overturn a decades-old law. Enjoy.

And others have tried doing just that regarding partisan political activity. Pulpit Freedom Sunday is an annual event during which pastors declare their preferred political candidates from their pulpits. The day is sponsored by the "Alliance Defending Freedom," formerly known as the Alliance Defense Fund, an arguably conservative group (and defined by the Southern Poverty Law Center as a hate group)[335] seeking to overturn political restrictions on churches and pastors.[336] Hundreds, perhaps thousands, of ministers proclaim from their pulpits on this particular

---

[334] 26 U.S.C. §7611(a)(2).

[335] "The SPLC lists ADF as a hate group because it has supported the idea that being LGBTQ+ should be a crime in the U.S. and abroad and believes that is OK to put LGBTQ+ people in prison for engaging in consensual sex. It has also supported laws that required the forced sterilization of transgender Europeans. . . ." From "Why is Alliance Defending Freedom a Hate Group?" Southern Poverty Law Center, April 10, 2020, splcenter.org/news/2020/04/10/why -alliance-defending-freedom-hate-group.

[336] See, e.g., Erik W. Stanley, "LBJ, the IRS, and Churches: The Unconstitutionality of the Johnson Amendment in Light of Recent Supreme Court Precedent," *Regent University Law Review* 24, no. 2 (2012): 237. The article's author served as legal counsel to the group, now known as the Alliance Defending Freedom.

Sunday openly partisan political declarations. And, so far, no one from the IRS has arrived in a black helicopter, though anti-war sermons by Episcopalians have raised IRS eyebrows.

The 501(c)(3) lobbying restrictions are vague, but the prohibition against partisan political activity is clear. Whether the barring of such political activity is an enforceable restriction on the free speech and religious exercise of members of the clergy is another question. It is a clear limitation: to state a preferred political candidate (or party) from the pulpit, or in a formal capacity, as a minister of a "church" is not allowed under 501(c)(3) requirements. To operate strictly within the law, one should not do so. And yet the IRS has repeatedly ignored the violations piled up on Pulpit Freedom Sunday.

The IRS has rarely revoked the tax-exempt status of a religious organization. The first court case involving a church was the Branch Ministries of New York.[337] Operating as the Church at Pearce Creek, Branch Ministries ran newspaper ads against then-candidate Bill Clinton who was running for U.S. President in 1992. The organization wrote in the advertisements: "Christian Beware. Do not put the economy ahead of the Ten Commandments."[338] It also claimed that Governor Clinton "supported abortion on demand, homosexuality and the distribution of condoms to teenagers in public schools." The IRS stepped in, again for the first time, and the revocation was upheld. The United States Court of Appeals from the District of Columbia Circuit ruled that merely having to pay taxes, effectively having less funds available

---

[337] Branch Ministries v. Rossotti, 40 F. Supp. 2d 15 (D.D.C. 1999), aff'd 211 F.3d 137 (D.C. Cir. 2000).

[338] Ibid.

for church operations, was an insufficient basis, even under RFRA, to warrant rescinding the IRS sanction.[339] The United States Court of Appeals for the Tenth Circuit reached a similar result for a religious organization engaging in political activities in 1972, though well before the complications of RFRA.[340]

These examples suggest that the IRS is on firm legal ground. But the trajectory of the Supreme Court plotted across its most recent decisions is pointing to a greater deference to free exercise of religious rights—an observation of the trend, not an endorsement of its potential results. The IRS might also be unable to get to the point of issuing a revocation under the Trump executive order, assuming that survives the Biden Administration, and the Congressional limit on such investigations. Given these factors, and the few cases of actual revocation by the IRS since 1954, a "church" organization is unlikely to face administrative action concerning political activity, barring taking out a newspaper ad decrying a political candidate by name.

And yet . . . and yet it is a bad idea to do so. There, I have said it.

Placing aside the U.S. Code and the ambiguous IRS directives for the moment, it may be worth pausing before a religious organization delves into partisan political activity. Meaning "Vote for Candidate A and not Candidate B," "Vote for Party X and not Party Y." The premise of this book is to *encourage* religious folks and organizations to express and to act on their moral values in public conversations, including taking public stances on legis-

---

[339] Branch Ministries et al. v. Rossotti, 211 F.3d 137 (D.C. Cir. 2000).

[340] Christian Echoes National Ministry, Inc., v. U.S., 470 F.2d 849, 856-7 (10th Cir. 1973).

lative matters and issues of social justice. But do such efforts necessitate expressions of *partisan* political allegiance or preference? That question may induce a spasm of disagreement in some of you, dear readers. But there it stands.

Otto Von Bismarck once said, "Politics is the art of the possible, the attainable—the art of the next best."[341] Politics are often a matter of expedience. They are not ideals taking an earthly form. In politics, bargains are made. And, speaking proverbially, it is not always God making the bargain. Time for a tangent.

There were three major destinations for passengers from Southern Italy during the great migration of the late nineteenth and early twentieth centuries. Ships left for Boston, New York, and Buenos Aires. Part of my family ended up in Boston—here I am—while another branch ended up in Argentina. My grandfather's first cousin, Antonio, was born in Argentina and entered the priesthood. He climbed up the hierarchy of the Catholic Church, eventually becoming in 1959 Archbishop of Buenos Aires and head of the Military Ordinariate of Argentina, which means head Catholic religious leader to the Argentine military. His coat of arms hung in my house for a time.

While in seminary, I was performing some research about this fellow. A classmate was peeking over my shoulder and noticed what I was doing. She remarked that Cardinal Antonio Caggiano, my first cousin twice removed, was a less than saintly figure— those were not her words, but I am trying to keep this a "family" book. Cardinal Caggiano, then a mere bishop, is alleged to have been involved in deposing President Juan Peron. He allegedly

---

[341] No, it was not Evita Peron (or Tim Rice and Andrew Lloyd Webber).

assisted in the resettlement of French and Italian fascists to Argentina—the story goes that he would not facilitate the migration of Nazi Germans not because of political sensitivities but because they were Lutherans.

He also laid some of the intellectual and religious groundwork for the right-wing dictatorship that assumed power in the 1980s. For example, he wrote the introduction to a book entitled *Le Marxisme-Léninisme*, written by Jean Ousset, a founder and key figure in *Cité catholique*, a Traditionalist Catholic organization (i.e., anti-Vatican II).[342] Cardinal Caggiano's remarks were staunchly anti-Marxist and could be interpreted as approving extreme political responses to left-leaning movements. Having the religious leader of a nation, and its military, greenlight all-out war against contrary social and political voices could lead to trouble.

And it did. In the 1980s, and after Cardinal Caggiano's retirement in 1975 and death in 1979, the "Dirty War" began in Argentina. Backed by U.S. resources, the military junta controlling Argentina waged a secret civil war against socialists, left-leaning Peronists, and other political dissidents. Thousands were detained, tortured, and "disappeared." The long shadow of these events continues to darken Argentinian society to this day.

Religion can and should engage with the social issues facing a society. Religion should not become merely one more outlet for

---

[342] The Second Ecumenical Council of the Vatican, also known as Vatican II, made sweeping changes within the Catholic church, including liturgy, use of Latin in services, church practices, etc. It has been perceived as a liberalizing effort, at least in its historical context, and has been a point of contention within the Church since its promulgation in 1965. For original documents, see "Documents of the Second Vatican Council," La Santa Sede, vatican.va/archive/hist_councils/ii_vatican_council/index.htm.

a political organization. When a religious movement becomes synonymous with a political party, right or left, both parts become lesser for the association. The political party walls itself off from a broader constituency and the possibility of wider and deeper engagement across such religious lines. And the religious movement may become hostage to the changing political realities of social programs, military interventions, or economic crisis.

Why? Because politics is often the art of the possible, meaning expedient, meaning self-serving, meaning indifferent to the consequences as long as they fall chiefly upon others. One critical purpose of religion, if I may so grandly opine, is to keep an eye upon the transcendent values that hopefully undergird a people, a society, a nation. Such values must not be expediently written off to meet the fleeting political conditions of an election cycle. Such values should not be sacrificed to accomplish self-serving goals or to feed self-serving desires. And such values should never be built upon the open or effective oppression of others, whether to fund one's enjoyment or to fuel the expression of one's fiery or even hateful sentiments. Again, when the religious seek to take the reins of power in the name of religion, a terrible bargain is being struck.

In the Bible, Jesus travels into the desert, where he is tempted by the devil. First, Jesus is goaded in his hunger to turn stones into bread but responds that "One does not live by bread alone." Then he is urged to throw himself off the pinnacle of the Temple of Jerusalem, in confidence that angels would come down to save him. Jesus instead remarked, "Do not put the Lord your God to the test." And lastly, the devil shows to Jesus all the kingdoms of the world, saying that he could become ruler of them all if he would but bow down and worship the devil. And Jesus responds, "Worship the Lord your God and serve him only."[343]

Why not achieve one's religious goals by embracing political expedience? Why not help oneself, and one's religious compatriots, by offering and then receiving political support? Why not take, or create, opportunities in this life because someone has to be in charge and wouldn't it be best for it to be me and those religiously like me? One might just as soon ask, why not eat, why not fly, and why not rule the world—for some reason, Jesus did not make such choices.

I have no way of knowing what was going through my cousin Antonio's mind, for he was a man I never met. But I would assume that he had all the "correct" religious intentions behind his words and actions. He may have thought all the right thoughts that somehow led in the years to come to the arrest, torture, and death of thousands. He may have died before these events, but to call for a war of ideologies is implicitly to accept the casualties of the ensuing war.

Furthermore, placing partisanship into the pulpit is fundamentally a declaration of defeat. How so? A religious organization hopefully has as a part of its mission the articulation and sharing of its values. These are the issues we care about, these are the values we cherish, these are the morals we hold dear. If for some reason the people in the "pews" have not heard those over and over again, something is amiss. If they do not remember them, something is similarly wrong. Because if after all that work, the people of the congregation do not have a sense of

---

[343] Matthew 4:1–11; Luke 4:1–13.

how to respond to those issues, to live out those values, or to navigate those morals, there has been a significant breakdown in communication.

If in turn there is no such problem, why would there be a need to get into *partisan* political declarations from the pulpit? That does not mean avoid preaching about those values or those issues. If there is a field of candidates and there are variations among them, as with a political primary, is it truly the role of a religious group to spoon-feed the answers, to forestall the choices? If there is a choice to be made, prepare the people to make it; do not make it for them. This not only addresses the IRS limitation on partisan activity, it also avoids the problematic situation of placing a religious group in one partisan corner of the patch when the moral landscape requires broader organizing for change.

Some examples: the right to bear arms and the right to an abortion.[344] These are legal rights supported by lines of Supreme Court cases. And yet they are also vigorously opposed by segments of society. As such, some believe the right to bear arms should be tightly controlled and regulated. Others believe the ability to have an abortion should be either nonexistent or limited to a tiny number of cases. Two distinct legal rights are objected to on different moral grounds, but both challenged because they are believed to threaten the lives of others.

The right to bear arms, or to own firearms for personal protection, has been upheld by a series of cases such as *District of Columbia v. Heller* and *McDonald v. Chicago*.[345] The end result of

---

[344] We'll tackle the tough stuff some other chapter.

[345] 554 U.S. 570 (2008) and 561 U.S. 742 (2010).

these two cases is that the Second Amendment now applies to the states, much like when the First Amendment was applied in the 1940s. These recent cases also effectively emphasized the latter half of the amendment to the exclusion of the rest: "A well-regulated militia, being necessary to the security of a free state, *the right of the people to keep and bear arms, shall not be infringed.*"[346] Arms may therefore be possessed and used for lawful purposes.

A stark distinction, however, might be drawn between a legal right and a moral justification. The right to own a gun is in contrast to the morally acceptable uses for it. Hunting and target practice aside, the primary result of *Heller* and *McDonald* is that guns may be possessed for self-defense. Therefore, to exercise that specific aspect of the right to bear arms there will likely need to be an assessment of the legality of usage, the conditions of its possession, or even the capacity of the user to be rightfully in possession of the weapon given their mental state or criminal past. The Supreme Court left the door open to all these policy matters in its decisions, including regulating the types of guns and ammunition.

And yet, the political arguments over the Second Amendment swamp those legitimate considerations. Any perceived infringement of the right to bear arms is portrayed as a slippery slope toward confiscation. The political process has become a zero sum game in which any effort to regulate guns is not only suspect but a betrayal of fundamental rights enshrined in the Constitution, though admittedly only enshrined since 2010

---

[346] Emphasis added.

when the Second Amendment was for the first time applied to a state rather than the federal government. There is no argument over this later point (though when did that phrase ever stop an argument?).

As a legal/political dispute, there has been little success by proponents of gun control. Shooting deaths have racked up alarmingly—in schools, theaters, workplaces, etc. And yet the outrage is bled away through delay or displaced by some other crisis or headline. No matter the body count, there does not seem to be any dent made in the political armor shrouding the issue.

So why not shift tactics? Why not ask whether it is *morally* acceptable to use guns? Again, there would likely be less of a moral dispute that guns used for hunting are permissible in all but the rarest of cases, assuming no bald eagles or pandas. Vegans might well differ. The same nuanced argument could be offered for target or sport shooting, though owning an armory might test that theory. The more important question underlying this raging dispute is under what moral theory is it ever permissible to kill another human being? Leaf through the scriptures of one's religious tradition, as applicable. Tick off the commandments, or their equivalents, to see under which conditions "Thou *shalt* kill."

I would not presume to speak outside of the Christian tradition. But within that not inconsiderable slice of U.S. religious society, there are vanishingly few circumstances under which a Christian may kill another human being. Given a broad reading of the teachings of Jesus, there may be *no* circumstances under which killing another human being is permitted. Church authorities tried over the centuries, in a tightly controlled way, to excuse killings during combat under "just war" theories. But one would be hard-pressed to apply those in a dark alley. And even the very ownership of a handgun might violate the spirit of that balancing of harms.

The point of this argument is not to publish a handy pamphlet to be used during a mugging. It is to suggest that having a legal right to do something, like *own* a gun, is not the same as having a moral right to do something, like *use* the gun. And even having a handgun for self-defense is far different than owning an assault rifle or high-capacity ammunition clips. Those devices exist to help kill many people, to hold off some expected onslaught of attackers, or to wage war against an army or the government. Again, not a potential outcome acceptable to Jesus of Nazareth.

It is worth noting that the Second Amendment bears close resemblance to one provision of the English Bill of Rights of 1689. This document sought to ensure the right of Protestants to bear arms in response to the actions of a Catholic monarch. Not a cozy outline for communal tranquility. Moreover, implicit in that prior right in England was the desire to maintain the option for rebellion against the government, a legal stance that might also run afoul of Biblical expectations, assuming that is a concern.[347]

Similarly, abortion is an enduring fault line within U.S. politics. It was legalized nationwide under the 1973 decision, *Roe v.*

---

[347] "Let every person be subject to the governing authorities; for there is no authority except from God, and those authorities that exist have been instituted by God." Romans 13:1. Personally, I am not a fan of this line from Paul, but if you happen to be someone with a tendency for quoting Romans (or Leviticus) for certain purposes, and against certain *people*, then this line from scripture should find its way onto the kitchen refrigerator as well.

Wade.[348] Since that time, support and opposition to abortion have roiled elections and embittered public debate. Once again, on the one hand there is a legal right. Efforts to overturn or to hem in that right have been a lawyers' cottage industry for decades and across many jurisdictions. On the other hand, there are moral arguments to be made about when life begins and what responsibility a mother, and society, has to the yet-to-be born.

Moral arguments against abortion often stand in the background while opponents use the legal mechanisms of society to stop or to ensure access to abortion. Against abortion, laws are passed requiring additional (or unnecessary) tests, mandating extra (or dubious) medical information, and specifying extended (or unnecessary) waiting periods. This ongoing debate even helped to spawn the *Hobby Lobby* decision, somehow making for-profit corporations into religious decision makers. The net effect of these legal struggles has often been to restrict access to non-abortion-related medical care for anyone with a uterus.

Like the right to bear arms, abortion seems to be a take-no-prisoners effort. And in the process of taking sharply defined sides, the ability to assess the moral dimensions of these policies has been cast aside. Any divergence is a catastrophic loss, leading to absurdities like laws requiring efforts to rescue ectopic pregnancies.[349] The battle lines become drawn between "pro-life" and "pro-choice," as if one side has become the defender of all life

---

[348] 410 U.S. 113 (1973).

[349] An ectopic pregnancy involves a fertilized egg developing outside the uterus, like in the fallopian tubes. It is not only medically impossible to save, but it is a highly dangerous condition for the parent, potentially leading to infertility,

and the other the bastion of all freedom. If we as a society could sidestep the feverish rhetoric and focus on the underlying moral questions, and legal policies framed by those morals, it would be an entirely different debate. And, yes, that observation may stray perilously into the outskirts of naïve, but here's hoping.

A supposedly pro-life position that does not correspond to helping women with unplanned pregnancies is a matter of being "pro-birth." Pregnant people may need access to healthcare, daycare, and job training, but somehow these are never forwarded as "pro-life" positions. To be fair, some religious groups are far more holistic in defining support for future children and parents.And yet if universal healthcare, affordable daycare, and greater access to higher education or vocational training became the norm, the number of abortions in the United States would plummet.

Conversely, there are ethical questions about reasons for or timing of abortions, such as choosing genders (i.e., aborting girls versus boys) or seeking a late-term abortion. On that latter point, viability is already a key factor in determining whether an abortion may occur, as per *Planned Parenthood v. Casey*,[350] and the medically acknowledged date for likely viability has changed dramatically since 1973. Abortion during the first trimester is legally far different from the second or third, but that existing restriction is rarely spelled out in public debate or public policy making. This being the case, a viable fetus might be protected, and abortion restricted, even in cases of rape or incest. And as

---

infection, or even death if untreated. snopes.com/news/2019/12/06/ohio-ectopic-pregnancy-bill/.

[350] 505 U.S. 833 (1992).

the range of viability potentially expands, so might the tightening of the timing of abortion under the *existing* Supreme Court decisions. At what point does the legal right to an abortion have to give ground to the viability of a fetus? And yet, if a pregnant person has no healthcare access to those life-saving medical advances trending toward viability, how can the state mandate what they cannot do?

Making moral arguments rather than taking partisan political stances does not make the social issue easier. It does however help to humanize the other side from being an opponent into being a person. Further, it places the conversation onto a level of greatest weight and deepest conviction. Even with issues of life and death, autonomy and public safety, the ability to articulate a clear ethical vision will be effort well spent, compared to the intractable battles to date on such issues as gun control or abortion. Call it the "chicken soup" theory of public policy: what could it hurt?

And with these examples in mind, congregations should not be in the business of partisan politics per se—it is really not our strong suit or our reason for being—but should remain doggedly engaged with and advocate for the social and moral *issues* that matter dearly to them. In the same sense, members of congregations should not inflict their political musings upon the wider body during a service, in the newsletter, or at a table at coffee hour. It is overly expedient, it is terribly self-serving, and it is an unfair use of that time and that place. And overlaying the religious with the political will ultimately weaken both, as religious folk cut corners to service a political agenda and political folk become beholden to the demands of smaller constituencies at the expense of the needs of the larger society.

Organize around values, plan around issues. Make it clear to people, within and without, what those values entail and those issues require. Do not choose the candidate or the party for them—that is their work to do. Instead, speak clearly and communicate passionately about what matters to you all religiously. Not only will that comply with the law, it will honor the audience and treat them with the care and dignity they deserve.

CHAPTER 22

Conclusions

IT HAS BEEN SAID that law is frozen politics.[351] Extending the metaphor, that would make the U.S. Constitution a glacier: ancient, slowly moving, a fixture of the landscape. Until recently for glaciers. Until the climate changed. Then the glaciers began to melt, and the oceans began to rise. I am growing to dislike that metaphor.

The Constitution can be changed by its terms. The Amendments are testament to that. And yet it is not easy to change the Constitution. It often takes some crisis, some scandal, some great movement to prompt a revision. Even extreme circumstances do not always bring about such change because changing the Constitution seems like changing the DNA of a nation. What rough

---

[351] Roberto Mangabeira Unger, *Politics: The Central Texts, Theory Against Fate* (New York: Verso, 1997).

beast slouches toward Bethlehem to be born, or in this case from Washington?[352]

Even as the words of the Constitution remain the same, the interpretations applied to them have varied greatly over history. Ask the average American about the separation between church and state, and you would likely get a range of answers. Some might decry the lack of prayer in school. Others might be concerned about the inroads of certain religious groups into the workings of government. Ask the average lawyer the same question and the range of opinions would probably be similar, though their grasp of the technicalities would be better.

I have also asked that question of my fellow clergy members, and I was extremely surprised to find that they knew little more about these laws than the average person on the street. That was an unexpected result given that the separation of church and state is part of their job. Hopefully, this book will provide to those interested at least a crash course in the basics, some examples for consideration, and even a few stories for sermon-writing.

The Constitution changes slowly, but the law surrounding it can change unexpectedly. The Supreme Court has become something like the "Chancellor's foot" discussed earlier, an arbitrary measure of the current officeholder's desires. Using two centuries of divergent legal possibilities, members of the Supreme Court can choose how to imprint personal biases—political, religious, or philosophical—onto the malleable contours of First Amendment law. Do they prefer the stringent provisions of the *Reynolds* case, sending a Latter-day Saint to jail for polygamy?

---

[352] Lovingly cribbed from "The Second Coming" by William Butler Yeats.

Then they might latch onto that thread and opine somewhere in the realm of *Smith*, siding with federal drug laws rather than Indigenous religious practices. Or do they embrace the more expansive protections of Free Exercise as in *Cantwell*, allowing Jehovah's Witnesses to proselytize more freely and quite pointedly? Then they would seek to emulate the *Sherbert* and *Yoder* cases, expanding the acceptability of sabbaths beyond Sunday and allowing Amish children to opt out of schools in the eighth grade.

The same pendulum has swung back and forth for the Establishment Clause. Originally, state-sponsored religions were fine, yet they fell out of political fashion in the early 1800s. But state sponsored education continued to deliver a specific brand of religious content, meaning homogenized Protestantism, and courts somehow declare it nonsectarian. This caused literal riots and furious political battles, prompting dissatisfied Catholics to build a separate school system.

When Christian prayers and Bible readings were removed from the public schools in the mid-twentieth century, it in time helped spawn a new wave of departures into private schools and homeschooling, this time filled with Evangelical Christians. These population shifts in the schools also coincided with waves of white flight from urban areas in the 1950s and 1960s. The racial and religious components of these twentieth-century divisions mirror the racial, ethnic, and religious components of the nineteenth-century political battles during the Reconstruction period. The resegregation after the Civil War had both racial origins and religious elements. Similar splits among urban, suburban, and rural populations in the U.S. have similar origins and elements to this day.

The public schools were walled off from religion, making some happy and leaving others seething. Years later, the Supreme Court began to mold Establishment Clause cases to remove concerns about entanglement, as in the *Lemon* test, and to replace it with the language of "neutrality" and "tradition," teeing up new social struggles over religion.

Purported "neutrality" allows a legislative body to build a bland-sounding law of general applicability that in practice supports religious groups, as seen in school-voucher cases like *Zelman*. Tradition permits a government body, and the courts, to seize upon some historical precedent and declare even new practices to be legally permissible. Prayers can be said at the start of public meetings because Congress did so in the 1700s, leading to the *Town of Greece* decision. Monuments can depict Christian crosses or the Ten Commandments because their religious weight has faded with time and are lost in secular context, as in *American Legion* and *Van Orden*. Even long-standing prohibitions against funding religious institutions have fallen away as set forth in *Trinity Lutheran*. Depending on one's perspective, this litany of changes could be a cause for celebration or alarm.

One less frequently voiced worry about the mingling of church and state is the effect it might have on either institution. This fear is that the state will not be guided by "religion" as a grand virtue but will instead become infiltrated by a single religion or a cartel of religions seeking influence over the lives of all citizens. One fever dream of recent years has been the prospect of Islamic "sharia" law being adopted or recognized in the United States. Placing aside the unreality of such concerns, the most direct way of addressing that worry would be to assure a sturdy wall separating church and state, religion and the law. This would avoid the prospect of religion standing in the place of law, regardless of which religion tries to influence the government.

And is it any better to have religion under the management of government? Imagine for a moment that one religious group had control over the public schools, as was arguably the case with generic Protestantism in the nineteenth century. If the content was from one religious denomination, many would complain. Dilute the content down and it becomes less objectionable to some, but far less meaningful to others who sincerely hold those religious beliefs. Having a government committee literally write a prayer of sufficient blandness to pass as vaguely religious, as in the *Engel* case in the New York public schools, verges on the offensive to anyone who considers prayer to be more than a homeroom recitation followed by announcements for the day. When nativity scenes need to be surrounded by reindeer and Santa Claus, the sacred is made profane, and that is no different for a forced Lord's Prayer rattled off with disinterest on the way to algebra. Government has absolutely no business in the business of prayer.

As mentioned previously, the law is not common sense. It is not the current mindset of a person who grew up in a certain place at a certain time. Rather, the law is complicated. For that reason, lawyers and judges spend years in school and decades honing their practice. That same could be said for religion—it is a life's work and a deep vocation. The typical member of the clergy cannot rattle off the requirements of the *Lemon* test or assess the shifting jurisprudence of the First Amendment. And the same could be said for the average person trying to grasp the intricacies of scripture, the mysteries of the divine, or the way to officiate a wedding.

And yet, members of Congress, state legislators, judges, and even justices of the Supreme Court somehow find themselves yearning to pick sides, deciding that the religious traditions of the 1700s should be carried forward as legal models for current government practice. Perhaps it would entail financially supporting houses of worship and religious schools in a manner soundly rejected across the country over a century ago, when arguments over such practices tore communities apart and literally started armed conflict in the streets. It might take the form of allowing people to discriminate against fellow citizens as a function of religion and therefore forcing someone not of that religion to be shut out of a business or a doctor's office for who they are (or who they love).

The Supreme Court's decision in *Smith*, freeing the government from catering to every religious objection, has a certain appeal. That freedom comes at the cost of religious groups who cannot follow their respective traditions, like the Native American Church and peyote. It would also prevent the result in the *Hobby Lobby* case, assuming Congress did not go handing out religious exemptions willy-nilly. This would be a "high wall" model of Free Exercise, leaving religious folks equally dissatisfied but also equally protected.

Under RFRA and RLUIPA, religious groups have a distinct advantage, making the finality of legislation less clear and the business of the courts busier. The freedom offered to those groups comes at the cost of those who do not share their religious beliefs but who must contend with the fallout, like the employees losing health benefits in the *Hobby Lobby* case. That would represent a "low wall" model of Free Exercise, meaning support for the religious on the public's dime, and the courts' time, including for groups across the religious spectrum.

High wall versus low wall models also affect Establishment Clause cases. No support for religious purposes versus open support through generic programs: one excludes evenly, the other includes by allowing religious groups to draw upon such government support (e.g., *Trinity Lutheran*). The opening of this door is not necessarily only wide enough to let the preferred candidates through. How long before the Satanic Temple tries to fund a preschool with school vouchers or build a playground with public funds? And if government tries to close the door for one, how can it avoid closing the door for all?

The height of the wall of separation gets higher and lower depending upon the laws Congress and others pass and the choices made by the courts. "Choices" because there have been higher and lower thresholds of separation throughout the history of the nation. Lift up one legal tradition as in *Reynolds* and matters change one way, lift another like *Sherbert* and they shift again. The Supreme Court can, with a jurisprudential straight face, make these starkly different choices and effectively rend the fabric of American society.

We are in a "low wall" phase of this legal evolution. Religious groups can find protection under RFRA and RLUIPA, which are notably federal statutory laws and not constitutional rights. These can be changed by Congress, but for now they could allow religious liberals and progressives to challenge federal laws to, for example, protect asylum seekers, brush aside limitations on their mission and ministries, and challenge the effects of federal policies that infringe upon their beliefs. The criteria of "neutrality" and "tradition" are broad enough to let in quite a range of possibilities. Want a menorah, or a May pole, on your New England town common? Seeking funding for your homeless shelter expressly for the LGBTQ community? Trying to reflect your religious tradition in the military chaplain corps, the uniforms of public safety officers, or in the ministries available to prisoners? Under these laws, there are many possibilities, if not any guaranties.

Every few decades, the laws surrounding the First Amendment seem to change. Sometimes those changes are ushered in by pivotal events such as the Civil War. At other times, they are the result of incremental shifts, as evidenced by the methodic steps taken by the conservative wing of the Supreme Court since the 1980s. The wall of separation between church and state is now far more porous, filled with legal gaps and indirect workarounds.

Like a tectonic plate in the earth's crust, things have shifted along fault lines of politics and tradition. Energy builds and suddenly an earthquake shakes the foundations of the law. It would be hard to slide the land back into place after a quake, and in the same manner it would be difficult to rewind the clock to the prior precedents of the First Amendment. Even when Congress tried with RFRA and RLUIPA, the results were mixed. Instead, it may be the wisest course of action to turn into the skid, the obligatory advice one gets at the start of any New England winter. Even as the First Amendment seems to slip away from what is familiar, it may be time to adjust the steering wheel and see where it might take us.

Conclusions

It may not be the most natural reaction for religious liberals to talk about religion, let alone pester the neighbors with one's religious identity. It may not be the most comfortable position for religious progressives to use the levers of institutional power to express their moral values and achieve their social objectives. Neither group, however, has the luxury of sitting out the fight as our society skids along between liberal and conservative, progress and tradition, equality and inequity.

How does one envision such a change?

The United States is at a turning point. The moral and philosophical foundations of our society are in question. It is like a raft in a storm, lashed together by those foundational elements. It is terrifying to consider the raft falling apart, but it may also be an opportunity to introduce something new into its construction. There have been many social changes over the past decade, let alone the past 50 years. Those changes need to be cemented into place. Any sense of progress one might feel for having helped foster such changes, of equal rights or economic justice, will be fleeting if those changes are allowed to be sidelined or cast aside. If the United States is to be a more diverse, more equitable, more just place, it will require the steady efforts of people who are dedicated to achieving and to protecting such progress. And our country has for two centuries especially protected and empowered religious folks in that work.

And so, hopefully, this book stands as an introduction to that legal tradition enshrined in the First Amendment. Hopefully, these sketches from history and religion offer a flavor of past conflicts and an understanding for future challenges. And, perhaps, the meager arguments set forth will spark some ideas and suggest a few possibilities.

As repeatedly set forth above, the answer to every legal question is "It depends." Strangely enough, that is also part of the answer to every social problem, every public controversy, and every societal challenge. The answers depend on who shows up, who rises to the occasion, and who stands ready to make a great work possible. The answers to all those questions and more depend. . . . They depend upon us.

Selected Bibliography

Books

Failinger, Marie. "United States v. Ballard: Government Prohibited from Declaring Religious Truth." In *Law and Religion: Cases in Context*, edited by Leslie C. Griffin. New York: Aspen Publishers, 2010.

Farrelly, Maura Jane. *Anti-Catholicism in America, 1620–1860.* Cambridge University Press, 2018.

Gordon, Sarah Barringer. *The Mormon Question: Polygamy and Constitutional Conflict in Nineteenth-Century America.* Chapel Hill: University of North Carolina Press, 2002.

Green, Steven K. *The Bible, the School, and the Constitution: The Clash That Shaped Modern Church-State Doctrine.* Oxford: Oxford University Press, 2012.

Harris, Mark W. *The Historical Dictionary of Unitarian Universalism.* Lanham: Rowman & Littlefield, 2018.

"John Calvin: Reply to Sadoleto." In *The Protestant Reformation*, edited by Hans Hillerbrand, 162. New York: Harper Perennial, 1968.

Massa, Mark, ed. *American Catholic History: A Documentary History.* New York: NYU Press, 2017.

McLoughlin, William. *New England Dissent 1630–1883: The Baptists and the Separation of Church and State, Volume I.* Cambridge: Harvard University Press, 1971.

Papa, Stephan. *The Last Man Jailed for Blasphemy.* Franklin: Trillium Books, 1998.

Patrick, John J., and Gerald P. Long, eds. *Constitutional Debates on Freedom of Religion: A Documentary History,* Westport: Greenwood, 1999.

Sarna, Jonathan. *American Judaism: A History.* New Haven: Yale University Press, 2004.

Schappes, Morris, ed. *A Documentary History of the Jews in the United States 1654–1875.* New York: Citadel Press, 1950.

Slater, Nelle, ed. *Tensions Between Citizenship and Discipleship: A Case Study.* Cleveland: Pilgrim Press, 1989.

Wright, Conrad. *Three Prophets of Liberal Religion: Channing, Emerson, and Parker.* Boston: Skinner House, 1986.

Periodicals

Aguilera, Jasmine. "Humanitarian Scott Warren Found Not Guilty After Retrial for Helping Migrants at Mexican Border." *Time,* November 20, 2019.

Alther, Lisa. "They shall take up serpents," *New York Times,* June 6, 1976, nytimes.com/1976/06/06/archives/they-shall-take-up-serpents -serpents.html.

Doyle, Heather Beasley. "On Religious Grounds." *UU World,* August 19, 2019, uuworld.org/articles/religious-grounds.

Jordan, Miriam. "An Arizona Teacher Helped Migrants. Jurors Couldn't Decide if It Was a Crime." *New York Times,* June 11, 2019.

Lerer, Lisa. "Abortion Is New Litmus Test for Democratic Attorneys General Group." *New York Times,* November 18, 2019, nytimes.com/ 2019/11/18/us/politics/democratic-attorneys-general-abortion.html.

Selected Bibliography

Ohlheiser, Abby. "The Satanic Temple's giant statue of a goat-headed god is looking for a home." *The Washington Post,* July 1, 2015.

Phillip, Abby. "Oklahoma's Ten Commandments statue must be removed, state Supreme Court says." *The Washington Post,* June 30, 2015.

Van Orden, Bruce A. "George Reynolds: Loyal Friend of the Book of Mormon." *Ensign,* August 1986.

Journals

Bartkowski, John P. "Claims-Making and Typifications of Voodoo as a Deviant Religion: Hex, Lies, and Videotape." *Journal for the Scientific Study of Religion* 37, no. 4 (December 1998): 559–579.

Betancourt, Sofía, Dan McKanan, Tisa Wenger, and Sheri Prud'homme. "Claiming the Term 'Liberal' in Academic Religious Discourse." *Religions* 11, no. 6 (2020): 311. doi.org/10.3390/rel11060311

Butler, Jonathan. "From Millerism to Seventh-day Adventism: 'Boundlessness to Consolidation.' " *Church History* 55, no. 1 (March 1986): 50–64.

Catches, Vincent. "The Native American Church: The Half-Moon Way." *Wicazo Sa Review* 7, no. 1 (Spring 1991): 17–24.

Gomez, Michael A. "Muslims in Early America." *The Journal of Southern History* 60, no. 4 (1994): 682.

Knox, Zoe. "Jehovah's Witnesses as Un-Americans? Scriptural Injunctions, Civil Liberties, and Patriotism." *Journal of American Studies* 47, no. 4 (2013): 1089.

Levy, Leonard W. "Satan's Last Apostle in Massachusetts." *American Quarterly* 5, no. 1 (Spring 1953): 35.

Neem, Johann N. "The Elusive Common Good: Religion and Civil Society in Massachusetts, 1780–1833." *Journal of the Early Republic* 24, no. 3 (Autumn 2004): 386.

"No More Deaths: An Interview with John Fife." *Reflections* 95, no. 2 (Fall 2008): 48.

Rhodes, John. "An American Tradition: The Religious Persecution of Native Americans." *Montana Law Review* 52, no. 1 (1991).

Rives, Nathan S. "'Is This Not a Paradox?' Public Morality and the Unitarian Defense of State-Supported Religion in Massachusetts, 1806–1833." *New England Quarterly* 86, no. 2 (June 2013): 232–265. doi.org/10.1162/TNEQ_a_00277.

Sarna, Jonathan D. "The Impact of the American Revolution on American Jews." *Modern Judaism* 1, no. 2 (1981): 149.

Stanley, Erik W. "LBJ, the IRS, and Churches: The Unconstitutionality of the Johnson Amendment in Light of Recent Supreme Court Precedent." *Regent University Law Review* 24, no. 2 (2012).

Turley, Richard E., Jr. "The Mountain Meadows Massacre." *Ensign* 37, no. 9 (September 2007).

Van Wagoner, Richard S. "Mormon Polyandry in Nauvoo." *Dialogue: A Journal of Mormon Thought* 18, no. 3 (Fall 1985): 68.

Whelan, Charles M. " 'Church' in the Internal Revenue Code: The Definitional Problems." 45 *Fordham Law Review* 885 (1977).

Zygmunt, Joseph F. "Prophetic Failure and Chiliastic Identity: The Case of Jehovah's Witnesses." *American Journal of Sociology* 75, no. 6 (May 1970): 931.

Index

315

Index

Cantwell, Russell, 147

Cantwell v. Connecticut (1940),
    147–150, 166, 191, 193, 303

capitalism, 3, 194

Carroll, Daniel, 64

car sales, 23–24

Case, Thomas, 76

Catholics and Catholicism. *See also*
    Irish Catholic immigrants;
    schools, Catholic

    and abortion, 181–182

    anti-Catholic messages, and
        Jehovah's Witnesses, 147,
        148–149

    anti-Catholic riots, 121–122, 141

    in early U.S., 55–56, 58, 74–80

    and politics, 133, 289–290

    and religion in public schools,
        121–124, 129, 134

    and Santeria, 215–216

    and translations of the Bible, 113

Catholic World (magazine), 141–142

cellmates, 233

Charles I, 78

Christian Legal Society, 221

Christian Spiritists, 224

"Christian," used as generic term of
    virtue, 45, 128–129

churches. *See also* politics, church
    and; separation between
    church and state; state-
    approved religion, (dis)
    establishment of

    IRS investigations of, 285–286

    restrictions on lobbying activities
        of, 284–285

churches as sanctuary

    Church of the Covenant, 266–270

    and legal considerations,
        271–276

    in medieval Europe, 263

    in 1980s, 264–266

Church of England, 43, 44, 53, 59, 75,
    186

Church of the Covenant in
    Centerville, 266–270

*Church of the Lukumi Babalu Aye,
    Inc. v. Hialeah* (1993), 215–219,
    285

City of Boerne v. Flores (1997),
    222–223, 235

civil law, 25–26

civil rights, 7, 29, 30, 62, 194–195

Civil War, 87

    and Congress's power to interfere
        with states, 94

    conscription for, 107–108

    and Dred Scott decision, 92

    and political parties divide, 109

Clarke, Harold, 231

Clinton, William, 287

Colorado Civil Rights Commission, 30

common law, 25, 26

commonwealths, 118–119

Commonwealth v. Kneeland (1838),
    161–166

communal ownership of property,
    81, 89, 97–98

communion, 232–233, 239

compassion, 268

Congregationalists

    Calvinists, 50, 76

Index

Index

Index

Index

Index

Index